Praise for *Rescuing Ladybugs*

"Reading *Rescuing Ladybugs*, I am struck by the warmth and skill of Jennifer Skiff's writing and the profundity of her message. I am reading it slowly because every single chapter makes me want to get out of my chair and go do more for animals. Thank you for the inspiration!"

— **K. Dawn,** DawnWatch

"The rising public anguish over the state of the natural world, the suffering of humankind and of our fellow creatures, is informed and affirmed by the many voices in Jennifer Skiff's book. *Rescuing Ladybugs* is an exceptional book — a clarion call to awaken our empathy, ignite compassionate action, and help recover our humanity in these dystopian times. It should be required reading for all high school students and will inspire all who care in their communion with other sentient beings."

— **Dr. Michael W. Fox,** author of *The Boundless Circle: Caring for Creatures and Creation*, www.drfoxvet.net

"Everyone will love *Rescuing Ladybugs*. With a perfect balance of memoir, stories, and testimonials, this remarkable book and the heroes in it will make you laugh, will make you cry — and, more than anything else, will invite you to become a member of the kindest, most joyous, and most rewarding movement on the planet: the compassion movement."

— **Natasha Milne,** coeditor of *One Hundred & One Reasons to Get Out of Bed* and host of *My Home Planet* podcast

"My heart responds to Jennifer Skiff's book because animals and humans are connected — we help, teach, he?¹ ___ ¹ ___ ___ _____
Please read *Rescuing Ladybugs*, learn, and ___
nect with and help our family of animals
— **Dr. Bernie S. Siegel,** author of

Praise for *The Divinity of Dogs* by Jennifer Skiff

"A perfect read for dog lovers and those wishing to adopt. An uplifting collection of stories about people who have had other-worldly experiences through their relationships with dogs."

— *Shelf Awareness*

"This is an uplifting book, perfect for this time of year. Many of these true stories are heartwarming and filled with pure joy — exploring the kind of innocent and absolute joy dogs offer and inspire."

— *Chicago Tribune*

"You don't have to be a pet lover to fall in love with these stories. *The Divinity of Dogs* captures the unconditional love and loyalty of dogs and delivers it with one big wet kiss."

— **Carole Tomko,** president of MyDiscovery

"*The Divinity of Dogs* is a fascinating read, bringing to life the very special, sometimes incredible, aspects of dogs, with whom we have the privilege to share our lives."

— **Clarissa Baldwin,** chief executive officer of Dogs Trust

"Tissue alert, but in a good way.... All these inspiring 'touched by a dog' true stories are heartwarming."

— *USA Weekend*

RESCUING LADYBUGS

For further information, review copies, or
to schedule an interview, please contact
Monique Muhlenkamp at
415-884-2100 ext. 15 or email
monique@newworldlibrary.com

Also by Jennifer Skiff

The Divinity of Dogs:
True Stories of Miracles Inspired by Man's Best Friend

God Stories: Inspiring Encounters with the Divine

RESCUING LADYBUGS

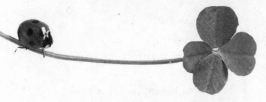

Inspirational Encounters with Animals

That Changed the World

JENNIFER SKIFF

New World Library

Novato, California

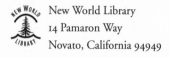
New World Library
14 Pamaron Way
Novato, California 94949

Text design by Tona Pearce Myers

Library of Congress Cataloging-in-Publication Data
Names: Skiff, Jennifer, [date]– author.
Title: Rescuing ladybugs : inspirational encounters with animals that changed the world / Jennifer Skiff.
Description: Novato, California : New World Library, [2018] | Includes bibliographical references and index.
Identifiers: LCCN 2018020105 (print) | LCCN 2018025537 (ebook) | ISBN 9781608685035 (ebook) | ISBN 9781608685028 (alk. paper) | ISBN 9781608685035 (ebook)
Subjects: LCSH: Animal welfare—Anecdotes. | Animal rights—Anecdotes.
Classification: LCC HV4711 (ebook) | LCC HV4711 .S55 2018 (print) | DDC 179/.3—dc23
LC record available at https://lccn.loc.gov/2018020105

First printing, September 2018
ISBN 978-1-60868-502-8
Ebook ISBN 978-1-60868-503-5

Printed in Canada on 100% postconsumer-waste recycled paper

New World Library is proud to be a Gold Certified Environmentally Responsible Publisher. Publisher certification awarded by Green Press Initiative. www.greenpressinitiative.org

10   9   8   7   6   5   4   3   2   1

*For Ann Clemons, my snake-loving, bird-calling,
four leaf clover–picking, ladybug-rescuing mother.
Through your eyes, mine were opened.*

Contents

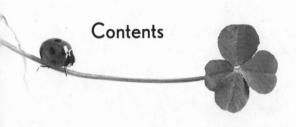

INTRODUCTION

When we were all children, the ladybug and butterfly stirred feelings of delight, puppies were heavenly, and farm animals made us happy. Our parents taught us that the ladybug — the tiny, red-shelled animal with black spots — brought good luck when she landed on you and that we should gently blow her away so that she could return safely to her family. The story nourished our natural empathy and set us on a path to feel compassion for all animals. We were being taught one of the greatest lessons in life: that kindness for others has rewards.

In 1998, I had an experience with a bear that confirmed that lesson and changed my life. I was in Asia, in the country of Laos, conducting research for a book I wanted to write. Most of the people in Laos are Buddhists, and I became immersed in the teachings of Buddhism. The religion — sometimes considered a philosophy — suggests that when people do good things, good consequences will return to them, and when people do bad things, bad things will happen. Karma. Buddhism also teaches compassion and instructs people to live in a nonharmful way, never killing or causing another being to suffer.

I felt clarity finding a spiritual practice based on compassion. But I was soon reminded that religious teachings don't guarantee enlightened ways, when I stumbled upon a merciless situation in a cultural park.

I was slowly making my way down a dirt trail at the park, having stopped to read a plaque about Buddha, when my boyfriend yelled, "Jenny, don't come down this path." Of course, I did. What I saw weakened my faith in humanity. Black-and-white Asiatic bears, identifiable by the trademark cream-colored collar across their chest, were imprisoned in five cages placed around a statue. Set on concrete slabs, the bell-shaped chambers were constructed of thick iron bars reaching six feet high and four feet wide. They were so small that the bears' bodies were pushing through the spaces between the bars. There was no protection from the glaring sun, no trees to offer shade. The bears were confined in metal straitjackets, forced upright with nowhere to turn.

I walked up and stood before one of the bears. He was crying and rocking, with one paw pushed completely into his mouth. Our eyes locked and we connected. In that moment, I felt his suffering. That's when he reached for me, extending his arm beyond his iron prison. He showed me his paws, blistered from cigarette burns.

The sadness grew louder. All around me, the bears were crying. I turned in a circle, my heart racing. They were in hell, all screaming for help. My knees buckled and I grabbed a handrail. That's when my boyfriend said, "Let's go, Jenny. There's nothing to be done here. You can't save every mistreated animal in the world." I understood what he was saying. But something in me irrevocably changed. In fact, I experienced an epiphany, a profound spiritual realization that, not only could I do something, but I must.

There are countless times throughout our lives when we're

presented with a choice to help another soul. My experience with the bears, whose complete story I tell in chapter 1, was the first of many situations in remote parts of the world where I was shown suffering and chose not to look away. I'm not alone. Many of us are confronted with injustice every day and choose not to look away. This book tells the stories of people who had an experience with another animal that affected them so profoundly it caused them to act.

I wanted to write this book for several reasons: to profile the good work being done by people to help other species, to inspire others to act, to document the current state of exploitation of animals, and to illuminate the interconnectedness of all species.

These extraordinary people — most of whom I'm lucky enough to call friends, whose unexpected encounters and nonverbal communication with other species motivated them to action — are leaders in what I call the compassion movement: the collective quest to alleviate suffering for all forms of life. *Rescuing Ladybugs* will take you around the world to experience the awe-inspiring and enlightening connections these leaders have had with animals of all shapes and sizes, from the nearly invisible pteropod to the savanna elephant. You'll learn how empathy motivated them to create sweeping changes that have ultimately benefited all species — including ours. All the stories are true. Some may be difficult to read, describing injustices, but I hope they fuel your compassion. My hope is that the stories will inspire and support your own intuitive guidance to do what's right when confronted by wrong.

This anonymous quote, often attributed to Martin Luther King, speaks to that idea: "Never, never be afraid to do what's right, especially if the well-being of a person or animal is at stake. Society's punishments are small compared to the wounds we inflict on our soul when we look the other way." I believe that we know instinctively what's right, and when we act on that instinct, we feel good; acting compassionately creates happiness in our own life.

The process involved in creating this book was challenging. My Australian publisher stipulated that, as part of a two-book deal, this had to be a memoir. It took me a year to figure out how to write a memoir that was meaningful, entertaining, and important. Throughout *Rescuing Ladybugs*, I share my personal journey with animals and tell some of the stories that have inspired me to action; these encounters often led to my connections with the amazing heroes in this book. As for how this book was put together, with a few exceptions, all the first-person stories were told to me directly through a combination of in-person, Skype, and email interviews, which I edited into single accounts. In a couple of stories, I combine my interviews with reprinted, previously published statements from other sources (and I cite those additions). In only one case is a personal account entirely from another source (Guy Stevens, from his book *Manta*). Every profile is introduced by a short story about how I met the person, and each includes a biography of the person's work, followed by a question-and-answer with them. Every story has been fact-checked by the person who is profiled.

Rescuing Ladybugs is about our collective journey to create positive change in the world for all species by breaking the barriers that cage and separate us. It's about the love that unites all species and shows how nurturing that connection helps all creatures to thrive. When we allow ourselves to experience this connection, we raise our consciousness, ignite our purpose, and become a force for good. The result is the awakening of our soul and the gift of an enlightened happiness that cannot be broken by the cruelty of a few.

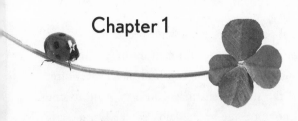

Chapter 1

BUDDHA AND BEAR

The Joy in Compassion-Driven Intervention

There are times in your life when you're presented with a choice: You can help another soul or you can look away. Such moments are pivotal — the decision you make changes lives forever, including yours. My game-changing moment came in March 1998 in Vientiane, Laos.

• • •

Vientiane, Laos

I stepped off a plane in Vientiane with my Australian boyfriend, Jon, and into another world. A rush of warm, humid air welcomed us, and instantly, the tension that came with entering a communist country seemed to dissipate.

Laos is landlocked by China, Vietnam, Myanmar, Thailand, and Cambodia. Poor and underdeveloped by Western standards, it's rich with people who choose, because of their religion, not to strive for monetary gains. The majority of people are Buddhists and are raised to cultivate wisdom and kindness while practicing compassion for all living beings.

Despite its peaceful population, or perhaps because of it, Laos has been the center of political battles for centuries. The most recent conflict had brought me here: the communist takeover after the Vietnam War and the subsequent mass murders of up to one hundred thousand Hmong people by the Lao People's Democratic Republic (LPDR).

I knew some of the refugees who'd made it out alive. They'd immigrated to the United States; many had opened nail salons, small grocery stores, and Vietnamese and Thai restaurants. While escaping, they'd lost family, friends, and even children. Moved by their bravery, I wanted to write a book that would lift the veil on Asian immigration to the United States while highlighting the human rights injustices in postwar Laos.

Thavisack Vixathep greeted us at the airport with a repeating handshake and toothy grin; he asked us to call him Tom. He was slim, around five feet tall, with short, shiny black hair. Tom was my government minder, an escort to make sure that as a journalist I didn't overstay or overstep my welcome.

Tom led us to a blue Mercedes-Benz sedan. As we climbed inside, he warned me I was not permitted to ask questions about the Vietnam War, reeducation camps, forced repatriation, the former Royal Lao family (many of whom had been murdered), genocide, or refugee camps. I tensed. Jon rested his hand on mine.

The first stop on our guided tour was Pha That Luang, a Buddhist temple described in tour books as the most important monument in Laos. On the outside, the reflection of the sun on the temple's gold-covered stupa and pillars was blinding. The feeling on the inside was just the opposite, calming and cool. In an alcove, the base of a gold leaf–covered statue of the sitting Buddha was adorned with fresh flowers and burning candles. In a far corner, a group of

Buddhist monks with shaved heads, their bodies wrapped in orange cloth, sat on the floor in meditation.

I already felt a connection with Buddhism. Its teachings make sense to me, as they do to the nearly 500 million people around the world who consider themselves Buddhists. Followers of Buddhism, often called the religion of compassion, commit to a life of nonviolence toward all animals and to eliminating greed from their lives. As I watched the monks, I was excited to be in a country where so many people were leading conscious lives.

Away from the main attractions of government buildings and temples, the real Vientiane felt like a small town. Motorbikes carrying entire families sped past our car while little girls in school uniforms of white shirts and navy blue skirts gathered together on street corners, eating pineapple skewered on sticks like it was ice cream. Shuttered apartments — reminders of the French occupation of Laos in the early 1900s — looked out over brightly colored fruit stands at every turn. Electricity poles and wires littered the horizon, while open sewers and dirt roads were a reminder that little had changed for decades.

That evening, as the sting of the heat disappeared with the sun, Jon and I were left alone to stroll a few blocks from our hotel to the banks of the Mekong River. Pretty young women with long, shiny jet-black hair and tiny frames beckoned us to their food stalls. We walked on, arm in arm, until an old man approached, offering two plastic chairs in a secluded spot under a tree. Jon ordered two Lao beers and we settled in, enjoying a view of Thailand, thirty-five hundred feet away on the other side of the glistening Mekong. Music filtered from a window on the nearby street, children laughed at the river's edge, and sparrows swarmed, welcoming the end of the day. The sunset was crimson red, created by a haze of smoke from cooking fires.

I was happy, swept into the moment with a cold beer and a new relationship. I'd met Jon eighteen months before, in Casablanca,

Morocco, while on assignment for CNN, during a party at the US consulate's residence. Two days later he unexpectedly burst into my life again.

At the time, I was scouting a location to shoot video of food markets. Local women in brightly colored robes with head scarves were perusing the outdoor stalls, shopping for their families' dinner. But what most intrigued me were the homeless street dogs, who followed at a safe distance. They looked up, eager to make eye contact with any person who might provide a scrap of sustenance, but it was as if they were invisible. No one took notice of them.

I'd witnessed this same street dog problem in other countries and gotten into the habit of packing boxes of dog biscuits when I traveled internationally. I reached into my bag, crouched to the ground, and one by one the market dogs cautiously approached and gently took a biscuit from my hand.

I was so caught up in the moment that I hardly noticed the man standing behind me until he said in an Australian accent: "If you were my girlfriend, I'd charter a plane so you could take these dogs home with you."

I turned and there was Jon, haloed by the sun, with a golden head of curls, freckled skin, and a contagious smile.

Now he and I were sitting together in Asia, contemplating the mighty Mekong, the source of life for billions of animals, sixty million of them human, and a silent witness to some of the world's greatest crimes against humanity. From where I was sitting, it was easy to visualize the tens of thousands of people who'd swum across the river to Thailand in 1975, while fleeing the communist regime. As I imagined the terror of that crossing, I wondered if writing about their experiences could actually prevent future wars, as I'd hoped. The world's knowledge of the Holocaust hadn't put a halt to mass killings. Genocide had occurred in Bosnia from 1992 to 1995, and it was currently happening in Rwanda. As I watched a large tree being swept downstream by the current, I wondered what power I had, if any, to create change.

• • •

The next day, Tom picked us up at 9 AM to take us to the National Ethnic Cultural Park, twelve miles south of Vientiane. I'd expressed an interest in learning about the history of the country, and he'd assured me I'd find what I was looking for there. Since the communist government still controlled Laos, I didn't expect to find what I was seeking — information on the Vietnam War and the mass exodus of refugees that followed. But I was eager to see what the government made public.

As we walked through the gates, it was apparent we'd entered a forgotten place. Kiosks were shuttered, footpaths were overgrown, and there were no signs of staff. Tom quickly apologized that it appeared closed and invited us to walk the grounds.

It was oppressively hot and the jungle was alive with the wing-snapping rattle of millions of cicadas. The noise was loud and yet simultaneously calming. I sauntered down a dark path that led to a moss-covered statue of an elephant. As I admired it, a bird landed on the elephant's trunk. It was a bright green parakeet, with a red beak and matching neck ring.

"Hello," I said, hoping he'd mimic. "Hello," I repeated. He nodded and extended his wings, ruffling them with a shake. He nodded again, let out a screech, and flew down the path. I followed, pushing past a patch of hanging vines to find him bouncing on a palm frond. As soon as I approached, he screeched and flew farther down the trail, out of sight. Then Jon yelled from that direction.

"Jenny, don't come down this path!"

"What is it?" I asked.

He didn't reply.

I proceeded cautiously until I reached a clearing. In the middle was a ten-foot-high statue of a smiling Buddha head surrounded by a circular dirt pathway. Jon was off to one side, standing in front of a six-foot-high bell-shaped cage with thick iron bars.

"Don't look," he warned.

The parakeet let out a screech and I looked up. He was on top of the cage, nodding as I walked closer. My eyes dropped.

A black Asiatic bear was imprisoned in a cage he'd physically outgrown. The cream-colored half-moon marking across his chest — a hallmark of Asiatic black bears — was broken in the center by a line of dark brown hair. He had a long snout and rounded ears that stood upright, each the size of a man's hand. One arm dangled outside the five-inch space between the bars, while the whole paw on his other arm was stuffed into his mouth. His eyes and the fur below them were wet, and he was rocking on his feet. When he saw me, a muffled cry erupted from his throat and his free arm reached for me. I moved closer, inches from his reach, and looked into his eyes. He was sobbing, trying to catch his breath like a child after a long tantrum. His eyes held mine. In that moment, telepathically, he conveyed his suffering to me.

I looked around his feet for signs of food or excrement, proof he'd been eating, but saw neither. A plastic pail of stagnant green water was behind him, but I couldn't tell if it was within reach. My eyes went to his again, and he lifted the arm that was outside the bars, turning it over for me to see the palm of his paw. There were five circular blisters, bubbled and red, on the pads, along with other spots of scar tissue. He cried out as I looked from the blisters back to him.

"You like bear?" Tom asked in his pidgin English.

"This is an unacceptable situation for any animal," Jon answered.

"Bear happy. Nice bear," Tom said, grinning.

"No. Bear not happy. Bad water," I said. "Bear is sick," I said, pointing to the blistered paw. "Who takes care of this bear?"

Tom's smile vanished. "I find man," he said, and walked away.

My eyes followed Tom, and it was only then that I saw the other four cages, all circling the Buddha, all imprisoning bears. I must have been so focused on the first bear that I shut out everything around me. Now it was as if someone had turned up the volume and all I heard were the sounds of despair. I turned in a circle, my heart racing, feeling anguished and desperate. The sun was unforgiving, burning. My knees buckled and I grabbed a handrail.

At that moment, Tom arrived with a man wearing a conical straw hat, a light brown long-sleeved shirt, and sarong pants. He was carrying a handmade wide-bottomed whisk broom. "This man is keeper of bears. He's friend to bears," Tom said.

I asked whether he spoke English, and Tom shook his head.

"Will you translate for me?" I asked.

Tom nodded.

"To keep bears in this small cage is not good. This water is bad water. Where is the food? And what is wrong with his paw?" I said, pointing to the blisters.

Tom interpreted the questions, and the two men launched into a discussion. The bear stopped crying and focused on their conversation, his eyes on them, his ears turned in their direction, one paw still in his mouth. I wondered if he understood their language. I couldn't. I could only read their expressions, and they were serious.

After a couple of minutes, the bear's keeper scurried away, and Tom turned to me and Jon.

"This bear has been here since baby. Some other bears," he said, pointing to cages nearby, "brought here by people who keep for pet, like dog, until they grow too big. They ask park to take care of them, and people pay money to see them. Man who take care of bear likes bear very much but say, never enough food for them."

As Tom talked, the keeper returned with a bucket of fresh water. He poured it into the green water, only serving to stir the algae.

He looked at me and smiled, clearly hoping for praise. I wanted to thank him but held back. The least he could do was to give the animals fresh water, and he hadn't. Not today and clearly not before.

"What about his paw?" I asked the keeper, pointing to the blisters.

We may not have spoken the same language, but he knew what I was asking. He answered and Tom cringed.

"This is where people burn bear with cigarettes," Tom said, mimicking the way a person would crush a cigarette butt in an ashtray.

My throat swelled and my eyes welled with tears. I turned to the bear and our eyes locked. With a despair that permeated my being, I physically felt his suffering.

Jon's voice interrupted. "Let's go, Jenny. There's nothing you can do. You can't save every mistreated animal in the world."

"No," I whispered, my eyes still connected with the bear. "But I can help the ones I come across."

In that moment, locking eyes with the bear, I experienced an epiphany, a profound spiritual realization that not only could I do something, but that I must. Fate had brought me here for a reason. I turned back to the bear. Wordlessly, I promised I'd help and asked him not to give up.

As I walked toward the exit, I stopped at each cage, took a photograph, and gave each bear my promise. When I looked back, the keeper was pushing a wheelbarrow, half-filled with vegetables, in the direction of the bears, and I experienced a moment of satisfaction. Yet I knew the gesture was meant to appease me; it wasn't based on any lasting compassion for the imprisoned animals.

As we walked toward the car, Tom suggested the bears were probably poached as cubs — victims of the illegal wildlife trade — and had been "saved" by the park. I didn't buy his story. The way the cages had been positioned around the Buddha statue was intentional; these animals were an attraction.

"Why does the government run the cultural park?" I asked.

"Government runs everything," Tom said. "But there is no money. We try to get tourists here because they bring money. I hope you might write story to bring people here and maybe that money help bears."

With those words, the path forward became clear, and I resolved to follow it. The key to unlocking the cages was to convince the communist government that there was a financial incentive in treating their native animals with compassion.

"Will you help me talk to the government about this situation with the bears? Will you work with me?" I asked.

Tom placed his hands together in prayer and bowed. When he lifted his head, he was smiling. "Yes. We work together. Thank you, Miss Jenny."

Before leaving Laos, I presented Tom with a handwritten letter of introduction to Nousay Phoummachanh, a minister secretary for the government and deputy director of the National Ethnic Cultural Park. It extended my gratitude for inviting me to visit. It included my credentials, a description of what I'd witnessed at the park, and a personal offer to provide advice on how to build the country's tourism trade.

• • •

Mount Desert Island, Maine, USA

I returned from Laos with a redirected purpose. Back home in Maine, I tacked a photo of the first bear I met on my office wall. His cries were embedded in my memory, and I decided to call him Fri, the Lao translation of "free." His rescue was now my priority.

Within days, a fax arrived from the Ministry of Information, Culture, and Tourism in Laos, a response to the letter Tom had delivered. It justified the condition in which the bears were found by stating that there were costs associated with the care of the animals but that money to feed them would be welcome. It also said the government would welcome help to increase tourism to Laos.

My thoughts raced. How could I help increase tourism to a communist country and also free the bears? Laos is naturally beautiful; it has a warm climate and is home to wild elephants, bears, and exotic birds. Those qualities attract tourists. Caged and tortured animals do not. Ultimately, I wanted the bears rehabilitated and released into the wild, but I knew that wasn't possible. There were no rehabilitation centers for large animals in Laos. There was only one solution.

That night I called Tom, whose role with me had changed from minder to government liaison. I told him that when people travel, they want to leave a country with a positive impression, yet the poor treatment of the bears went against everything Laos, and Buddhist culture, stood for. I suggested the creation of a sanctuary where the bears from the cultural park could live on several acres and where tourists could view them from a distance. Then I offered to build it.

Tom seemed excited by the idea and suggested the Laotian Ministry of Defense might be the correct office to grant land for a sanctuary, not the Ministry of Information, Culture, and Tourism. He offered to meet with representatives of both departments.

Two weeks later I received a fax from the Ministry of Defense. It read:

Dear Miss Skiff,

The Department of Defense will make land available if you will build a sanctuary for bears. Thank you for your interest in Lao tourism.

Lao PDR

It was almost too good to be true, too easy. I was skeptical and excited all at once. I had easily cleared what I'd thought would be a major hurdle. The next step was to find the person to build it.

Through research, I discovered Victor Watkins. In 1992, while working for the World Society for the Protection of Animals (WSPA; today known as World Animal Protection), he'd initiated the first international crusade to help captive bears. The campaign, called Libearty, worked in conjunction with other animal welfare groups to end the practice of dancing bears in Europe and Asia, bear bile farming in Asia, and bear baiting in Pakistan. The campaign's goal was to expose the exploitation of bears in an effort to get public and government support to end these cruel practices.

Victor had also helped design and build the first bear sanctuary in the world, which had enabled the Greek and Turkish governments to eradicate the use of dancing bears in their countries by providing a home for confiscated bears. Victor Watkins was my man. I picked up the phone and called him in London.

Victor was sympathetic to the cause, but I didn't have him at "hello." I explained my intentions to liberate the bears in Laos. When I finished, Victor peppered me with questions: Who would build the sanctuary? Who would pay for staff costs and ongoing food and medical supplies in a third-world country where many people didn't have those amenities? I had no answers, but I was sure of one thing: I was talking to the single person who could help.

As he politely wrapped up our conversation by wishing me well, I panicked.

"Please, may I meet you?" I asked.

"I'm afraid I can't commit to a project like this, but yes, we can continue the conversation. I'll be at the Karacabey Bear Sanctuary in Bursa, Turkey, next month. It's a permanent home for former dancing bears. Can you meet me there?" he asked.

I looked at my calendar. I was scheduled to be reporting for CNN from a Greek island off the coast of Turkey. It was meant to be.

I called Jon in Australia and asked if he wanted to meet me in Turkey.

• • •

Karacabey Bear Sanctuary, Bursa, Turkey

The combined scent of pine and cedar hit me like a spray of per-fume as I stepped out of the car at the Karacabey Bear Sanctuary, nestled high in Bursa's mountains. Victor was waiting, and he em-braced me like a long-lost friend. He was younger than I expected for someone with his accomplishments. He looked like he was in his late thirties and had light brown hair and a neatly trimmed beard. He was casually dressed in a collared, short-sleeved shirt and jeans.

As we toured the facility, Victor explained that it had been built in 1993 for a single purpose: as a place to release dancing bears kept illegally in Turkey by displaced Roma populations, often deroga-torily referred to as gypsies. The moment the sanctuary was ready, Victor had led a late-night raid to rescue a dozen European brown bears held captive in Istanbul. The mission took eight hours as po-lice and veterinarians worked together to tranquilize the bears, cut their chains, and load them into crates — all during a downpour. After another six hours of traveling, the bears were safely in Karaca-bey, free from their torturers.

The bears were big, over six feet tall when standing. Most of them were covered in light brown fur with rounded, upright ears. I found it hard to comprehend that these beautiful animals had ever been under the control of human beings. But as Victor explained, most of them had been stripped of their defenses. Their keepers had burned holes into their snouts with blazing metal rods so they could be controlled by a nose rope or ring. Their teeth had been knocked out and their nails removed. And they had been beaten into submission.

In the outdoor enclosure, I could see ten bears. Some were playing together while a few were in rough shape, mentally. One was walking in circles and two were rocking, exhibiting the same behavior I'd noticed at the cultural park in Laos. Victor explained that they suffered from a form of posttraumatic disorder.

The root of the cruelty and suffering they'd endured was an age-old problem: poverty. After centuries of persecution in Europe, many Roma people didn't have homes or jobs. Some stole bear cubs from the wild because they knew people would pay to watch the bears dance. If people hadn't paid, the abuse wouldn't have continued. It is the same as when people pay to take selfies with chained elephants, captured dolphins, tethered monkeys, or lion cubs. Money drives exploitation.

"Let's talk bear sanctuaries," Victor said. "Write this down. It's what you need to know."

I fished a notepad and pen from my handbag and wrote the following:

1. Sanctuary should include natural bear habitat/forest.
2. Fence. Can be weld-mesh fencing or stone walls. 2–3 meters high. Fence foundations must extend 1.5 meters deep. Bears dig.
3. Protective barrier. Electric fence. Charge must be 7,000 volts. To prevent bears from going out and people from getting in.
4. Buildings for staff.
5. Quarantine den for newly rescued bears for adjustment period.
6. Enclosure should be 6 hectares or 15 acres to house 30 bears.
7. Must have: freshwater pools, trees for climbing, dens for hibernation, and areas of shade. Perfect setting is in natural forest.

"The male bears will need to be sterilized before going into the enclosure together," he said. "You will want to have a vet clinic on-site. How confident are you that you can secure the land?" he asked.

"That's the good news," I said. "The government has agreed to give three acres."

"For how many bears?" he asked.

"Five."

"It won't be enough. Once it's built, people will want to surrender bears to you. When you build it, they come."

"Will you help me build it?" I asked.

"Follow me," he said. In his office, he unrolled a blueprint of the Karacabey Sanctuary.

"You need a drawing to work from. Use this one," he said. "What are you thinking it will cost to build?"

"I've been estimating around eight thousand US dollars for the enclosure. To be honest, I didn't even think about other buildings."

"Triple that," he said. "Can you raise that kind of money?"

"I'll have to," I replied.

An hour later, it was time to go. As Victor led me to the parking lot, I was upset but tried not to show it. He had given me drawings to build a bear sanctuary, but I hadn't been able to secure what I wanted: a commitment from him to help. With a lump in my throat I took his extended hand, covered it with both of mine, and thanked him for the plans, his time, and his advice.

I rolled down the car window to wave good-bye, and Victor lifted his finger into the air. He approached the window and leaned in.

"You go raise the money. I'll be in touch," he said.

• • •

Perth, Australia

The sun was shining when I landed in Perth. Eight months had passed since meeting Victor in Turkey. I was in Australia to visit Jon and to raise the rest of the money for the bear sanctuary in Laos. So far, in my purse, I had $6,000 and fifteen pieces of donated jewelry, which I intended to auction. The money came from an American friend who donated a portion of one night's proceeds from her restaurant. The jewelry was a gift from a couple of dear friends who, when asked for help, reached into the depths of their jewelry boxes and presented me with seldom-worn rings and necklaces.

Jon was confident his Australian friends would be generous if we threw a good party. I loved the idea but wasn't sure how to pull it off. I knew very few people in Australia who might help. I did, however, have faith. Past experience had proven to me that when you set forth to right an injustice, you will find yourself surrounded by good people willing to help.

And that's what happened. The first person I approached was Theresa Smith, a California girl married to an Australian and one of my first friends in Perth. Years before, for her fortieth birthday, Theresa had invited me and her friends to take surfing lessons, and we'd remained friends ever since. Theresa was popular, often hosting parties at her mansion in the exclusive suburb of Peppermint Grove, and I figured she'd know the best way to organize the party. Over a cup of tea under a giant peppermint tree, I showed her the pictures I'd taken of Fri and the other bears. She studied the photographs for ten seconds and then turned them facedown on a table.

"I need to introduce you to Jayne Middlemas," she said. "You'll like her. We'll need a committee."

The next day I met Jayne, and as she studied the photograph of Fri, she smiled and said, "I'll be on your committee. I'll handle the money and accounting."

The next morning at a beachside café, I met Bill Woolley and his fiancée, Lindi, by chance. I didn't even have to show Lindi a photograph. She joined the party committee on the spot after hearing what I'd seen in Laos.

At the end of that first week, Taury Wainwright, a sweet-natured, beach-blonde girlfriend of one of Jon's business partners, had also raised her hand to help. Taury, a decade younger than the rest of us, had many friends who were famous Australian footy players, and she promised to get a young, hip crowd to the party.

We decided to ask Ian Love, the owner of the popular restaurant CoCo's, if he would host the party. Jon knew Ian and arranged a meeting, and Ian quickly agreed. He had two dogs and was an animal lover, and he threw in a substantial discount on food and drinks.

Miraculously, a team of bear warriors had materialized, all eager to end the suffering of five souls they'd never met.

Five months after the formation of the committee, the glamorous event and jewelry auction caused a frenzy of generous bidding that raised $17,500. Combined with the $6,000 I already had, the sum totaled the exact amount Victor had said we needed to build the sanctuary.

I could barely contain my excitement when I called Victor with the news. He had good news, too. His organization, WSPA, had given the nod to oversee construction of the sanctuary. In addition, he'd reached out to the Thai Society for the Conservation of Wild Animals (TSCWA) to see if it would assist with the project. Apparently, TSCWA had received many complaints about the neglected bears at the Vientiane National Ethnic Cultural Park. Not only were they willing to help us, but they offered to sterilize the bears and relocate them to the sanctuary once it was built.

Like an unstoppable wave, the movement to uncage Fri and the other bears was a powerful force of energy. Good was prevailing, and I was overwhelmed by the generosity of people from all parts of the world who were working to right this terrible wrong.

• • •

Mount Desert Island, Maine, USA

Approximately six hundred days after I met Fri, I received a large manila envelope in the mail. It was a letter from Victor, telling me the bears were finally home in their new sanctuary. The news was bittersweet. Two of the five had died while awaiting rescue.

I stuck my hand in the envelope and pulled out two photographs. One showed a medical team standing over sedated bears on stretchers. Another was a shot of a bear in a wooden crate being transported on the flatbed of a truck. Tears welled in my eyes as I studied the pictures and thought of the bears I hadn't been able to save. As I reached for a tissue on my desk, a third photograph dropped from the envelope and to the floor. I picked it up and my spirit lifted. It was Fri — recognizable by his unique, broken half-moon chest marking. He was standing upright, rubbing his back on a tree. He was smiling.

When I first touched down in Laos nearly two years earlier, I'd been searching for justice and compassion for human beings. I left the country with something else: a clear understanding that all animals, human or otherwise, deserve life and are entitled to freedom. The experience was enlightening. I was shown that as difficult as it is to witness the cruelty that often comes with rescue, the reward in helping a defenseless soul is immeasurable.

• • •

The first bear sanctuary in Laos was built by WSPA, TSCWA, and more than a hundred people, primarily from the United States and Australia, who generously funded it. Today, the Laos Wildlife Rescue Center is home to twenty-four bears. It is operated by the Wildlife Friends Foundation (WFF), a Thailand-based charity founded by Edwin Wiek.

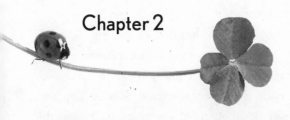

Chapter 2

PORCUPINE, MONKEY, ELEPHANT, PTEROPOD

The Power of the Collective Voice

Perth, Australia

"Come and see dragons with me! I understand they've just eaten a Japanese tourist. Isn't that wonderful?" Guy joked in his posh British accent. Guy was calling from Bali, Indonesia, and paused, presumably to take a drag from his ever-present cigarette. "If you come, I promise not to order suckling pig at any of the local establishments."

I first met my most eccentric friend when he was Guy David Greville. Then he became Lord Brook, and he was now Guy Warwick, the Earl of Warwick. Behind the façade of his often sarcastic, sometimes shocking, but always witty repartee, he was a highly intelligent, deeply caring man whose friendship I cherished. While our views on animal welfare oftentimes differed, he supported my advocacy and had, more than once, let me use stays in his Spanish villa as an auction item to raise money for charities.

Guy was also one of Jon's closest friends, and he wanted Jon and me to go on vacation with him and his partner, Natalie Bovill, to the island of Flores, Indonesia, where he was thinking of buying land. He was enticing me with the promise of seeing Komodo dragons.

I'd been intrigued by the giant lizard since reading the book *Last Chance to See* by Douglas Adams and Mark Carwardine, about unique animals on the verge of extinction. Guy knew this, since we'd once seen a Komodo dragon together at a Balinese zoo, and indeed, I couldn't resist the thought of seeing a "dragon" in the wild. Eight weeks later, in 2013, Jon and I met Guy and Natalie in Bali, where we boarded a small plane for the hour-long flight to Flores.

The entry to the island couldn't have been more spectacular. As we flew over hundreds of uninhabited lush, green, volcanic islands, where high cliffs dropped to white beaches that bled into turquoise water, a calm washed over me.

• • •

Island of Flores, Indonesia

A smiling man with light brown skin and dressed in a khaki-colored uniform introduced himself as our driver and proceeded to take us on a twenty-minute, hold-on-to-someone-to-stay-upright bumpy ride to Jayakarta Suites, a four-star hotel on the southwestern tip of the island.

As we turned into the resort's palm-lined drive, Guy exclaimed sarcastically, "Oh no! I'm afraid monkey is on the menu." As we drove past a clump of metal cages, I looked back and noticed someone was chained to a tree.

"Is that a monkey?" I asked.

"Yes, and a menagerie of others are tucked away in the back garden," Guy replied, then teased: "Apparently, I've chosen hotels badly. We've landed in the only one where they keep the meat on the premises."

A few minutes later, while the others walked into the hotel, I went in the opposite direction.

I stopped near the monkey who was chained to the tree. Around his neck was a chain-link collar inside a clear plastic tube. His hand reached out to me and his mouth opened to speak, but he made no sound. He picked up a Kit Kat candy wrapper and showed it to me, pleading for another. I looked around for a caretaker. There was no one in sight.

The sound of honking geese caught my attention: Four white birds with orange-colored bills stood in the corner of a five-by-five-foot enclosure, beckoning. As I approached, they became excited, waddling back and forth in their small space. Directly above them was another cage: In it was a porcupine and an empty clamshell. Neither cage contained food or water.

Three feet away was another, larger enclosure, about sixteen square feet. The four sides were mesh wire, and the floor was concrete. In it, eleven monkeys on short chains were clipped to the wire walls in such a way that they couldn't reach each other or the floor. They were all clinging to the wire mesh. The floor beneath them was immaculate, with no sign of feces. Like the other cages, there were no food or water feeders.

As I scanned the scene, all seventeen animals fell silent, staring at me.

"I'll be right back," I said.

In the lobby, I passed Jon, Natalie, and Guy, already dressed in swimsuits and sarongs, on their way to the pool. I headed for the front desk and asked for the hotel's manager. The young man didn't speak English, and my Indonesian was limited to basic niceties. After a brief interchange that involved me mimicking a monkey, I understood that the manager, Mr. Agus Tabah Wardhana, was away for the day. I was given an appointment for the next day at 2:30 PM.

I walked into the dining room and through the swinging doors of the kitchen, where I was again forced to play charades with a chef who spoke little English. Ten minutes later, I left carrying food for the animals: a bucket of rice that I understood was for the geese and another bucket of sliced fruit for the monkeys and porcupine.

First, I stopped at the gray-colored monkey who was chained to a tree and handed him a slice of watermelon. He snatched it from my hand, took a bite, and responded by drawing his lips back into a huge, toothy smile.

Nearby, the geese honked for my attention, pleading to be released. The presence of a nearby pond, and their inability to get to it, must have been torturous. I tossed the rice from the bucket into their enclosure through the wire.

The sign on the porcupine's cage read "Twinkle." I took a slice of watermelon to a corner of the cage and pushed part of it through the wire.

"Twinkle," I called.

The porcupine's nose lifted but he didn't leave his corner. I walked around and dropped a piece of the fruit through the wire in front of the quilled animal. He sniffed at and quickly took it, his milky-white eyes revealing his blindness. When he finished, he turned to me, asking for another piece. I obliged. For a nocturnal animal, his situation was dire. He had no water, no den, and nothing to shade him from the hot, blinding sun.

The gray-colored monkeys were long-tailed macaques, named because their tails are longer than their bodies. In Indonesia, they're also called crab-eating macaques because they swim and dive for crabs. I have interacted with macaques on many occasions in Bali; they are omnivores, and females dominate their social groups.

They were fearful as I neared, quickly snatching the fruit I offered and devouring it while keeping their eyes on me.

A man appeared, carrying a broom. He smiled at me and nodded, seemingly pleased at what I was doing. I assumed he must be the animals' caretaker.

"Where is the water?" I asked, knowing he probably didn't understand English.

I looked around. There wasn't a hose; just an empty bucket outside the monkeys' enclosure.

"Water," I asked, pointing into the bucket. He didn't seem to understand. I picked an empty water bottle out of a trash can and pretended to drink. He smiled, walked away, and returned ten minutes later with an unopened bottle of water, which he handed to me, apparently thinking I was asking for myself. I unscrewed the cap, unlatched Twinkle's enclosure, righted the clamshell, and filled it with water.

Now the man smiled and nodded; he understood. He left again and returned with a bucket of water, putting it into the enclosure with the geese. I pointed to the monkeys, and he pointed at the water bottle I was still holding. Confused, I gave it to him. He proceeded to walk around the monkey enclosure and toss spurts of water in each animal's face. The monkeys recoiled. Only one opened his mouth, catching a bit of the water thrown at him. The others went without.

The next morning, after a restless night, I waited for the restaurant to open. I had a coffee and a glass of pineapple juice, then swept the buffet of fruit and bread and took it to the animals.

This time, when I called Twinkle, he greeted me like a lost friend, running toward my voice. I pushed a piece of cantaloupe through the wire. As I watched him eat, I wondered if I might be standing too close. I'd pulled plenty of quills from the faces of dogs who'd interfered with porcupines. I understood the pain Twinkle was capable of delivering, but I couldn't help but tempt fate. I put my index finger through a hole in the wire and scratched the top of his head. To my surprise, he leaned into the scratch like a dog.

Tempted to release the geese, I didn't, fearful that this unauthorized act would interfere with the negotiations I hoped to have with the hotel's manager. Instead, I fed them the equivalent of a loaf of bread.

As I neared the monkey enclosure, the tiny creatures with big eyes reached their arms through the metal bars, hands open, begging for a morsel of food. I walked around the cage quickly, handing each one a piece of watermelon, cantaloupe, or banana. They snatched the fruit with one hand, while holding on to the wire with another, and ate hurriedly.

I still hadn't formulated a strategy for my meeting with Mr. Tabah, the hotel's manager. I didn't know what I was going to ask him to do. The previous night, I'd asked Guy for advice; he speaks fluent Indonesian and has lived on Bali for a good part of his life. Guy warned: "Indonesians will tell tourists one thing and do another. They know that you will leave. If that menagerie is bringing them money, they will not shut it down."

Mr. Tabah, a tall, thin man with a high forehead and wearing wire-rimmed glasses, greeted me with a handshake in the hotel's foyer at 2:30.

"I understand you are concerned about the monkeys," he said. "How may I assist you?"

"Yes. I'm concerned for the monkeys, the geese, and the porcupine," I replied.

"Why don't we walk to them and talk along the way," he suggested, motioning toward the door.

As we walked, I made a point to summarize my credentials: I had decades of experience working directly with animals in shelters and sanctuaries, among other things, and perhaps most of all, I had 150,000 animal-loving social media followers. Mr. Tabah seemed to understand that these followers represented a powerful force.

"Mr. Tabah, you have a very beautiful, special hotel," I said.

"Thank you," he replied.

"But I'm very disappointed to see such poor treatment of animals. It has ruined my vacation, not made it better. People come here to see animals in their natural habitat, enjoying life — not caged."

"I understand what you're saying." He nodded.

"You do?"

"Yes. You are not the first person who has complained," he said. "Many have complained and noted their displeasure when reviewing the hotel. But this is a complicated situation. This zoo was started by the man who started the hotel, and he's been very proud of it. It has been a difficult subject to discuss with him."

Mr. Tabah stopped between the porcupine and monkey enclosures. "We do our best to take care of these animals."

"With respect, Mr. Tabah, there is no food or water in these cages, the monkeys are chained even inside the cage, and the porcupine doesn't have a log to sit on or shade to protect him. He's probably blind because of the sun exposure. And these geese — why are they even in here?"

"The geese are here because hotel guests complained of the noise they made at night as they walked the grounds. The porcupine, Twinkle, was part of the original zoo. We had another porcupine, his friend, that died. The monkey cage started with a few, and then people gave us their pet monkeys. They fight if they're unchained." He paused. "Miss Skiff, I am interested in what you have to say. What is it that you suggest we do?"

In that split second, as I looked into the eyes of the geese, who were watching intently and seemingly listening to our conversation, I decided to go for broke.

"Let's release these monkeys back into the jungle. I'd like to build a proper enclosure for Twinkle, and I suggest you either find a good home for the geese or release them during the day if they are only causing problems at night. You won't have to worry about feeding them because they will forage. In fact — why don't we give that a try now?" I asked.

Mr. Tabah turned to a man who was gardening nearby and

spoke to him in Indonesian. The man walked to the cage and un-latched the gate. The geese pushed open the door and sprinted across the lawn to the edge of the pond. Then, for what seemed like five minutes, they drank, scooping water with their bills and tossing it down their throats by lifting their heads into the air.

"Thank you," I said, touching my hand to my heart. "This makes me happy."

"I agree with you," Mr. Tabah said, turning toward the monkeys. "I understand people don't want to see this. But I don't think we can release all the monkeys."

"Why?" I asked.

"It is not something I am able to discuss with you," he replied, looking serious.

I understood that I needed to be careful and respectful. I didn't know the politics of the hotel's zoo, but I could see he was genuinely considering my request. "I understand. How many do you think you would consider releasing?" I asked.

He wrung his hands, looking beyond the monkeys, lost in thought.

"I will have to get permission from our office in Jakarta. I would like to work with you. We will have to wait and see. If we are able to release monkeys, are you available to do this on the day after tomorrow?" he asked.

"I sure am," I smiled.

In the lobby, as we parted, he asked me to call him Agus, and I bowed with my eyes closed and hands clasped, symbolizing my gratitude. "*Terima kasih*," I said in Indonesian: "Thank you."

I found Jon, Guy, and Nat on the terrace having cocktails.

Guy winced when he heard about my exchange.

"I'm sorry to disappoint, darling Jen, but they'll never do it. I've lived here for thirty years. They want to please you, but there's nothing in it for them." He paused and took a long drag from his cigarette. "Are you terribly disappointed?"

"I have hope, Guy," I said. "I *hope* you're wrong!"

As I watched the sunset, my eyes canvassed the islands. The sea's color was changing with the light, shifting from turquoise to an indigo blue. Despite the calm water and comforting colors, I remained anxious about what lay ahead.

That night I called Dr. Barbara Royal.

A good friend, Barb had a thriving veterinary practice in Chicago and was one of the few vets I knew who worked with exotic wildlife. I needed her advice. I explained the situation — I might soon be re-releasing monkeys into the jungle after years of captivity, monkeys destined to die otherwise — so how could I ensure their survival?

Barb asked if they could be taken to a rehabilitation center to prepare them for a release. When I explained this wasn't possible — this remote island had no wildlife centers — she instructed me to feed up the monkeys. Then, on the day of their release, I should leave them near a source of fresh water and fruit and nut trees, along with a three-day supply of fruit.

The next day, after a massive monkey feeding, Jon convinced me to join a morning boat excursion to visit parts of the island not accessible by land. We left the quiet seaside village of Labuan Bajo on a twenty-eight-foot runabout and were immediately transported to another world. Emerald green hills jutted from turquoise water, and white beaches lit the way.

We hugged the coast for two hours, never seeing other people. The coastline was pure, untouched by development, and yet, beneath us, I was surprised to see that much of the coral was bleached white. We learned that it had been destroyed by dynamite fishing, an illegal practice where dynamite is thrown into the center of a school of fish. The dead or stunned fish float to the surface of the water and are easily collected. Just like development destroys habitat, dynamite was killing life-sustaining ecosystems.

On the way back, we detoured to a tiny, white island that

appeared in the distance like a diamond on a bed of aquamarines. As we neared, it became clear that the oasis was created by a heap of shells. We anchored and jumped overboard. Underwater, the sea floor was like a jewelry counter of the most magnificent shells. I picked up an empty, chambered nautilus. I'd never seen one in the wild before, and holding it to my chest like a treasure, I rose to the surface, closed my eyes, floated on my back, and said a prayer for the monkeys.

When I arrived at the hotel, there was a message from Agus. He wanted me to meet him in two days at 7 AM. There was going to be a monkey release.

The next morning I fed the animals and set off on our planned adventure to see dragons on Komodo Island (a story I tell in chapter 3). Then, at dawn's first light on the day of the promised release, I tentatively walked out of the hotel and saw a flurry of activity near the cages. My heart lifted. Six men were standing by the large enclosure wearing uniforms of collared shirts with khaki pants. The monkeys were inquisitive, eyes wide, peering between the cage wires. Nearby, the back of a small pickup truck was stacked with four wooden crates.

Agus greeted me.

"Nine of the monkeys will be released today. Three have to stay," he said.

"This is wonderful news," I said. "How will you choose which monkeys stay?"

"I was hoping you could help me with that decision."

"Are there any that were born here?"

"Yes, there is a mother who gave birth to two while she has been with us," he said, pointing to the mother, who hissed, showing her teeth. "She came from the forest, but not the babies."

"Then, if three are to be left behind, it makes sense that she stays with her babies. Their chances of survival are less than the monkeys who have come from the forest," I said, regretfully. "May

I ask a favor? When the others have been released, will you please take the collars off the remaining monkeys so they can move around and play in the cage, and may I work with your staff to repair this monkey cage and the porcupine's, too?"

"That would be nice of you," he replied. "I'm very happy to accept your offer."

Agus then gave instructions for the work to begin. One man opened the enclosure door, unchained a monkey from the wire, and placed him on top of a wooden crate in the back of the truck. He held the monkey while another man lifted wire cutters to the monkey's neck. The monkey, to my surprise, bowed his head to facilitate the removal of his steel burden. It was as if he knew what was about to happen and offered no resistance.

After ten minutes, the men finished cutting the rusty chains from the monkey's neck, and then they carefully lowered him through a top hole in one of the crates. Immediately, the monkey reached his tiny black hand, whose long fingers resembled my own, through the slats. I offered my finger, and like a baby, he took it.

One by one the metal collars were removed and the monkeys were put into the transport crates. The door to the enclosure was closed, leaving the mother and her two children behind. I went to her to apologize, and she hissed at me. As I got into a van, I thought about how I deserved that for leaving her behind.

The caravan into the jungle included two small pickup trucks carrying the crated monkeys, a third truck with staff, and a van with Agus, Jon, and me. We stopped once briefly at a makeshift market where a man was selling fruit from a blue tarp on the ground. Jon and I purchased all his bananas and other fruit, which we added to the supply of food we'd brought from the hotel.

As we traveled into the mountains, the sun revealed a wet and glistening, lush green countryside. We were taking the monkeys home, to the place where they'd been kidnapped, and I was filled with hope for them.

After an hour, the caravan stopped at an unlikely bend on a winding mountain road.

"This is it," Agus announced.

We got out and unloaded. While teams of men lifted the ends of each crate, others bundled tarps with the fruit and carried them on their shoulders. Agus led the way as we formed a single line and descended into the jungle, following a mountain stream down a steep, slippery hill until the sunlight disappeared, blocked by the canopy of trees.

Birdsong was all around us. I looked up to see them but the birds were elusive. But I did see an abundance of mangosteen, *duku*, *salak*, and star fruit dangling from the trees. Agus had assured me the release site had plenty of fruit, leaves, roots, and bark, all the foods that would make up the majority of the monkeys' diet. As we walked deeper into the tropical forest, it felt like we'd entered an Eden for monkeys.

Agus stopped at a place where the water pooled. The crates were gently placed on the ground within five feet of one another, and as Barb had instructed, the fruit was placed near the crates.

The monkeys peered through the slats. They were silent, as if holding their breath in anticipation. I lifted my camera and, in unison, the men opened the doors. The monkeys shot from the crates like bullets from a gun. Within three seconds they were gone. I was left with only one image on my camera — a shot of the men with their hands on the crate doors, and the blurred, ghostlike images of the monkeys in flight.

I looked up, searching the canopy, but they were nowhere to be seen. We lingered briefly, taking in the moment and the beauty of the place, and then left, leaving the crates and food behind.

Back at the hotel I plunged into the pool, and then joined Jon, Guy, and Nat for lunch. Guy was surprised and pleased when I told him of our unexpected adventure.

"What about the other poor creatures you've left behind," he teased. But there was a cutting truth in his words. I had to make it better for those who were left behind. So when they headed off for a motorbike excursion, I went back to the enclosures.

Two men from the hotel staff met me there, and mixing pidgin English with a bit of Indonesian and a lot of pantomiming, I explained what I wanted to do.

We left together and arrived back at the cages an hour later with several long, thick ropes, planks of wood, buckets, bamboo mats, and one semi-hollowed log I'd found on the edge of the property.

We started with the monkey enclosure. The monkeys remained chained in the same places, and they watched with keen interest as we hung ropes from one side of the cage to the other, put up a tire swing, created wooden perches, and positioned accessible water wells using repurposed milk containers.

We started renovations on Twinkle's enclosure by unrolling a used bamboo blind, spreading it over most of the exposed wire in his cage. He stayed in the cage while we did this, never threatening. Instead, he was inquisitive, his head in the air and his nose active. When we finished the floor, he stepped on it, took another step, then another, and then danced, lifting his feet and turning in circles with obvious happiness. It may have been the first time his feet had touched a flat surface since he'd been taken from the wild, and his excitement was contagious. We all laughed as he pranced around the cage.

I lured Twinkle away from the door of the enclosure with a piece of watermelon. As he nibbled on it, one of the men moved the four-foot-long, two-foot-wide log into a corner of the cage. Then I walked to the corner of the cage behind the log and called Twinkle's name.

Twinkle headed toward me but was blocked by the log. He stopped, sniffed, and lifted his foot, touching the wood, assessing the intrusion. Then it was as if something deep inside his soul triggered a genetic understanding of the log's purpose. He ran around it several times, his joy apparent, and started excitedly digging into its center.

Finally, the three remaining monkeys were, as Agus had promised, released within their enclosure. I watched as the metal was cut from their necks and felt their relief. I thanked the men with a traditional bow and said, "*Terima kasih.*" The men thanked me in return, and I held myself back from giving them an American high five. I didn't have to. We were all clearly pleased by our accomplishments.

When I returned a few hours later, at dusk, the geese were still in the pond, two monkeys were playing on a rope, a third monkey was sitting on the tire swing, and Twinkle, my dear Twinkle, was asleep inside his log.

At sunrise the next morning, I sat down in the restaurant in a chair facing the Flores Sea. The same familiar waitress, a young lady with long, shiny black hair tied back in a ponytail, greeted me with a coffee and a generous plate of cut fruit. She was smiling.

"*Terima kasih,*" I said.

"I know what you do," she said in English as she placed the cup and plate on the table and stepped back. Then she put one hand over her heart and said, "Thank you, Monkey Lady."

I smiled and nodded, feeling overwhelmed by her gesture.

A few moments later, a waiter approached. He stopped a few feet from me, and when I looked up at him, he stood at attention, beat a fist on his chest above his heart twice, and said, "Monkey Lady."

As he turned away, another man approached and did the same thing, followed by another waitress who clasped her palms together in front of her chest and bowed. "Thank you, Monkey Lady," she said.

As she walked away, my eyes followed. Gathered near the kitchen door, the staff were watching me. I waved, prompting smiles and nods in return. And then it hit: a rush of emotion. My eyes filled with tears, my face flushed, and I nodded my thanks with a quivering smile.

Their demonstration fell like a ray of sunshine on a stormy day. Their hearts, too, had been pained by what they'd witnessed.

On the path to do what's right, we're never alone. My experience has been that when we speak for those who cannot, an army builds and walks with us. In rescuing the monkeys, I did not lead the charge. Instead, I was only one last voice of reason, one that followed, and helped facilitate, what many others, both hotel guests and staff, had wanted before me.

Afterward, I stayed in touch with Agus by email. His replies were always short, but he let me know the animals were fine and the hotel was following the feeding regime I'd suggested. Then, six months after the monkey release, I received an unexpected email. Agus was very pleased to tell me that he'd closed the hotel's zoo permanently, and the three remaining monkeys in captivity — the mother and her two children — had been taken to the release site and set free. The four geese had been placed in a welcoming home. The only sad news was that Twinkle the porcupine had died.

For me, I felt some relief knowing that the unnecessary suffering Twinkle had endured was over. I only hoped he'd died peacefully, in his log. My brief relationship with a porcupine had shown me that gentle souls come in all forms and that they, like us, can experience joy. Without his prickly exterior, Twinkle was a dog, imprisoned in a cage, yet grateful for the smallest kindness. I trusted his soul was now in a better place.

That night the stars were bright in the Southern Hemisphere. Each person who'd spoken out on behalf of these animals had also, unwittingly, raised the already-present consciousness of the zoo's keeper, Agus Tabah Wardhana. Sure, the threat of lost tourism dollars to the hotel may have influenced the first release, but the second act — the shuttering of the zoo — was fueled by compassion. It was further proof of the transformative power that is created when we raise our collective voice to demand change.

Jo-Anne McArthur

MONKEY

I met photojournalist Jo-Anne McArthur on Facebook. I was surfing my feed one day and was stopped by an image. Instantly, the photograph of a pig's eye peering through the steel ventilation hole of a transport truck made me gasp. That one eye conveyed so much of the pig's despair. I shuddered. A tear dropped. My index finger clicked on the link, and I was taken to We Animals.

A lightbulb went off when I saw Jo-Anne's name. She initiated the project called We Animals to document the plight of "the invisibles," as she calls them: animals used for food, for clothing, in research, and for entertainment. We'd both been profiled for our animal welfare work in the book *One Hundred & One Reasons to Get Out of Bed* by Natasha Milne and Barbara Royal, and I was intrigued to learn more about the investigative photojournalist and author, who'd been the subject of the highly acclaimed documentary *The Ghosts in Our Machine*.

In one photograph, Jo-Anne had been able to tell a story that would have taken me a week to write. She has a profound ability to affect people with images so that they're moved to create change, and one of her gifts to the world is a database of photographs that she offers for free to campaigns dedicated to ending animal suffering. With her unique talent, Jo-Anne shows us the world, perhaps not as we'd wish it, but how it truly is, and provides us with plenty of opportunities to change it.

Her awakening came when she was twenty-one years old and on a hiking trip with friends in Ecuador. While walking through a mountain village, the young Canadian came across a monkey chained to the side of a building. As tourists gathered to snap pictures, using the monkey as a prop, she turned her lens on the helpless animal to document his sad story.

• • •

Baños, Ecuador

I can't remember a time when I didn't want to be around animals. It wasn't just that I loved animals, but I had a deep curiosity about them, as well as concern for them. For me, being with animals has always given me instant joy. I could even describe it as relief.

My parents let me be the way I was with animals even though they didn't feel as I did. We had birds at home, and I didn't want them caged, so they allowed me to let the birds fly around when I persisted in asking if they could be let out in the house. My sister and I also had rabbits and guinea pigs that we loved, but they were relegated to live in the garage, which made me sad. When the neighbor's dog, Duke, a shepherd/Rottie mix, barked and cried endlessly from being left outside throughout the year, I asked the neighbors if I could walk him. They agreed, and to this day I can recall the happiness I felt — and Duke's, too.

What I learned as a young person is that animals, whether wild or domesticated, are fascinating individuals, and that often, they need our care or reverence but aren't getting it. It wasn't until later in life that I learned that I could channel that concern for animals into transformative actions.

When I was twenty-one years old, I had an experience with a macaque monkey that changed my life. At the time, I was a student at the University of Ottawa, in Canada, studying human geography and English literature. I was on a hiking trip in the Andes Mountains in Ecuador, South America, with two friends from school. We were on our second day of a two-day hike and had spent most of it in the clouds on the lushly green volcanic mountain Tungurahua.

That afternoon, we made our way to the popular tourist town of Baños to spend the night. As we entered the town, passing houses, I stopped when I noticed a group of people had gathered around a building. As I got closer I realized they were looking at a monkey who was chained to the bars of a windowless sill. He was alone and vulnerable, perched between a concrete block and a pillar with no water or food source. His hair was a mixed color of gray and tan with a dark crown on his head. It struck me that he had absolutely nowhere to go but that sill.

The sight of him had attracted attention, but not in a good way. People were stopping to have their pictures taken with him. He responded by straining against the chain to reach into their jackets and bags for food. And he found it and quickly ate it, causing laughter.

I stopped to take photos as well. This was an epiphanic moment for me. While everyone was taking photos because they thought the situation was funny, or unique, or cute, I took pictures because I thought that what I was witnessing was terribly cruel. It dawned on me at the time that if I took photos, I could share them and somehow change his situation. I wanted to show this picture all around so that people would react with sadness and dismay. This wasn't funny or unique or cute! This was an animal living as a slave.

This short encounter made me realize that I saw animals differently from how many other people did. I saw both individual creatures and their circumstances. I wondered about their history — where they came from and where their family was.

This was also a moment when I realized I could use my camera for change. Until that time, I'd been searching for "my story." That's what photojournalists do: We search for stories. But more so, we look for something that is ours, something we can return to, something we care deeply about. I realized that no one was photographing animals the way I did, the way I could.

After this revelation, I started turning my camera toward animals as much as I could. I call these "the invisibles." They are the animals who are right in front of us, and yet we fail to see or really consider them. A project began to take shape. I knew I wanted my animal work to be called *We Animals*. It would be a reminder that we are *all* animals — different but with so much unexplored commonality. My goal was to take photos that bridged the gap, that brought us closer to the experiences of our animal kin, in hopes that maybe we'd learn to treat them better, to respect them, to not abuse them or see them as objects, as "other."

I became really driven by this project because I saw that very few photographers were documenting "the invisibles." While it's perfectly fine to photograph cats and dogs or the charismatic megafauna on the cover of *National Geographic*, who was looking at the billions of animals we keep in factory farms, fur farms, labs, and the small cages of roadside zoos? So many of these animals are totally out of sight. That's part of why we sort of go along on our merry way, eating them, wearing them, using cosmetics that are tested on them. We don't see, we don't know. I resolved to lift the blinders by taking pictures. By going to the places no one gets to see, such as pig farms in Spain, mink farms in Sweden, sheep sale yards in Australia, and slaughter- houses in Tanzania and Canada.

My work devastates me. Seeing hens crammed into cages so small they can't turn around, standing on their dead cage mates to alleviate the pain in their feet from standing on wire flooring. The pigs unable to turn around in gestation crates. The foxes in fur farms gnaw- ing at the bars until their gums are raw and infected, trying to find a way out. I wanted to save all these animals, but I couldn't. I've met hundreds of thousands of them now. The best way I could help them was by making their lives and their suffering known. I've learned that perseverance is an important part of what we all do in life, especially when it comes to creating social change.

After years in the field on all seven continents — okay, I didn't land on Antarctica, but I bobbed around it on a Sea Shepherd boat for three months! — this work has opened my eyes to the immense suffering of animals. When you're faced with it — with thousands of animals crammed into one stinky, urine-saturated barn — and you look into their eyes and they look into yours, the suffering becomes real. It's tangible, and it's worse than any horror movie. I get to leave, but they can't. And this is all because there are so many of us — and so many of us wanting cheap meat without thinking about where it comes from.

Like us, nonhuman animals experience all sorts of complex emotions, from jealousy to fear to silliness. Lots of animals have a fun sense of humor. But I've witnessed them locked up all over the world, and their eyes look at you full of questions. That's the thing about these animals: They have all the questions and we have all the answers. They seem to ask, *What are you doing to me? Are you going to hurt me? Are you going to take away my babies? What's next?* Some animals are despondent. Others remain wild, or brave, and try to fight against their confines. I'm not sure which makes me sadder.

Yet I have hope. It's an exciting time to be an animal rights photojournalist. The work — mine and others' — is being published, discussed, and recognized. Finally, people are starting to look, and see, and change.

• • •

Jo-Anne McArthur is an award-winning photojournalist, author, and humane educator. Her incredible work has been used in investigations, campaigns, protests, and academic pursuits around the world. It has contributed to the shuttering of animal-breeding facilities and has been used to create animal-protection laws. She offers the free use of her images to animal welfare organizations.

Jo-Anne is the author of *We Animals*, a book based on her life's work, and a second book, *Captive*. Jo-Anne's other initiative is the Unbound project, where she highlights women on the front lines of animal advocacy. Photographs for the We Animals project have been shot in more than fifty countries and have contributed to more than two hundred global campaigns to end the suffering of billions of animals.

Have you ever rescued a ladybug?

No, but I do remember saving a dragonfly who was drowning in a lake. He spent a half hour on my hand, drying himself off.

Name three things that make you happy.

Animals. Learning. Loving.

What one book, documentary, or speech has had a profound effect on you?

There are many animal documentaries that I'd recommend, starting with *Blackfish*, *Sharkwater*, *The Ghosts in Our Machine*, *The Last Animals*, *Carnage: Swallowing the Past*, and the wonderful books by Marc Bekoff, Carl Safina, Peter Singer, Lori Gruen, and so many others.

Regarding your food choices, how do you describe yourself?

A joyful vegan.

If you had one message to deliver to others, what would it be?

Every choice we make matters and affects the lives of others. The status quo keeps us on this mindless path, unawakened to what's happening behind closed doors. The kinder choices, those that take into account the lives of others, are always the right choices, and those choices will always feel good.

We're so lucky to exist on this improbable, living earth but for one tiny moment in time. We strive for happiness and for lives of purpose and meaning. We seek comfort and peace and freedom from harm. In that, we differ little from the other lucky animals who inhabit this beautiful place. If we can all make kindness and compassion a priority in our day-to-day lives, and if we can treat all others the way we hope to be treated — with kindness and care and respect — we'd be one big collective step closer to a world where we can all live free from harm.

If you had one wish that was guaranteed to come true, what would it be?

All forms of animal exploitation would end today.

What advice do you have for people who say that they want to help animals in need but are too debilitated by what they witness?

Animal abuse is an absolute emergency for billions of innocent victims, and each of us can step up to help end it. We can end it by not buying and consuming their bodies. It's a way of curbing, not only animal cruelty, but climate change, pollution, and the global food shortage. If we're hurt, debilitated, or paralyzed by what we witness, we can just change what we eat.

Carole Tomko

ELEPHANT

I met and became friends with one of the "most influential women in cable television" in 1989, in New York City, before she reached that level of recognition. Carole Tomko and I had been hired by Cable News Network (CNN) cofounder Reese Schonfeld and former CNN vice president Ted Kavanau to help run a nightly national news program called *Crimewatch Tonight*. Carole was the production unit manager, and I was the assistant managing editor, big roles for two girls in their twenties. When the show ended, I went to CNN and Carole went to the Discovery Channel, where she began changing the world.

Carole was a multitasker the likes of whom I'd never seen before, and her work ethic undoubtedly helped her rise at the company. I remember a sleepover at her home in Bethesda, Maryland. It was 9 PM, and while I sat in her kitchen, catching up over a glass of Chardonnay, she simultaneously screened a TV show and responded to emails. Over the years, I proudly watched my friend hold positions as president and general manager of several networks and divisions at Discovery Communications.

In 1997, shortly after the launch of Animal Planet, Carole became its executive producer and director of development and production. The rest is history. The channel shed light on the mystery and lives of other species, making inroads to animal programming like never before. The channel confirmed what many of us already knew: that television viewers like animals enough to support a channel entirely devoted to them.

In 2013, after more than twenty years with Discovery, Carole went to work with Microsoft cofounder, philanthropist, and visionary Paul Allen and his sister, Jody, as the general manager and creative director of their company, Vulcan Productions. The mission of Vulcan is to "find smart solutions for some of the world's biggest challenges," and Carole's job is to share and help make progress on those solutions. Vulcan brings together commercial, philanthropic, research-driven, policy-based, and innovation ventures under one roof, creating a new model for driving awareness and change. Storytelling is one of the tools in the company's vast toolbox.

Like the writers, photographers, and editors who work with her to create meaningful documentaries, series, multigenre content, and social media campaigns, Carole is an unsung hero. And for as long as I've known her, she's been happy with that. Ego doesn't drive her. The power to create meaningful change does.

• • •

Okavango Delta, Botswana

When I was offered a job at the Discovery Channel, it was a fledgling cable network. I loved the content and jumped at the chance. Eventually, we launched Animal Planet, and I became the head of development and an executive producer on a series called *The Crocodile Hunter*. This position was the start of my journey with — and dedication to — wildlife.

Unlike many others, I didn't have any one epiphany with animals that changed my life. I guess you could say that a feeling of intense obligation and responsibility snuck up on me. As I've learned more about the environment, the oceans, and wildlife conservation and have had a chance to travel, I feel a growing need to protect the planet for future generations by sharing the story of what's happening to it. But in 2013, I did experience a profound connection with an elephant that has continued to inspire me.

To create change in the world, you sometimes need proof that there is need for change. This was the case in Africa, where research-ers have estimated that elephant populations are declining at a rate of twenty-five to thirty thousand annually. The Great Elephant Cen-sus [GEC] was a global collaborative effort — initiated and funded by Paul Allen — to count the largest living terrestrial animal on the planet, the African savanna elephant. It was the first-ever pan-African census of savanna elephants and was a massive undertaking, span-ning eighteen countries. It took more than ninety scientists, six NGOs, and dozens of conservationists on the ground nearly three years to complete.

In 2013, while the philanthropic division of Vulcan was launching the GEC, I learned there was a pregnant elephant at a place called Abu Camp, located in the Okavango Delta in Botswana, Africa. The camp is part research/conservation station, part rehabilitation center for orphaned elephants, and it's an amazing safari lodge. The herd is free-roaming for most of the day. When they're in camp, visitors pay for the privilege of spending time in close proximity to them, which in turn pays for the elephants' care. I had just started working at Vulcan and knew how rare it was to capture natural history footage of an elephant being born in the wild, so when I learned an elephant named Kitimetse was about to give birth, I sent a crew to capture this important moment.

I coordinated the crew from my office in Seattle, and on a starry, moonless night in November, our amazing partners and crew filmed Kiti giving birth at Abu Camp. Kiti's labor was long, so the team had plenty of time to debate the calf's name. Eventually, they chose Naledi, the word for *star* in Setswana, a local native language.

We filmed with the latest infrared cameras, and even though the human eye couldn't see a thing, the cameras helped us witness some-thing extraordinary. Kiti delivered Naledi in the middle of the night. While trumpeting and performing what appeared to be elephant celebrations, Kiti kicked dirt all over the newborn. At first it wasn't clear why she was doing it. Then it became obvious. She was trying to cover up the smell of a new baby so other animals wouldn't know and come near.

When I first saw the footage, it was overwhelming. It's one thing to hear that an elephant is giving birth. It's another thing to see the actual footage and watch how the herd treats her. They were all present for the birth. Even wild elephants who were familiar with the Abu herd, but didn't live with them, came to be part of the event.

We didn't plan to make a documentary about Naledi, but six weeks after giving birth, Kiti died unexpectedly, orphaning Naledi. Cathy, the matriarch of the herd, miraculously started lactating even though she had never given birth to her own calf. But she didn't have enough milk and didn't know how to take care of the baby. Naledi couldn't get enough milk and her health began failing. Luckily, Dr. Mike Chase, the biologist and zoologist assigned to oversee the Abu herd and who was present at Naledi's birth, was still on hand as part of the elephant census work. He intervened and established a plan to save her life. Wellie Jana, a manager at the camp, was assigned the full-time, round-the-clock job of bonding with Naledi, to entice her to drink milk from a bottle. It took weeks, but eventually Naledi came around.

Naledi's story kept delivering so many twists and turns that we decided to keep shooting as her life unfolded and progressed and she was eventually reintroduced to the herd. As filmmakers, we were presented with a beautiful intertwining of two stories: a young scientist tackling a massive undertaking of a pan-African survey with partners across the continent, and this single baby elephant struggling to survive. The result was a documentary called *Naledi: A Baby Elephant's Tale*. When you watch it, it's hard not to be in awe of the handlers who dedicate their lives to this herd and to Abu Camp for its work bringing awareness to elephant issues.

It was a busy time. While working on Naledi's story, we were collaborating with two other teams to produce the documentaries *Mind of a Giant* and *The Ivory Game*. While filming the latter, Richard Ladkani and Kief Davidson placed themselves squarely in the middle of the ivory trade to tell the stories of the activists who are in the field trying to stop poaching and the trade from Africa to China.

When I look back, 2016 was the year of the elephant. We

produced three documentaries on elephants in one year with the goal of striking at both the supply of and the demand for ivory products.

Working on these films at the same time gave me three concentric perspectives of elephants. Naledi's story is emblematic of the struggle of the African elephant and is a story of hope and inspiration. *Mind of a Giant* reveals the intelligence of these incredible creatures and their complex consciousness. And *The Ivory Game* follows the ivory trafficking route from Africa to China. *Naledi* showed the devotion of many to save one elephant, while *The Ivory Game* outlines the destruction caused by the people who poach one elephant every fifteen minutes, just for its tusk.

Meanwhile, the Great Elephant Census wrapped up. After nearly three years of work, Vulcan released the results in September 2016. The data showed that savanna elephant populations declined by 30 percent between 2007 and 2014. This makes it clear that the current rate of decline, at 8 percent annually, puts this iconic species on an unsustainable trajectory.

As a team, we learned that by combining storytelling with philanthropic investment, technology-driven innovation, and policy, we can transform audiences from viewers into engaged activists who want to address the critical issues of our time. I've learned there are lots of solutions, many of which provide a positive economic impact. The solutions include shifts in personal behavior, responsible consumer choices, and influencing governments to act.

At my job, we have a hashtag we like to use: #onlyatVulcan. What we accomplish truly could only happen at a place like Vulcan. When you think about what Vulcan sets out to do, the scale and the scope of it, it's mind-boggling. I certainly didn't know it when I accepted the position, but it's clear to me that this is exactly where I am supposed to be. It's a privilege to work under the leadership of Paul Allen and with a team of incredible leaders who don't know the word *impossible*. They are all there because we are tackling issues that many others consider impossible, and they are in a constant state of learning and curiosity. I can't imagine doing any job other than producing stories that move people.

• • •

Research from the Great Elephant Census became the necessary fuel to ignite countries and their representatives to take action against the illegal ivory trade. Within two weeks of the release of the findings, the International Union for Conservation of Nature (IUCN) called on countries to close their domestic ivory trades. Within a month, all 180-plus member nations of the Convention on International Trade in Endangered Species (CITES) not only agreed that legal ivory markets must be closed but they shut down a measure that would have allowed one-time-only sales of ivory stockpiles. Within three months, the Chinese government vowed to end the ivory trade in its country by 2017.

Unlike people who had an epiphany with a single animal that caused them to take action, Carole says her path has been consistent and steady. Her connection with animals most often starts when she meets the human beings who are working to protect them. Naledi, now weighing in at over two thousand pounds and described by her caretakers as being rambunctious with a loving personality, remains with her herd in Botswana. Carole has been able to share her connection with the elephant by producing the documentary *Naledi: A Baby Elephant's Tale*. In just a few short years, she has also helped deliver many more award-winning projects: *Racing Extinction, The Ivory Game, Ocean Warriors, Mind of a Giant, Unseen Enemy, Body Team 12, We the Economy, We the Voters, #ISurvivedEbola*, and *STEP*.

As a strategic thinker with the privilege of working for a philanthropist and visionary, Carole brings scientists, researchers, conservationists, NGOs, government agencies, and protectors together. The result has been documentaries, series, and social media and impact campaigns that excite, educate, and motivate people to seek global change for all animals — including humans.

Have you ever rescued a ladybug?

I've rescued ladybugs when they were trapped inside by opening the window and letting them out. Sometimes, when they've been crawling on the wall, I've used my hand as a transport, letting them crawl on it and delivering them to a railing outside. I've always been told ladybugs are good luck. I believe it!

Name three things that make you happy.

My family, including my parents and my kids, Nicholas and Grace. My parents taught me the importance of getting back up after you fall down, which was particularly important since I was a gymnast growing up! My kids have taught me about joy and looking at the world through a lens of wonder and curiosity. Walking the beach rejuvenates me, no matter where I am. I can hear myself think after a good walk on the beach. And lying on the ground with our two dogs, Roo and Louie, just sticking my face in their fur and massaging behind their ears.

What one book, documentary, or speech has had a profound effect on you?

There's no single book that has had a profound effect on me, but I do remember reading *Reflections of Eden* by Biruté Galdikas and being moved by her story. Similarly, Terry Grosz's book *Wildlife Wars: The Life and Times of a Fish and Game Warden* was powerful.

Being knee-deep in the documentary world, it's hard for me to think of just one doc. A good documentary can define problems and drive awareness of an issue. A great documentary reaches you not just in your head but in your heart. It inspires action and creates impact. My job is to create tools and stories that reach audiences from students to influencers and policymakers.

Regarding your food choices, how do you describe yourself?

A conscious eater focused on sustainability. While I was working with Louie Psihoyos, he radically changed my view on seafood and of course red meat. While I haven't fully given up either, I have drastically reduced my consumption and consider which brands and products I purchase to ensure my choices are not degrading the environment.

If you had one wish that was guaranteed to come true, what would it be?

For a global wish: world peace. For a selfish wish: that Nicholas and Grace will live full and healthy lives, be agents of change, enjoy every high and low of their lives, and that they'll pass along both a love of exploring this amazing planet and the message of the planet itself to their heirs.

What advice do you have for people who say that they want to help animals in need but are too debilitated by what they witness?

You don't need to be in the field to help animals. There is an endless list of ways people can help. My contribution is using storytelling to drive awareness and behavior change. Others contribute with technology or by helping with policy change. The simple act of sharing is so powerful and creates a ripple effect. Every day we make choices with what we eat, purchase, and consume and with how we live. If everyone was more conscious and purposeful with their choices, they would help the environment — and therefore animals. And we can all help support those who are dedicating their lives to animals by sharing their stories or financially supporting their work.

When people get behind saving another species and they become stewards for the environment, it creates a powerful sense of community.

Susan Rockefeller

PTEROPOD

There are angels in our waters. They are small and difficult to see, but their divine grace has kept our oceans healthy for an eternity — until now. For one dedicated filmmaker and conservationist, these often-unacknowledged little miracles put the delicate balance of life into perspective and have given her an unfaltering desire to ensure their survival.

I met Susan Rockefeller (then Susan Cohn) while sailing in the Tyrrhenian Sea — off the northeast coast of Sardinia, Italy — in the summer of 2001. The occasion was a thirty-five-day cruise to celebrate the joint birthdays of our mutual friends Dun Gifford and David Rockefeller Jr. (then Sue's fiancé and now her husband). Within hours of meeting, Sue and I had donned goggles and were underwater, exploring. When we emerged, treading water, we talked about all the trash we'd seen — plastic, toilet paper, and bottles — and how few fish.

We soon discovered our common interests. Sue was a documentary filmmaker and writer, and I was an environmental television producer and journalist. We were sailing on separate boats, but at sunset, we came together to discuss marine life and the politics of saving the seas. We also took time to sing, dance, and laugh — a lot — which cemented our enduring friendship.

Sue was raised in Larchmont, New York. Her earliest memories are of the beach, where she remembers watching seabirds run up and down the shore, in sync with the ebb and flow of the waves. She's always been sensitive to nature, and she spent most of her childhood outside, connecting with frogs and toads. Inside, she kept gerbils, hamsters, and guinea pigs, which she believes was testament to her parents' tolerance for childhood curiosity. Her parents were kind to all animals and people and made a point to teach her about empathy in a simple but profound way: not only through their words but through their actions.

Following graduation from college with a degree in environmental studies, Sue moved to Alaska to live with Inuit and Iñupiat communities in Shungnak on the Kobuk River, north of the Arctic Circle, as well as in Selawik and Kotzebue. In these villages of hunter-gatherers, she introduced people to new vegetable-growing techniques that would help lengthen their short growing season. Those techniques enabled them to supplement their meat-based diets with vegetables throughout the year. The three years Sue spent with Inuit communities proved life-changing for her. She saw directly how keenly people are connected to other animals, plants, the ocean, and the climate, and how we rely on these connections for our existence.

One of the many things I admire about Sue is her thirst for knowledge. She's a voracious reader, always interested in who is making the world a better place and how they're doing it, what they think, and what they know. Her insatiable curiosity means her free-thinking mind is always evolving. Sue's game-changing, deep connection with another species didn't happen until she was fifty years old, and it wasn't in person. It was, however, the piece of a puzzle she didn't know she'd been searching for.

• • •

New York City, USA

There is an ethereal animal called a pteropod that lives in our oceans. At just one to two centimeters long, these tiny zooplankton are sometimes called "sea angels" because of the two large wings (also called parapodias) on their feet. I didn't know anything about this sea snail until I was fifty years old. When I finally learned about them, they changed my understanding of the balance of life.

I was curled up on the couch of my New York City apartment reading "The Darkening Sea," an article by Elizabeth Kolbert in the *New Yorker*. The piece was about the effects of climate change and ocean acidification. It referenced the pteropod as a species that was seriously affected by both. An award-winning environmental journalist, Kolbert explained that pteropods are a critical building block for food in the marine ecosystem and that they're a source of food for many fish, as well as the ocean's largest animal, the blue whale.

Ocean acidification — caused by too much carbon dioxide being released into the atmosphere — is devastating the pteropod population, along with that of many crustaceans, by causing their calcium exoskeletons, or shells, to become thin and brittle. Kolbert stressed that if acidification continues, the pteropod could lose its ability to produce its shell and, therefore, could cease to exist entirely. The effect of their demise would be disastrous for the world.

Kolbert's research and her compelling writing struck home and took me back to Alaska, where I'd lived in my early twenties. I saw the awe-inspiring northern lights. I watched caribou herds and their newborn calves grazing on the expansive tundra. I witnessed schools of shimmering chum salmon headed upstream by the thousands to spawn. It gave me a perspective on life rooted in ecological abundance, indigenous wisdom, and profound gratitude for this miraculous planet we call home. I understood what Kolbert was illustrating — the importance of saving what is most precious and most vulnerable. I was touched by the fact that so many other animals depend on this tiny creature for life. I realized that if these beautiful, almost angelic, creatures are at risk of disintegrating, the consequences would have momentous ripple effects. This realization rocked my understanding of climate change and ocean health. All of a sudden, I felt keenly the plight of the pteropod, the taxing pressure to survive in an ocean environment that's too acidic. I began to comprehend that humanity's greed and overuse of fossil fuels had created an environment that could lead to the collapse of our oceanic ecosystems. It was apparent that we needed to prevent any further increases in CO_2 emissions if we wanted our planet to thrive.

This moment of enlightenment came when I fully grasped the reality of what was going on in the oceans — that life is an intricate web and that each creature on this earth has an intrinsic beauty and purpose. There is small and invisible life on this planet that supports us all. The pteropod is one example of these often-unacknowledged species, and there are countless more, ranging from microbes that support soil health to the millions of marine creatures in the sea.

Reading Kolbert's story put everything in perspective for me. It was the piece of a puzzle that fit together with everything I'd learned about ocean acidification up to that point. The message of the article was clear: The simple pteropod is a crucial building block, and the beauty and bounty of our oceans are dependent on these tiny creatures. When I realized this, I was inspired: I wanted to protect this fragile web of life. The realization also motivated me. I wanted to keep our earth more vibrant and beautiful, to celebrate life in all its forms, and perhaps most of all, to be thankful for all beings, big and small. With the human population of our planet expected to reach nine billion by 2050, I wondered how we could protect those beings, reverse the trend toward the extinction of species, and give hope to the intricate and mysterious web.

Alongside two close friends, I decided to coproduce a film called *A Sea Change* to educate others on the effects of carbon dioxide on our waters. Specifically, the film documents how the pH balance of the ocean has changed, with a 30 percent increase in acidification since the beginning of the Industrial Revolution. It cites experts who predict that at the current rate of increase in carbon dioxide emissions, acidity will continue to rise in kind. They say that over the next century, the world's fisheries will collapse into a state that could last millions of years.

Following *A Sea Change*, I produced a second film about our oceans. *Mission of Mermaids: A Love Letter to the Ocean* links the myth of the mermaid to ocean health. It's a poetic ode to the seas and a plea for their protection. With the objective of igniting global conversation about ocean protection and conservation, I created a line of message-inspired jewelry. To keep the conversation going, and to highlight the work being done by people driving positive change, I founded *Musings*, a digital magazine, to address complex global issues in an easily digestible format. The magazine profiles thought leaders in entrepreneurship and responsible innovation who provide inspirational calls to action.

I joined the board of the nonprofit Oceana in 2011. The group works to save oceans using sound scientific research and global advocacy. This work has been extremely rewarding because you can see the effects of being on a team of people with the same mission.

Thanks to that one moment of enlightenment inspired by the pteropod, I've become truly passionate about helping others understand the fragility of our ecosystem. I live each day in wonder and mystery, thrilled by the beauty and bounty of this earth. I hope to demonstrate how we can bring back its bounty and resilience by moving toward a greener economy and giving our oceans time to rest and rebound from our relentless extraction of fish. Humans are encroaching into so many environments that much of our biodiversity is at risk. We need everyone at the table to help celebrate all aspects of life, to connect with empathy for all animals, and to work together to protect this precious place we call home.

• • •

As a documentary filmmaker, writer, and artist, Susan Rockefeller uses the power of storytelling and art to inspire awareness and to mobilize action across a range of environmental and philanthropic causes.

As a conservationist and ocean advocate, she is creating global change that helps animals and human beings. Since its founding in 2001, Oceana has achieved close to two hundred victories and protected more than 3.5 million square miles of ocean.

Have you ever rescued a ladybug?

As a child, I would muck around ponds and the woods near my home and collect frogs and take care of them. I also once took care of a bird with a broken wing. When it comes to rescuing ladybugs, I have only done so metaphorically. I am inspired and moved to protect those other ladybugs — the pteropods and the millions of creatures on this earth who do not have a voice to protect themselves.

Name three things that make you happy.

Family, art, and nature.

What one book, documentary, or speech has had a profound effect on you?

My Traitor's Heart by Rian Malan. It is one of the most honest autobiographical accounts of living in South Africa and is chillingly brilliant in its honesty about race, apartheid, and the human heart. As for a documentary, I would say *The Salt of the Earth* about the work of photographer Sebastião Salgado.

Regarding your food choices, how do you describe yourself?

I am a flexitarian. My diet is 90 to 95 percent plant-based and the rest is mostly grass-fed meat, wild salmon, local lobsters in Maine, and pasture-fed chicken, eggs, and artisan cheeses.

If you had one message to deliver to others, what would it be?

To be on a journey to lead with love and protect what is precious to you.

If you had one wish that was guaranteed to come true, what would it be?

That we all learn to lead with love and have empathy toward ourselves and all sentient beings.

What advice do you have for people who say that they want to help animals in need but are too debilitated by what they witness?

Start with one small action. Once you're on the path, you will meet others who will support you and give energy and the conviction to do more. Take one step at a time and begin. It can start with rescuing a ladybug; it can start with helping a blind person cross the street. Start small and connect. Open your heart and see where your path will take you.

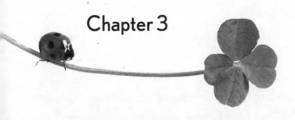

Chapter 3

DRAGON, MANTA, ORANGUTAN

Preservation for the Good of All

Komodo Island, Indonesia

There's only one place in the world where the man-eating Komodo dragon still lives in the wild: in the archipelago of the Lesser Sunda Islands in Indonesia. The prehistoric monitor lizard is said to have evolved from a species of lizard that originated in Asia forty million years ago. Fossils in Australia prove it took its current form while living there. Then, around fifteen million years ago, at a time when the Asian and Australian continents were still connected, it moved north into Indonesia. But when the oceans rose, it divided the continents, and the Komodo dragons became stranded on some of the most remote islands in the world. Today, according to the International Union for Conservation of Nature (IUCN), the lizard is a vulnerable species, with only three thousand left in the wild. They are known to live on the islands of Flores, Gili Montang, Gili Dasami, Rinca, and Komodo in the Flores Sea.

In 1980, in an effort to prevent the dragon's extinction — and to preserve the biodiversity of the region, both on land and in the water — the government of Indonesia created Komodo National

Park. The dragon is threatened by the increasing encroachment of people and, according to park officials, the poaching of Timor deer, the dragon's primary food source. Surrounding these islands are some of the richest marine environments in the world, featuring coral reefs, mangroves, and seagrass beds. The thriving ecosystems are home to more than a thousand species of fish, dugong (similar to manatees), sharks, manta rays, whales, dolphins, and sea turtles.

In 2013, I was in the middle of an unexpected monkey rescue at the Jayakarta Suites hotel on Flores Island (see chapter 2) when my friend Guy Warwick convinced me to take the day off so he could make good on his promise to take me to see Komodo dragons in the wild. Though Komodo dragons still live on Flores, the best place to see them is the national park on Komodo Island, which is a day-long roundtrip boat ride from Flores.

We left from the seaside town of Labuan Bajo; the group included my husband, Jon; Guy and his partner, Natalie Bovill; and our mutual friend Gonzalo Sanchez Villa, who captained the boat, since he'd made the trip before.

With bags stuffed with towels, snorkels, chips, sandwiches, and soft drinks, we climbed aboard a rented twenty-eight-foot runabout and were greeted by the moldy, rotting fish stench characteristic of a well-used, rarely cleaned boat. The smell was so putrid we considered asking for another boat but decided we didn't have enough time. The roundtrip to and from Komodo would take all day, and we needed to get going. However, aside from the smell, the day was perfect: the sun shining, the temperature 95 degrees, and the water a spectacularly clear aqua blue. For two hours we sped among lush green, volcanic mountains jutting from the sea, passing only two other boats on our journey.

At Komodo, we entered a bay lined with a white sand beach and beyond that a rocky landscape. As the boys tied the boat to the wooden pier, I scanned the long beach with its backdrop of rocky hills. The scene was eerily quiet and void of other people, like some-thing out of a *Planet of the Apes* movie.

Admittedly, I hadn't done much homework before the trip. I had assumed, since Komodo is a national park, that there would be facilities, an element of structure, and safety measures. I was wrong. We were about to become live bait for one of humankind's few predators.

Guy relished the natural tension of the moment and began spouting unsettling facts designed to scare us, most likely details gleaned from a book by naturalist Sir David Attenborough that he'd read when he was twelve. Guy is the most well-read person I've ever met, and I've long suspected him of having a photographic memory. He was in his element, using his twisted sense of humor to set a hair-raising tone as we hiked into unfenced dragon territory.

"They've eaten lots of tourists and attacked God knows how many others," he said casually, as we walked a narrow dirt trail to a tiny building marked with a Komodo National Park sign.

"People rarely survive attacks," he added.

A park ranger named Maday greeted us outside the building. Guy conversed with him in Indonesian, and he relayed that the fee, if it included a ranger escort, would be 1,150,000 rupiah, or about 120 US dollars. "It's forty-five dollars if we want him to come with us," Guy said. "Give it to him!" we responded.

When Maday then grabbed a six-foot-long pronged stick as if it was a loaded rifle, my confidence in his protection was dashed. Jon and Gonzalo obviously had the same thoughts because they im-mediately took the two remaining sticks that were propped against the building.

As we set forth on a guided nature tour to see Komodo dragons in the wild, four words kept repeating in my head: "Lions, tigers, and bears."

Guy took the lead with our guide, conversing in Indonesian

and English; Jon and Gonzalo paired behind them; and Nat and I followed, clinging to each other.

"Maday says not to go off the path alone," Guy relayed. "Apparently, a Japanese tourist left his tour group on a photo-taking mission and was eaten. Also, he says a German tourist disappeared here. They can't prove he was eaten because a body was never found, but they did find his glasses."

A minute later, after more conversing with Maday, Guy turned to us again, grimacing.

"Sadly," he said, his British accent dragging the word, "a native boy was attacked in 2009 and didn't survive. He was only eight and had stepped into the bush to have a wee."

"Shut the fuck up," someone said, and we all laughed.

"There," Maday said enthusiastically, pointing past a field to our right.

Like a bunch of prairie dogs, we stood on our toes, peering into an area of scrub twenty-five feet away. The bushes were moving, and I could see a tail, but whatever was going on was just far enough away to be hidden from view.

"Follow," the guide said, stepping into tall grass.

Guy, Jon, and Gonzalo did as instructed while Natalie and I stayed behind.

"They're nuts," she said.

"Absolutely nuts," I said. "But are we more stupid standing here by ourselves? They've got the sticks."

"Good point," she said, wincing before taking a step into the grass. I grabbed the back of her shirt and followed.

One thing I did know about Komodo dragons was that they render their victims helpless by holding them down with sharp, curved claws and by piercing their bodies with knife-like teeth while depositing poisonous venom and deadly bacteria.

I was petrified. My mother had often warned me of the dangers of following others, saying, "Just because Johnny jumps off a bridge doesn't mean you should." She was adamant I rely on my own intuition and common sense. As I followed the crowd directly into a den of prehistoric, two-hundred-pound, ten-foot-long, flesh-eating lizards, I instinctively knew I was being stupid.

Ten steps later I witnessed a frenzy. The desperate, glazed eyes of a young deer were looking through me as three huge dragons ripped her body apart. The boys were intrigued by the sight, while Natalie and I were horrified. I never had the stomach to watch predator-prey nature programs, and this one was live. Still holding Natalie, I turned from side to side like a spectator at a tennis match, scanning the brush and grass for more dragons that might be heading for us. Another fact I'd read on the Smithsonian's website: Komodo dragons can sense prey up to 2.5 miles away. They knew we were there.

The feeding dragons ranged in size from six to eight feet long. They were gray-colored and looked like just what they were, giant lizards. The deer's beautiful head jerked back and forth, and I could hear her bones break. I couldn't help imagining the deer's perspective: what it must feel like to be the hunted, and how frightening it would be to live on an island overrun with real-life monsters.

"Can we get out of here?" Natalie asked.

"Please," I begged.

The boys reluctantly turned and we continued down a dirt trail. Now everyone was on guard: alert and aware of the stupid situation we'd chosen to put ourselves in. Jon protectively took my hand.

Over the next hour, we walked a loop path and saw several other dragons, once being forced to stop while a ten-footer blocked our path, its legs bowed and neck lifted, sensing our scents with its tongue. Had it wanted to, it could have given chase and might have outrun one of us. We stood, frozen in our spots, prepared to spring. Luckily we didn't have to. Eventually it sauntered into the brush and we ran past.

Maday concluded our dragon adventure by dropping us off at a drink kiosk. Dripping with sweat from heat, exercise, fear, and anxiety, we climbed the steps of the elevated platform and ordered one of only two drink choices, warm Coca-Cola or Fanta; then we sat down at a picnic table. It was soon apparent why the kiosk was elevated. Below us, dragons lazed in the heat of the afternoon sun like dogs on grass on a warm summer day.

Even more surprisingly, a deer grazed twenty feet from one dragon. The scene was surreal. The island's animals had found a way of coexisting, including humans. Indigenous peoples had suffered plenty of dragon attacks, and yet they hadn't decimated the dragon population. I wondered why.

The answer became clear as we walked toward the boat on our way to leave the island. Standing between us and the pier were around twenty men, their arms laced with strings of white, blue, and black freshwater pearls. As we neared, they surrounded, pleading for us to purchase a string from them.

The price of one necklace was the equivalent of about five dollars. That amount of money would feed an island family for a week. I purchased twenty to use for silent auction prizes at animal charity fundraisers in America and Australia.

In 1977, Komodo and the islands and water surrounding it were designated by UNESCO as a biosphere reserve, since the region contains one of the world's richest marine environments. Komodo National Park was established in 1980 to protect the dragon populations on Komodo and the neighboring islands, mainly in the interests of science, to study evolution. Then, in 1991, the over 540,000-acre area was named a World Heritage Site. The designations serve to protect a host of species under threat, from the dragons and the Timor deer (who are threatened by poaching) to whale sharks and seahorses, who are being overfished. Because of all the efforts to preserve species while creating sustainable tourism, we were about to witness something extraordinary.

By 2 PM, we were back on the boat and the afternoon sun was peaking. The heat was unbearable, humid, and relentless; the air breathless and the sea calm and flat. Small puffs of cumulus clouds formed over distant islands but offered no respite from the searing sun. We neared Pantai Merah, or Pink Beach, known for its blush-colored sand created from a combination of limestone and foraminifera shells. We all wanted to dip in the ocean. While the beach was enticing, I'd read that Komodo dragons are good swimmers and will often launch from beaches on the island. To be safe, we decided to move to deeper water.

Gonzalo found a sandy spot at a depth of twenty feet. The moment he cut the engines, we were overboard.

Below, tiny fish the size of a thumb with colors that were off the charts of any spectrum swam by effortlessly, their backdrop a rainbow of pastel-colored corals. A sea turtle glided past an electric blue starfish splayed over purple coral. Striped angel fish meandered in pairs.

Gradually, our heads lifted from our underwater sightseeing, and as we treaded water, we chattered about our morning with dragons. Within five minutes, a swooshing sound caused us to turn, and we saw something that looked like a torpedo leaving the water. Airborne, the massive, black-colored animal flapped its wings before disappearing back into the Flores Sea.

"What was that?" I asked.

"That's a manta," Gonzalo responded from the boat's deck. "Did you see that span? It must have been twenty feet."

Within moments, in the same area, a second manta broke the surface with a magnificent display of aerial ballet, using its pectoral fins as wings.

There are few sights in the world that can render a person speechless. For me, this was one of them.

We quickly climbed the ladder of the boat solely to get a better view of the magic that was happening in our midst. Diamond-like sparkles danced on the top of the sapphire ocean as we stood silently in our bathing suits, goggles atop our heads, stirred to euphoria by the magnificent grace of this species.

We were rewarded — one last time — as the manta shared her joy and bestowed us with the gift of knowing that the work to protect one species benefits us all.

Guy Stevens

MANTA

The magical experience of witnessing the flight of a manta ray off Komodo Island was so exciting that it ignited a desire to know more about the species. In my search, I discovered the organization Manta Trust and its cofounder, Guy Stevens.

Stevens was born to nature-loving parents and grew up in the countryside of Dorset, England. As a kid, he loved dogs but says it was wild animals that really captivated him. At twelve years old, he was given a fish aquarium. The gift kindled an interest in fish. Over the next few years, he grew so obsessed with them that he became known to his friends as the "crazy fish guy." By the time he reached the University of Plymouth in Devon, England, his future was clear: He was going to become a marine biologist.

Stevens saw his first manta in 2003 while snorkeling at Lankan Beyru, a manta cleaning station in the North Malé Atoll of the Maldives. As he watched cleaner fish groom the skin, the gills, and even the mouths of the mantas, he became intrigued by the plankton-feeding rays and their massive twenty-three-foot-long spans. He declared then and there that he was going to study them. Since then, he's done that and much more. Stevens both highlights the animals' plight and works to protect them, collecting scientific data on the species to support arguments on behalf of their conservation.

Stevens describes mantas as the most graceful, gentle, and inquisitive animals in our oceans. He says they're extremely intelligent, with the largest brain of any fish, and with cognitive abilities among the most advanced of marine species. Despite this, mantas are threatened by fisheries and the gill plate trade — the buying and selling of their gill plates for use in traditional Chinese medicine. Like many marine mammals, they are also unfortunate bycatch victims, caught in nets set for other fish.

In 2008, while diving in Hanifaru Bay in the Baa Atoll of the Maldives, Guy created a lifelong relationship with a manta ray when he saved her life. He kindly gave permission to reprint this story from his book, *Manta: Secret Life of Devil Rays.*

• • •

Hanifaru Bay, Maldives

Every year I see dozens of manta rays with injuries caused by fishing line entanglements, usually because they've gotten accidentally caught up on lines set to catch other animals. While the hooks, which often get stuck in the mantas' mouths, rarely cause long-term injuries, the trailing line itself is the real danger. Manta rays regularly feed by somersaulting in tight loops. These backward flips wrap the trailing line around the manta's body, where it begins to knot and cut deep into the animal's skin, just like cheese wire. The result is often the loss of a cephalic fin, major scarring, or worse. The unlucky individuals who are unable to break free suffer a slow and painful death.

I have heard many stories about entangled mantas approaching and circling divers as if reaching out for help, allowing the divers to cut free their entanglements even though the manta must endure great pain in the process. This behavior runs contrary to the actions of most injured wild animals, who panic in fear of attack or greater injury in the presence of humans. With ever-growing reports of encounters between injured manta rays and humans, the implications for what appear to be such intuitively "clever" thought processes and actions by the mantas make me think deeply about one question: Just how intelligent are manta rays? I have spent thousands of hours in the water with mantas, and I have always felt there is more going on behind their big cow-like eyes than is generally believed. When I look into the eye of a manta and wonder what it is thinking, I often get the impression the manta is asking itself the same question about me.

While I hate to see any animal in distress, especially as a result of human actions, a part of me had always wanted to experience for myself an encounter with an entangled manta. In August 2008 I was diving among a mass-feeding aggregation of about a hundred manta rays. I noticed one of them was trailing a mass of fishing line and my heart began to race. Before I could react, the manta peeled away from the other feeding individuals and swam directly to me, circling within inches of my head. The manta was a ten-foot-long female, and as she moved closer I saw that her injuries were severe. The line was wrapped around her body several times, slicing a wound about twelve inches directly through her upper and lower jaw, deep into her gill, and backward into her head. The more she tried to open her mouth to breathe and feed, the more the line dug into her flesh.

My dive buddy had already surfaced, having run out of air. I was at forty-nine feet with very little air left myself, and my dive knife was on the research boat anchored more than three hundred feet away. There was no way I could untangle the thick knots of line with my hands alone. I needed a knife, but I was worried that, if I left the manta in such obvious distress, I would lose my chance to help her. But I had no choice; I had to surface and leave the manta behind. I swam back to the boat as quickly as I could. I exchanged my empty diving cylinder for the only other one that had any air left, but this one was still only about a quarter full. To make matters worse, it was beginning to get dark.

It took me fifteen minutes to get back down to the feeding mantas, and I was worried I had missed my chance. But the injured manta approached again and began to circle me. I swam closer and grabbed hold of the algae-encrusted line. I began to cut away the strands one at a time. Although I had to pull hard at some of the line to remove it from the deep lacerations in her head and gills, the manta remained calm throughout. Moving her pectoral fins just enough to keep herself from sinking to the seabed, she swam in a slow circular motion around me.

Within a minute or two I had removed all of the line, revealing the full extent of the appalling damage that had been inflicted by human actions. Some of the cuts were extremely deep. Even with all the line removed, the manta continued to circle me, but I had run out of air, out of light, and out of time. I had to leave. I quickly took a few photos of her and her injuries so I could be sure to recognize her again if she survived. Then I headed to the surface and back to the boat.

I will never forget that encounter. The connection and sense of achievement was rewarding for me, yet also extremely depressing. I hoped that she was able to survive her injuries, and I was encouraged by several more encounters with this same manta (now called Slice — MV-MA-1267) in the weeks that followed.

The most intriguing of these encounters happened while I was diving with about a dozen other divers, watching a group of more than a hundred feeding manta rays spiraling together in another mass-feeding event. To my surprise, one of the mantas peeled away from the others and swam directly toward me. As it passed overhead I saw the injuries and recognized Slice. She circled above me a few times before returning to feed with the main group of mantas. I was the only diver she approached, and I still don't really know what to make of this behavior.

As a scientist, I tried to rationalize and explain it logically. Maybe through association with divers at cleaning stations, the mantas think we can act as a kind of giant cleaner fish, removing fishing line and later helping to further clean the wound. But I cannot help thinking it was more than that. I think Slice recognized me and was curious to learn and interact more with this strange creature who had helped to set her free.

Whatever the truth may be, it made me want to learn even more about these graceful animals. I hope that over the coming decades, Slice will still be around to teach me more about the captivating world of manta rays.

This experience connected me more deeply with a species I was already interested in, and it increased my empathy toward manta rays and the marine world. It also left me saddened at humankind's destructive nature. Combined, these emotions distilled my desire to address the conservation challenges facing these species and their habitat.

• • •

In 2005, Guy founded the Maldivian Manta Ray Project (MMRP) with the goal of using scientific research and education to conserve the Maldives' manta population. His efforts led to the creation of several marine protected areas at key manta aggregation sites, including Hanifaru Bay, where he met Slice.

In 2011, his work was further rewarded when the Baa Atoll — a seven-hundred-square-mile area of coral reefs and islands in the Maldives that includes Hanifaru Bay — was designated a UNESCO World Biosphere Reserve.

That same year, Guy and Thomas Peschak cofounded the Manta Trust to conserve manta and mobula ray populations throughout the world. Their goal is to bring together scientists, researchers, and volunteers to work closely with tourism stakeholders, local communities, businesses, and governments to create community-based initiatives and government legislation to ensure sustainable futures for mantas and the people who live near them.

In 2013, Manta Trust, as part of a coalition of charities, achieved a successful listing of both manta ray species on Appendix II of CITES, an international agreement between governments to protect plants and animals.

A year later, the organization won another victory. At the Convention for the Conservation of Migratory Species of Wild Animals (CMS), protective legislation was enacted for all species of mobula and reef rays, along with multiple species of sharks, in the form of an environmental treaty supported by the United Nations Environment Program.

In 2016, the Manta Trust, working with nonprofits Planeta

Océano and WildAid and government departments in Peru, created the first national protection law there, making it illegal to kill manta rays in Peruvian waters.

Have you ever rescued a ladybug?

In England, we called them ladybirds, but I've since been Americanized and call them ladybugs. When I was a kid, I had a little square book, and it was a ladybug story that my mum read to me. She taught me about the seven-spot ladybugs and the two-spot ladybugs and also about the sex of ladybugs. She was always talking about the animals and flowers. I have rescued ladybugs when they've come out of hibernation and are trapped inside by opening the windows and letting them out.

Name three things that make you happy.

Reading, walks in the countryside, and spending time with my partner.

What one book, documentary, or speech has had a profound effect on you?

The Power of One by Bryce Courtenay.

Regarding your food choices, how do you describe yourself?

Ninety-five percent vegetarian.

If you had one message to deliver to others, what would it be?

Wildlife on our planet is disappearing faster than ever before. We are the instigators of species' extinctions and habitat destruction on an unprecedented scale. Life on earth is precious, so fight for all the species that do not have a voice. Take action now against the ignorance and apathy that is destroying this planet.

If you had one wish that was guaranteed to come true, what would it be?

To receive a donation to the Manta Trust that would be enough to cover the core staff and operational costs of the charity in perpetuity.

What advice do you have for people who say that they want to help animals in need but are too debilitated by what they witness?

There are many ways to help animals. If you cannot directly become engaged at the sharp end, then provide assistance to those who are.

Willie Smits

ORANGUTAN

The history of the world will, one day, be defined by the people who witnessed the tragedy of impending extinction and were able to turn humanity's destructive patterns into creative solutions. Willie Smits will be recognized as a genius who was moved to save one orangutan and, in doing so, discovered a way to save many species and entire ecosystems by convincing human beings to replace self-defeating economic exploitation with sustainable, life-enhancing conservation.

I was alerted to Willie by my friend Verna Simpson, cofounder of Humane Society International Australia.

"You have to meet Willie Smits," she said. "He's amazing and has the perfect story about an orangutan."

Verna had worked with Willie, a Netherlands-born tropical forest ecologist and microbiologist, to uncover and expose the illegal trafficking of wildlife in Indonesia, where he is a leading animal welfare advocate.

As promised, Verna introduced Willie and me to each other via email, but he never replied. I followed up with a couple more emails but still didn't get an answer. Irritated and yet intrigued, I buried myself in research about Willie. I discovered a man who is fluent in six languages and is leading a race against time to prevent the extinction of the orangutan, a species that shares 97 percent of our DNA. The more I learned about him, the more determined I became to tell his story.

Six months later, I tried a different approach and sent him a tweet. Much to my surprise, he responded and agreed to an interview.

To prepare for our talk, I watched Willie's TEDx talks, speeches, and interviews on YouTube. I also read hundreds of pages of papers he'd written about work to stop illegal logging, re-create rainforests, provide jobs for the poor of Indonesia, create laws to end wildlife trafficking, and so much more. I also read the book he wrote with Gerd Schuster and Jay Ullal titled *Thinkers of the Jungle: The Orangutan Report* — which is undoubtedly the most enlightening book ever written about the plight of orangutans. When I finally met Willie on Skype, he explained that his species-saving efforts started simply: when someone tried to sell him a baby orangutan.

• • •

Kalimantan, Borneo

My relationship with other animals started at the beginning. I grew up in the Netherlands, and for the first six years of my life I didn't speak to human beings. I only had the animals. My connection became apparent when I was just a year and a half old. I went missing for eight hours and was eventually found in a little hut, hugging the meanest dog in the neighborhood. I didn't want to let go of the dog, and he didn't want me to let him go.

When I was six, I developed an affinity for birds. By then, my parents had been told I was autistic, and they didn't mind that I began to spend all my spare time in the forests with the birds. When I was twelve, I wrote my first article about the behavior of owls, and for the rest of my teenage years, I rescued many birds that had fallen from their nests, nurtured them, and released them back out into the world, some successfully.

My dream was to become a veterinarian. That was my biggest passion. I loved animals and could communicate love better with animals than with people. There was only one place in the Netherlands that offered veterinary studies: Utrecht University. To pursue my dream, I traveled there to discuss admission. But on the day I went, it was raining, the train was late, and the bus didn't connect. When I arrived, the lights were out in the building, and there were a couple of very boring people with beards saying, "You won't have a chance. You won't get a job as a veterinarian." The strangers' opinions were so demotivating I went home and decided never to return to the city of Utrecht again. I ended up going to Wageningen University, where I studied tropical forestry, genetics, and tropical soil science.

When I was twenty-eight, I moved to the island of Borneo, at the request of the Indonesian Ministry of Forestry and with special permission from Wageningen University. A year later I was asked to work for Tropenbos International, a Dutch organization that researches tropical forests for nature conservation and sustainable use. Four years later, I had a family and was the father of two sons, with another on the way.

One October afternoon in 1989, I was shopping in an outdoor vegetable market in Kalimantan when I had an experience that changed my life. I was carrying my youngest son, Jan, in my arms and walking through the markets. The ground was covered with piles of fermenting garbage, plastic, vegetable pieces, and opened-up coconuts. It was a dirty, blackish mush. Everything smelled of rotting vegetables. It was very hot. All I wanted to do was to get the shopping over so I could return to the air-conditioned car. That was how I was feeling when some guy put a cage in front of me. A little orangutan was in it, staring at me, and that was the moment I was lost.

The man asked me to buy the baby orangutan. I said no.

But when I got home that afternoon, those eyes stayed with me. Those eyes. They were so sad. They penetrated me and got stuck in my soul. They were the force that led me back, the call for help. That was the connection that changed my life.

Around 8 PM, I went back to find the orangutan. The market was closed. It was dark. The cage was actually in the same place where the guy had been, but the orangutan was gone.

That's when I heard a sound, a gasping for air. I looked to the left and about four meters away there was a pile of garbage. The baby orangutan was on top of it. Near death, she'd been thrown away as a wasted product. She was not going to survive much longer.

I went to her and picked her up. As I did, the guy came out from under a table where he'd been sleeping and demanded I pay him. "Hey, mister, money, money," he said, giving chase. But I ran with her. I got in my car, held her in my lap, and drove.

When I got home, I met resistance. My then-wife said I wasn't allowed to "bring that dirty thing in the house." So I stayed outside with her and the mosquitoes all night long. She was in very poor condition, weak and dehydrated. I tried to force some lukewarm water with a bit of milk into her, and I massaged her belly and kept her warm throughout the night. Finally, the next morning, she started to breathe more regularly.

By the afternoon, she showed signs of gaining strength. She started eating a banana, and after that it was actually quite miraculous how fast she recovered. Maybe the hope let her live.

I named her Uce — ooh-chay — for the sound she was making as she struggled to breathe. She was with me for two weeks when word got out with forestry staff that I'd saved the life of a baby orangutan. That's when I was contacted by the wife of a staff member. She had bought an orangutan in a market and he was sick. She didn't know what to do. I agreed to take the second baby, who was called Dodoy.

Having Uce and Dodoy changed me. Over time, as I took care of the babies, I noticed there wasn't a lot of difference between them and my own children; they reacted in the same ways. As my children started talking, the orangutans were also developing. They had an inherent capability to understand human communication, even grammar and the kind of basic abstract thinking used in algebra.

I began to learn about the fate of many orangutans. They were being kept in the most horrible conditions, even used as prostitutes, while others were being eaten. I thought, *This is not right. This is injustice.* I looked at what the other orangutan projects were doing, but most of them had to do more with tourism and offering photo opportunities than with providing orangutans with a safe haven. I decided to do something myself, to protect my Uce and Dodoy.

I started by working with forestry officials to make it illegal to hold orangutans captive. While I was doing that, thousands of local schoolchildren came together to raise money to build an orangutan rehabilitation center.

But I knew it wasn't enough to rescue orangutans. The circle of death and exploitation would continue as long as their habitat was being destroyed. I had to protect that habitat so they had somewhere safe to return to. The only orangutans left in the wild were on the islands of Borneo and Sumatra, and their populations were declining rapidly.

Rainforests were being destroyed because of illegal logging and the global market for palm oil. Local people who needed to earn an income were cutting down trees for money or were burning down the rainforest to allow for palm oil plantations. Orangutans were in the way, but they also provided another source of income. Babies could be sold as pets, for meat, and for entertainment. Getting them wasn't easy. Their mothers, whom babies cling to for the first two years of life, were clubbed, axed, shot, or burned in order to pry their children from their arms.

Consumers around the world were participating in this destruction because many products — from peanut butter to lipstick to detergent and even ice cream — contain palm oil, but consumers usually don't know that. Most food labels just call it vegetable oil. As long as there was a market for it, the forests would continue to be burned for palm oil plantations, and the orangutans would be murdered. Rescuing orangutans wouldn't fix that problem.

I knew that for Uce, Dodoy, and other orangutans to survive, I had to combine economic development with conservation. People had to have a financial incentive not to destroy the forests and everything that lived in them.

I started realizing that sometimes you have to look for solutions in unforeseen corners of the science fields. The solution to my problem was the sugar palm. Sugar is a form of storable energy; it's a chemical battery that preserves solar energy. You can transport it easily and convert it into any kind of product that you need. For me, the sugar palm is truly the champion of photosynthesis, providing food, security, environmental protection, income, job creation, and climate protection.

The goal of my sugar palm project was to take land that had been decimated, reforest it with indigenous trees, and plant sugar palms in and around it to produce a marketable product while creating a safe, sustainable primate habitat. We called the first area of reforested land Samboja Lestari. It included some two thousand hectares (about five thousand acres) purchased and legally protected from future development.

Meanwhile, Uce and Dodoy were growing up. The schoolchildren had been successful in raising money, and Uce and Dodoy were moved into our new orangutan rehabilitation center to learn the skills necessary to survive in the forest. During this time, we planted a quarter of a million trees at Samboja Lestari. Many of the trees had been grown from seeds taken from orangutan feces found in the wild as a way to ensure their survival. Then sugar palms were planted around the perimeter as an income source for the locals and as a fire buffer.

Around the same time, my good friend Peter Karsono and I founded the Balikpapan Orangutan Society to protect the orangutan and preserve its habitat while working with local people. Today it's called the Borneo Orangutan Survival Foundation, still better known as BOS. The organization began by retraining people who'd previously made a living decimating rainforest and killing orangutans. Now they learned how to farm fruit, vegetables, and rattan.

During my work on Samboja Lestari, I discovered that you can actually rebuild a rainforest, restoring hydrology and rainfall and sequestering carbon dioxide in the process. The land was all grassland at first. In year one, we planted trees mixed with various cash crops for the local people. In years two and three, other crops — such as bananas, papayas, and pineapples — grew up between the still-small trees, taking over to provide income and jobs for people. Then the trees started reaching nutrients deeper in the soil, and that's your real capital. Then we saw the speed of tree growth picking up. The forest canopy started closing up and the clouds were coming back. The rainfall increased and the nutrients brought up to the surface were improving the growth of the new forest, and bringing with it biodiversity and jobs. With this project, we combine the power of nature and the power of technology. Today, in Samboja Lestari, more than 160 birds and many of the big predators are there, in just a small area.

As I was working on this project and making these important discoveries, Uce and Dodoy had been learning the skills to survive. Three years after I found baby Uce dying on the top of a pile of garbage, it was time to let her and Dodoy go.

I chose to release them in Balikpapan's Sungai Wain forest, a protected forest that provided an important part of the drinking water supply for the city of Balikpapan. I hoped that the dependence on the water by people would keep the forest protected. Nine orangutans were released together, and they spent the night in a cage we'd placed in the forest so they could get used to the trees and the smells and not rush off in various directions in panic. I wanted the release to be perfect, where the orangutans made a clean split with humans. I wanted to do it completely by the book, but it just didn't work that way.

From a distance, we opened the cage with a rope and they all got out quickly — except Uce. One of the other orangutans, Made, went right up into the trees and was getting fruit and coming back to show the others. It was lovely. But after an hour and a half, my sweet Uce wasn't doing well. She was still sitting on the cage.

I couldn't resist. I went to her and led her to a *Licuala* palm. With my Swiss Army knife I cut a leaf from its soft heart, ate some, and gave it to her. I stroked her for a while, and gradually she went up into the trees. She didn't want to go, but eventually she did.

Three and a half years later, after she had not been seen for three years, our staff found her, and I rushed to the jungle to check on her. When she saw me, she came out of the trees, took me by the hand, and led me into the forest to a *Licuala* palm. With her teeth, she ripped out a leaf from the heart of the palm and gave it to me. I almost had a heart attack because that was exactly what I did for her, cutting off a leaf of that very same species of palm, *Licuala grandis*. I truly believe that she was telling me, "I remember."

On another visit, she came down from the trees to show me something special. She had given birth, and she handed me her baby son, Bintang, who was terrified of me. When she had a second baby — Matahari, another boy — years later, she did the same thing. Uce's third baby is a girl we named Leica at the request of the photographer who first took her picture.

Dodoy has thrived in the Sungai Wain forest. He is a dominant male in the area and is likely the father of Uce's second son, Matahari. That's what we assume, having witnessed them mating. They have now lived in the forest for more than twenty-six years.

Today, Samboja Lestari — the former grassland that was returned to a rainforest — is also thriving. It's like a forest oasis, surrounded by vast coal mine areas that are devoid of life. The project proved that rainforests can be re-created, bringing back with them water and oxygen, the two things necessary for the survival of all species. But the pace of habitat destruction is faster than its re-creation. The survival of confiscated orangutans, bears, and other native species in Indonesia depends not just on us having available habitat to release them into but, most importantly, on us preserving the intact forests we still have left. Through my research, I learned that a hundred hectares of land can support just three adult orangutans. Today I'm working on a plan to restore over eight hundred thousand hectares (nearly two million acres) in Borneo. The plan will re-create the Samboja Lestari project on a vastly larger scale by harvesting biomass for energy, fertilizing the soil organically, creating new forests, planting sugar palms, providing jobs, and creating habitat for orangutans and other native wildlife.

Through Uce's eyes I've witnessed a disaster of epic proportions playing out in Indonesia. It's taken thirty years of work, but the solutions are now in place to save the orangutans — and also our own species. To do this, everyone has to participate. For me, it's easy. I receive love and gratitude from my orangutan friends all the time. When I can, I walk into the forest, switch off my own language, and wait. My friends sometimes come down from the trees and greet me with happiness and hugs. They are gifts to our world. In protecting them, we are ensuring the survival of other species, too — including our own.

• • •

Willie Smits has been called the one person on the planet who understands nature best. He is a forester, microbiologist, conservationist, animal rights advocate, wilderness engineer, and social entrepreneur. Driven by his love for orangutans, he's discovered the formula to restore a rainforest after its destruction.

Over the past thirty years, Willie has established 114 conservation projects in Indonesia, including setting up sanctuaries in twenty-eight locations throughout the country. He designed the Schmutzer Primate Centre at the Ragunan Zoo in Jakarta, Indonesia, a place for sick, injured, and blind orangutans who were confiscated from wildlife traffickers and have no option for release. Willie's design includes privacy glass that permits visitors to see the orangutans without being seen by them. At the end of 2017, he was asked to help redesign the whole zoo to improve animal welfare standards.

Willie has been named one of the top ten greatest social entrepreneurs of all time. He is an Ashoka Fellow, has been awarded the Satya Lencana Pembangunan Award for his reforestation work from the Indonesian government, and has received the Golden Ark knighthood from His Royal Highness Prince Bernhard in his native country of the Netherlands. In December 2017, the Indonesian government awarded his Masarang organization the Paramakarya award, which recognizes Indonesia's best medium-sized social enterprise.

Since his first meeting with Uce, Willie has facilitated the rescue of some thirteen hundred orangutans and has developed personal relationships with five hundred. He has supported the creation of laws to improve the protection and rehabilitation of orangutans and other species; has built rehabilitation facilities for their care; and has purchased otherwise destroyed land and re-created rainforest sanctuaries so they can have homes. He has also taught locals on the island of Borneo how to sustain themselves without participating in the destruction of rainforests for palm oil, the ultimate cause of the orangutan's collapse.

Despite his efforts, Willie says orangutan habitat is being destroyed at an unrecoverable rate. Orangutans are listed as a critically endangered species, meaning they're dangerously close to becoming extinct. While he's been working to preserve the species, up to 80 percent of the remaining orangutans living in the wild have disappeared. The survival of the species, Willie says, depends on the human race taking the plight of the species seriously and doing everything it can to help. He invites anyone reading this book to go to Borneo, to volunteer, and to be a part of the effort. Because, he says, once you communicate with an orangutan, you will understand the battle for the preservation of all species, including our own.

Thirty years after her rescue, Willie speaks of Uce adoringly. When asked about their relationship today, he smiles and says, "I love her and I know that she loves me."

Have you ever rescued a ladybug?

Yes. I had a huge collection of ladybirds actually, when I was six years old. I made drawings of them, the ones with two, four, and six spots, and the orange and red ones. There were so many. I think I had something like twelve species of ladybirds.

Name three things that make you happy.

The hugs of orangutans who come down from the canopy to greet me many years after their release to the wild. The smiles of people, especially in disadvantaged communities, when they realize they changed something for the better, and that it was really possible despite bad past experiences. Spending time with my grandchildren. I guess these might all be the same, and they are all examples of real love. In addition, I love my eureka moments, when an invention or idea is born.

What one book, documentary, or speech has had a profound effect on you?

The very first lecture I heard by R. A. A. Oldeman, a professor in tropical forestry at Wageningen University. It inspired me to do something with my life and to explore the tropical rainforests.

Regarding your food choices, how do you describe yourself?

I am a pescatarian. I do not eat meat. I try to eat healthy, preferably local organic food.

If you had one message to deliver to others, what would it be?

Giving up is no option.

If you had one wish that was guaranteed to come true, what would it be?

It's probably corny...but I would like to having the feeling, when it is my time to go, that I did something to leave this place better than it would have been without me having been there.

What advice do you have for people who say that they want to help animals in need but are too debilitated by what they witness?

I don't like to give advice. I just hope I may inspire others a little bit.

• • •

While I was working on Willie's story, I received an unexpected document from him. It was a letter he wrote in 2002 to a newly rescued and frightened orangutan whom he had met while walking around a quarantine compound one night when he couldn't sleep. When I read it, I felt humbled that he'd shared it with me. I was also moved to tears, grateful for the opportunity to get a real glimpse into his world. I asked Willie if I could share it with you, and he kindly agreed.

• • •

Samboja Lestari, Borneo

All of a sudden you wake up, frightened, having heard this noise in the dark of the night so close to your sleeping place. A dark shadow stands in front of you, and you move back to the wall and shriek. Who could this stranger in the night be? With your head pulled even deeper between your shoulders and your legs and arms tightly held to your small body, you carefully look back to me in the gray shades of this moonlit night. It's just me, a lonely man who cannot sleep after he heard Romeo, Jabba, and Papa call in the night. Their mighty voices still seem to tremble on in my chest. The longing and sadness in their voices make me want to sit and talk with a friend, just to feel a little understanding during a night that will last several more hours. The songs of the cicadas also seem sadder tonight. After all those years in darkness under the soil, now they're using their precious short time in the trees to find their mates and reproduce by singing with all their might. So here I am, a large stranger in the shadows in front of your cage, waking you from dreams I so much would like to know, to understand, to share...

I squat down close to your cage, and in the faint light I start to see your eyes and you see mine. I shriek while pouting my lips and moving my head slightly backward to tell you that it is okay, you do not need to be worried about this new person of the night. You answer me and slowly turn around toward me. I call you again and offer the back of my hand against the bars that separate us. I see your worried, interested eyes, and I feel so much warmth for you, so much pity that here you have to sit alone because the humans that robbed your mother's life also gave you the disease for which you are being treated in this small confined space. And you read my eyes and come toward me, keeping your eyes fixed to mine. Then you smell the back of my hand and gently taste it with the tip of your tongue. You have decided you want to know me, and I wonder what you will do next.

You look in my eyes again, and yours tell me you want me to touch you. Gently I scratch your jaw and the area behind your little ear. You look to the side and let me, but your head is still a bit low. You have decided to trust me, but we are not friends yet. You are lonely and need a friend as much as I do this sleepless night, so I caress your cheeks and the side of your fine fuzzy lips. Your lips are so incredibly soft, soft as the finest baby cheeks, and you turn your gaze toward my face. You are so beautiful, so soft, so gentle, and how much I want to ease your fears and pain. Then you smile, more with your eyes than your lips, and I wonder what your name is, where you came from. I want to know all about you, I want to get to know you. Why are you in this quarantine cage by yourself?

Again, you read my eyes. I cannot hide anything from you, not even in this sparse light. You see my feelings and now know it is really okay. You move my caressing hand to your belly, and I am happy to comply. You lean your head against my arm, holding it tight with your long leathery fingers, and for a few meandering minutes we both enjoy this cozy peace. Then you decide to ask me for help and gently you push my hand toward the padlock on your cage. I know you want me to open the lock but I don't have the key. I pull, I twist, I use force but to no avail, and you know I cannot open it, and when you make an effort yourself, you don't even try hard for you already know it cannot be done, for you have attempted it before. Still you gently push me with your arms stretched through the bars toward the other door and padlock and ask me to try this one, please. Again I oblige, and you feel the muscles in my arm getting hard and the shaking of your cage from the force with which I pull the lock. You sit back and so do I. I shriek and you acknowledge I tried. Then you look around, and from the corner of your cage you take an orange and give it to me. Gratefully I start peeling and we share several pieces. While eating, you look me in my eyes. Relaxed, these two lonely minds just enjoying the time together, tasting the sweet parts, both spitting out the slippery seeds, looking into each other's eyes.

Then you look to the trees behind me, and I know what you are saying. How nice it would be to sleep in your nest again, close to the warm body of your loving mother. I stand up and your slightly worried eyes follow my every step. I break off leafy branches and together we push and pull them to your side of the bars. Now that is a real smile! It is so much fun to arrange the branches and the leaves, to construct the nest. Your busy hands push and shove, pull and rearrange again. Then you smell the leaves and look intensely at them. You look at me and hand me a leaf. You bring it to my lips and show me that I should try it. Okay, I'll try. Hmmm, this leaf is bitter; also, the hairs on its surface are unpleasant to my tongue and an astringent feeling to the back of my tongue makes me spit out the leaf. You look at the fallen crumbled wet leaf just out of reach. Again, you offer me a leaf and ask me to try once more. Okay, but this one tastes just as bad. You ask me to open my mouth and gently take the piece from my lips and smell and taste it. Now you believe me and let it fall! See, it is bitter and no good. You look for another orange from your storage corner and peel it for the two of us. Yes, this helps to get rid of the bitter taste; you are so right. One piece for me, then one for you and again. You are so nice, so fair.

Then your eyes change, and you look me deeper in my eyes. I feel a shiver; what is it that you want, that you think? You ask me for my hand, and when I offer it, you gently guide it through the bars and unfold my fingers. Then gently, carefully so as not to scare me, you take my index finger between your lips and then deeper between your teeth. Slowly your mouth encloses my finger and gently you suck on my finger. Then harder, and you hold my arm in place with the long fingers of your hands. Then your eyes move up to the trees away from my eyes, and all of a sudden I feel shocked and I shiver. You are crying; you are so sad! No tears, but your eyes! They tell it all. What pain they show, looking up into those trees. Are you remembering your mother's breast, your beautiful exciting life up in the trees, her smile, her gentle touch? Tears fill my eyes, for I cry with you. How much I want to take away this pain, this suffering, but all I can do is to let you suck my finger while you think of times long gone. Who are you? What happened to you? I want to know!

After seemingly endless time in shared sadness you abruptly let go and turn away. You sit against the bars looking out the other side, your back toward me. When I stand up with cramped legs, you just shriek and barely look back at me. Do you remember the people who killed your mother? Do you need to be alone with your sadness, your frustrations? I need to get you out of that cage, make life better for you. You are so special; let me get to know you better. Clouds cover the moon, and when I walk away in the night, I hear you shriek. In a few hours, I will be back...

Chapter 4

DOG, CAT, CHIMP

On the Path to Do What's Right, You're Never Alone

Çeşme, Turkey

The sun was bursting into the hotel room, signaling a beautiful day ahead. And why wouldn't it be? I was waking up in Turkey with my boyfriend, Jon, by my side, looking at a view of the Aegean Sea.

It was 1998. We'd arrived at midnight, having driven six hours from the Karacabey Bear Sanctuary in Bursa, Turkey, where I'd attempted to convince Victor Watkins to help me build a bear sanctuary in Laos (see chapter 1). In twenty-four hours, I was expected on the island of Chios, Greece, to shoot stories for CNN. But today was mine to be with the man who'd flown all the way from Australia just to spend a few days with me.

We made our way to the breakfast room, where a generous, traditional European smorgasbord of breads, pastries, fruit, cereal, Greek yogurt, honey, hard-boiled eggs, and a large selection of sliced meats and cheeses was displayed over several long tables.

As Jon sipped a double espresso, he outlined the day's itinerary, which, since he was a foodie, revolved around a 2 PM lunch booking at a restaurant reputed to be the best in Çeşme. To start, we planned to stroll through the old village, where we would taste traditional apple tea and *lokum* — a soft, often rose-flavored candy known as Turkish delight. Excited for the adventure, we left the hotel and walked into the sunshine.

We immediately heard a commotion. Someone was yelling on the hotel's terraced patio, an extension of the dining room where people were eating. I stepped toward the noise. A well-fed woman was holding a piece of bread in the air and angrily yelling at a starving dog who was begging for food. The dog was skeletal and hairless, her blistering skin covered with bleeding, open sores. As the woman kicked at the dog, it cowered.

I stepped between them.

"Stop!" I said, lifting my hand.

Her eyebrows arched in surprise, and she said something to me in Turkish that I'm sure would have offended me if I'd known what it meant.

"What is wrong with you? Can't you see this dog is dying? Go away," I said, shooing her with my hands until she backed up. We didn't speak the same language, but she understood and left in a huff.

During the heated interchange, the dog had remained just behind me. I turned to her.

"It's all right, sweetheart," I said in a high-pitched voice.

Her tail wagged ever so slightly.

I looked at Jon.

"The buffet is closing in ten minutes. Be quick," he said.

Minutes later, I placed a paper napkin heaped with bologna, cheese, and bread in front of the dog, who had patiently remained standing next to Jon. She ate quickly, scanning the perimeter as if mindful the food could be taken from her. I watched in silence, aware she wasn't long for the world. I couldn't imagine the pain she was in and the suffering she was enduring.

When she finished, she stepped up to my bare leg, licked it, and then sauntered into the street.

I knew Jon was looking forward to a morning of tasting teas and candy, but I felt there was a reason the street dog had crossed my path. I just couldn't leave her to suffer.

"Change of plan?" I asked with a wink.

He'd seen it coming, a foregone conclusion. Always the doctor, he put up the usual protest: "Where will we find a vet? It's a stray and no one will want it — even if we pay for the medical bills. What if you get bitten? She's sick. What if you catch something from her?"

I smiled.

Resigned, he said, "Don't touch that dog, Jenny. Get something to wrap her in."

I borrowed a sheet from the hotel, and we set off on a mission to find the dog. We found her about ten minutes later in the corner of an abandoned market stall, lying on an old mattress. She lifted her head, acknowledging me, and then put it back down. I wrapped her in the white sheet and took her into my arms, immediately feeling her heat. She was burning up. She rested her head on my shoulder and looked up at me with gratitude. If she was supposed to be part of my journey and I was supposed to be part of hers, she was glad I'd finally come.

Jon hailed a taxi. The driver didn't understand much English, but he knew where we needed to go. He took us to an animal clinic, but the office was closed. The driver explained that this was the only veterinarian in town.

Between my pocket dictionary and the driver's pidgin English, I was able to convey the idea of an animal shelter.

"Yes!" he shouted. "I take you there."

As we set off, Jon looked at the exposed face of the dog who was wrapped in my arms like a baby.

"She looks like a sweet dog. Let's name her Lokumia, after the Turkish candy we're *not* going to taste."

After twenty minutes, the driver turned onto a bumpy, dirt road. As we tumbled along, my thoughts of anger toward a woman without an ounce of empathy for a starving dog melted as I became acutely aware that Lokumia's heart was pressed against mine and that our heartbeats, so close to the skin but separated by a thin sheet, were touching, pulsing against each other. Her eyes locked on mine, she pressed her head into my shoulder, and there was a telepathic exchange of love. She was safe and I was at peace. I felt the divinity within her and understood that while her body was broken, her spirit was luminous.

Another twenty minutes later, the taxi pulled up to a small compound where a hundred barking dogs greeted us from a large, fenced-in yard. A tall man with sand-colored hair and wearing a white coat greeted us and took Lokumia from my arms, explaining he was a veterinarian. We followed him into a small building, where he placed the dog on a steel surgical table. After examining Lokumia, he explained that she was near death, suffering from starvation, severe dehydration, and the worst case of mange he'd ever seen. She only had hours, maybe days, left to live.

Still, he was willing to see if he could save her. As if she were ours, he asked our permission to give her fluids. We agreed.

While the veterinarian prepared an IV drip, I stood next to Lokumia with my hands on the sheet that still covered her. Her eyes opened sporadically, checking I was there, but she didn't move.

While the doctor looked for a vein to insert the needle, he explained to us that the shelter was started by the dog-loving mayor of Çeşme and was staffed by German veterinarians who flew to Turkey and volunteered their time for month-long stints. Because of an abundance of strays, the dogs would never get homes but would live — while there was funding — at the shelter.

My heart sank. I looked at Jon. He read my mind.

"What would happen," he asked the vet, "if we wanted to keep her?"

The vet looked up from his work and beamed.

"Then," he said, "she will have a reason to live."

A happy energy filled the room as we agreed to take Lokumia — if she survived. The vet seemed supercharged and excited, hopeful for the dog who had just come into his care. He told us that he'd give her fluids to see if she responded, and if she did, he'd try a new drug to combat her mange.

We exchanged phone numbers, and I donated money for her care. As we left, I glanced into the eyes of the dog who, as she faced death, gave me her love, and I told her she was a good girl. I truly didn't expect to see her again.

A week later, I called the veterinarian from Greece. He was excited to hear from me and had good news. Lokumia was alive, she was responding to medication, and he'd formulated a plan. Once she was well, he would take her to Germany, where she'd be placed with a foster family who would look after her until she passed the quarantine tests necessary to travel. Then she would fly home to me.

A few months later I received a letter to let me know Lokumia was safe in Germany and living with her foster family.

Two weeks after that, I received another letter from the vet. He commended me for rescuing Lokumia, but he had news he hoped wouldn't be upsetting. The German foster family had fallen in love with her and asked if I would consider letting her go.

With tears of sadness and happiness, I called him and said yes.

I'd wanted to bring her home, to take care of her for the rest of her life. But I knew instinctively that she was where she was supposed to be.

My brief time with Lokumia would always serve as a reminder that when we come across situations in life that trigger our sense of right over wrong, there is reward in choosing right. The experience was also proof that when you're on the path to do what's right, you're never alone.

Chris Mercer

CARACAL

As kids, most of us were exposed to African wildlife through pictures in *National Geographic* or shows on public television channels or the Discovery Channel. But few of us have had the opportunity to visit and see wildebeests, lions, giraffes, and elephants on the African continent. Our exposure is limited to one-hour snippets, often depicting gory battles between predator and prey species. What is often missing is the predation of these beautiful species by humans.

As an environmental journalist, I've been exposed to distasteful practices against animals that typically don't receive media exposure because they're legal. One of these practices, prevalent in parts of Africa, is called canned hunting. It's an unethical game played by participants who lack a moral compass. Chris Mercer is leading the fight against it.

Mercer grew up in rural Zimbabwe (then called Rhodesia); he lived and participated in what he calls the hunting-fishing-shooting environment of the time. His constant companion was his bulldog, Tuppence, whom he called Tuppy. He describes his parents as having no interest in their children; he spent his fourth birthday in a boarding school. During school holidays, Tuppy provided much-needed companionship to a withdrawn and otherwise independent child.

When revolutionary and politician Robert Mugabe took control of Zimbabwe, a reign of genocide, corruption, anti-white racism, and human rights abuses ensued, and like so many other people, Chris fled the country.

Over a decade later, in 1992, the retired lawyer was enjoying a barbecue at a friend's house, when he met the compassionate, animal-loving Bev Pervan. She told him how she had crossed the Atlantic Ocean in a thirty-eight-foot sailboat, and he was instantly attracted to her adventurous spirit.

The two became a couple and decided to pursue Bev's dream of opening the only wildlife rehabilitation sanctuary in the Northern Cape province of South Africa. They built the Kalahari Raptor and Predator Sanctuary, and it was there that Chris developed a deep compassion for all living creatures — and a broad understanding of the bureaucratic complications involved in protecting wildlife.

At the time, canned hunting was a relatively new business, as was captive breeding, the industry that fed it. In short, animals such as lions were bred solely to be delivered to a fenced enclosure where they were shot or killed with arrows, their bodies taken as trophies. The shooter often paid between $15,000 and $50,000 to walk away with the claim that he shot a lion, rhino, or tiger in Africa.

To supply the hunts, captive breeders raise lion cubs. Because these breeders know that the practice would be condemned if people understood its true purpose, they call their breeding operations "sanctuaries" and claim the cubs are orphaned from the wild. They advertise for financial and volunteer assistance, and unwitting tourists, lured by the opportunity to help rescue and save the cubs, actually buy into the industry that is raising the lions to be killed.

Chris is the founder of the only animal welfare organization in the world, Campaign Against Canned Hunting (CACH), with the sole purpose of ending canned hunting. It was a connection with three wild cats and a battle to save their lives that fueled his determination to protect the innocent.

• • •

Northern Cape Province, South Africa

The phone call that changed Bev's and my life came from Noenieputs, a farmers' co-op store and filling station in the remote semi-desert, located hard up against the border with Namibia. One of the tough souls who farmed this harsh landscape phoned me to report he had captured three caracals. Caracals are wild, often fawn-colored cats with long, black-tufted ears, dark facial markings, and long legs. They are native to Africa and are often referred to as lynx.

I gathered he'd caught a female caracal in a gin trap — a steel-jaw mechanical trap — and her leg was broken. He'd also managed to catch two others, presumably the female's own half-grown kittens.

We arranged to meet the following day to pick up the cats and transfer them to the sanctuary. We faced a problem. It would be illegal for us to transport the caracals without a transport permit or to keep them without a captivity permit. It was a Thursday. We could never hope to get a permit granted within forty-eight hours, if at all, from the conservation office in Kimberley, the administrative capital of the Northern Cape province. They were closed on the weekend. The animals would be dead by Monday if left in the trap. I decided to fetch the caracals right away.

The farmer was waiting for me on my arrival. In the bed of his bakkie, which is a small pickup truck, was a wire mesh cage containing three hissing, spitting, terrified caracals. I could see that the mother's leg was badly shattered by the gin trap, but she looked alert and strong, and that was a good sign. I transferred them to the wooden box we used for carrying animals by placing it against the opening of their cage and sliding open the door.

The three cats fled their stressful wire cage into the welcoming security of the dark box, and I slid the door shut. I thanked the farmer for taking the trouble to give them a second chance at life — most farmers would have killed them out of hand — and set off for the long drive home.

As I drove, I phoned ahead to ask the local veterinarian if he could meet me at his surgery later and to warn him that I would not get there until after dark.

The female caracal's leg was an awful mess, and assisting the vet to operate on it was not pleasant. There is nothing glamorous about rehab work. Although deeply sedated, she still moaned in pain as the vet worked on her.

It was nearly midnight by the time I got home, too weary even to acknowledge the rapturous welcome of my dogs. Bev had prepared a special cage for the newcomers with food, water, and warm bedding. The female, still unconscious with her leg bound up like that of an Egyptian mummy, was gently placed in a brick building we'd converted into an intensive care unit. Then, at last, I could crawl into bed.

Some say no good deed ever goes unpunished, and we were soon to find that out for ourselves.

Monday came and went without any reply to our request for ex post facto permits. Then the officials faxed us a terse reply informing us that caracals were a declared "problem" species, and that according to an old provincial ordinance passed in 1957, it was compulsory to remove them from the environment, and that anyone who failed to do so would be committing a criminal offense. Their reply went on to advise us that we were to be prosecuted for our crime unless we euthanized all three animals forthwith and provided proof to a conservation officer that the animals had been "removed from the environment." In short, we were instructed to kill the animals or face prosecution.

Events moved quickly. The usually silent and unresponsive government department found an amazing ability to engage with us all of a sudden. Bev and I talked about how to react to the threat of prosecution. Killing the three caracals was out of the question; we would both rather have gone to prison if it came to that. We could have released the two young caracals, even though they were not really ready for life on their own, and then claimed that they had escaped.

The threat of criminal proceedings did not trouble us unduly. Although I was not a South African lawyer, I had spent half a lifetime in the courts, both as a prosecutor and as a defense lawyer in Rhodesia, and I had endured enough hardship so that the prospect of a little criminal trial in a magistrate's court held no terrors for me. If the department's intention had been to frighten us into submission, it had miscalculated badly. The sole effect of the threat was to stiffen our resistance to a conservation department that had proven itself as having no concern whatsoever for animal welfare.

Our reply to the threatening letter was to decline the instruction to euthanize the three caracals, but to suggest a compromise: If the department could find a safe facility for the animals — safe enough that we were confident they'd be going to a better home than what we could provide — then we would voluntarily surrender them. I could almost see the steam rise in the distance when our offer was received. How dare we question an official decision? Who did we think we were to try to impose conditions on official actions? Our offer was hotly rejected, and we were informed that the caracals would now be confiscated by conservation officials. We were also informed that we would be prosecuted for transporting and keeping wild animals without a permit.

The convoy arrived at nine sharp on the following Friday. And what a convoy it was, stretching back about a hundred meters. There were carloads of conservation officers, resplendent in their khaki uniforms. There were bakkie-loads of policemen, including a senior officer. There was a veterinarian, armed with darting equipment. And also, to our astonishment, the video unit of the South African police, all the way from Pretoria, five hundred kilometers away.

It is painful to record what happened next. The vet started firing darts into the trapped animals, who panicked and scattered in every direction. They climbed tree trunks in the enclosure and even climbed up the wire mesh. In their stress, they salivated excessively. Gossamer threads of foaming spittle, looking like spiders' webs, floated around the enclosure. The darts were ineffective and only partially paralyzed the animals; with hindquarters dragging, they tried to climb the wire mesh to get away. The darts themselves were far too big for such small animals and would certainly have broken bones had they not struck flesh first. But we did not know this at the time and thought the vet knew what he was doing.

While I filmed this spectacle of cruel ignorance, Bev was beside herself with grief. The sight of these precious little animals being so severely ill-treated was more than she could bear. Our blood pressure was going through the roof as we were forced to watch, helpless, this bungling incompetence. We offered to catch the cats ourselves, but the officials would not allow us to do so. It took a full two hours before the three little caracals were properly sedated and captured, and by then their body temperatures were so dangerously high that they had to be doused with water by the vet. The brutal capture finally over, the convoy drove away, taking our three bedraggled, unconscious little caracals with them. I was left trying vainly to comfort Bev, who was sobbing uncontrollably.

I'm a mild person, slow to anger, but I was more than mildly enraged over the appalling ordeal to which Bev and the three caracals had been subjected. After what we'd been through, we were never going to allow the matter to rest.

The following morning, bright and early, I was at the office of an attorney in Kimberley. The attorney took me straight to advocates' chambers to confer with counsel. The legal team would make an urgent application to the high court in Kimberley for relief. The day was spent in consultations and settling affidavits, and I drove the two hundred kilometers back home the same evening.

Days passed. Bev and I awaited news from our lawyers with anxious anticipation. Finally, the call came. We had won. The warrant of seizure had indeed not been worth the paper it was printed on. The judge had granted our order requiring the officials to go to Bloemfontein Zoo, where our cats had been taken, and fetch them to us — immediately. What elation! Bev shed yet more tears, only this time they were tears of joy.

The following day our caracals were returned to us. This time there was no grand convoy or official police video units from Pretoria. Just one lonely little bakkie driven by a junior official.

The cats arrived very subdued and sickly. We medicated them and released them back into the camp from which they had been so brutally snatched. They had been away for five days.

The three caracals had become quite famous, and the news of their return to the center was reported in the mainstream press.

Reports were all sympathetic to us and the animals. The confiscation had backfired badly upon nature conservation officials. The whole issue of problem animal control — and the complicity of conservation services in the widespread massacre of wildlife by farmers using unethical methods — had been projected into the public domain. It was not just in Kimberley. All conservation structures were now under public scrutiny like never before. Publicly humiliated, the conservation department needed a successful prosecution against us to reassert its power.

Charges were laid and we were summoned to appear in the Kuruman Magistrate Court. The trial was inconvenient enough for me, but for Bev it was sheer purgatory. She had so much emotional capital invested in the animals at the center, and she was terrified that the department would use a conviction as an excuse to close us down and euthanize all her beloved charges.

Suffice it to say that over a period of three years, and at great financial cost, we fought the callous officials to a standstill. While the officials were busy fighting us, Tripod, as we called the mother caracal, recovered from her amputation and became a friend. She lived in a large veld camp, characteristic of the area. It was about a hectare (or two and a half acres) with lots of trees, bushes, and tall grass. Sadly, she would have never survived in the wild.

I used to call Tripod just as one would call a house cat: I'd make kiss-kiss sounds every evening and sit near her on a bench while she hobbled out of the bushes and ate her food. Slowly she became tamer, and eventually she would saunter over to where I sat after feeding her and playfully sink her teeth into my rubber boots. I so enjoyed just being with her and watching her. She never gave me any trouble.

Tripod's two kittens were successfully released back to the wild when they were ready. We felt a huge satisfaction in watching them walk free, yet we were left with a sadness akin to bereavement for days after they left.

Over the years that followed, Tripod became the most marvelous surrogate mother for all the young caracals who came into our care. She was a calming influence on them, and like a mother cat, she would indulge in face-licking with the kittens. It gave me great pleasure to see them lying together during the heat of the day in the shade of the camel thorn trees.

Bev and I always regarded the ordeal of saving Tripod and her kittens as the best money we've ever spent. We took a stand on a moral principle and fought it all the way to the constitutional court. There have been many benefits from it, but none more rewarding than having saved the lives of the three beautiful cats whose only crime, to some, was living.

• • •

The three-year battle to save three caracals was the beginning of what would be a lifelong quest for Chris to help African wildlife. In 2005, he and Bev penned the book *Canned Lion Hunting: A National Disgrace*, and two years later established the Campaign Against Canned Hunting (CACH), an all-volunteer NGO that raises awareness of lion farming and canned hunting with the goal of ending the practices.

To tighten the noose on an industry known mainly to trophy hunters, Chris works to expose it. His proven theory is that when tourists and volunteers find out they're being duped by breeding facilities that are raising lions to be shot, they won't pay to participate. "If you don't feed the people who exploit animals," he says, "they go out of business." CACH initiatives that alert the travel industry to deceptive practices in lion walking, cub petting, and volunteer jobs at fake sanctuaries have won world conservation and ethical tourism awards.

In 2014, CACH participated in the Global March for Lions, a coordinated event to expose the cruel industry of captive breeding for canned hunts. Soon afterward, animal activist Donalea Patman persuaded the government of Australia to ban the import of lion trophies into the country.

Working in conjunction with other animal welfare organizations, the media, and filmmakers, CACH is creating awareness and change. Following the premiere of the film *Blood Lions: Bred for the Bullet*, France banned the import of captive and wild lion trophies in its country. And in 2016, the US Fish & Wildlife Service (USFWS) announced restrictions on the import of trophies taken from captive-bred lions in South Africa after some species of African lion were listed under the Endangered Species Act. However, in March 2018, the USFWS (led by the Trump administration) reversed this decision and again allowed lion trophy imports on a case-by-case basis.

Before Bev's passing in 2016, Chris and Bev cowrote two more books, *Kalahari Dream* and *For the Love of Wildlife*. The stories tell of their love for Africa's wild animals and the successful battles they've fought to protect them.

Have you ever rescued a ladybug?

Regret not.

Name three things that make you happy.

Living in beautiful natural surroundings in the Klein Karoo; living with animals; the love of family and good friends.

What one book, documentary, or speech has had a profound effect on you?

"The Bell of Atri," Henry Wadsworth Longfellow's delightful poem about the abused horse.

Regarding your food choices, how do you describe yourself?

Vegetarian.

If you had one message to deliver to others, what would it be?

That loving animals is not enough; you have to fight for them, regardless of the cost and the unpopularity it will bring you.

If you had one wish that was guaranteed to come true, what would it be?

A total ban on lion farming and canned lion hunting in South Africa.

What advice do you have for people who say that they want to help animals in need but are too debilitated by what they witness?

It is hard to do it on your own; you need a supportive partner.

Emma Haswell

GREYHOUND

Tasmania is an island state located 150 miles off the southeastern corner of Australia, edged by the Southern Ocean. It is spectacularly beautiful, with dramatic, rock-peaked mountains that drop into white beaches with aqua-blue lagoons; rolling, lush farmland; and an abundance of wildlife. I traveled there in 2014 with photographer Alex Cearns and her partner, Debora Brown.

Our first destination was the Tarkine rainforest, where we hoped to see a Tasmanian devil in the wild. Backcountry camping and hiking in a virgin rainforest without trails was amazing and grueling. We didn't see any of the almost-extinct devils, but we ran across the skins of enough poisonous snakes that, after three days, I was thrilled to climb down the mountain and head for Brightside Farm Sanctuary, the other purpose of our visit.

Located in Cygnet, Tasmania, Brightside was founded by Emma Haswell as a place where rescued farm animals could have the rare opportunity to live full lives in a natural environment.

As we drove through the sanctuary's farm gate, we saw lush, green hills speckled with grazing cows in the distance and arrived at a large barn near a house. Stepping out of the car, I was warmly greeted by two camels, five pigs, a turkey, and ten dogs. The sun was shining, and everywhere I turned there were animals, all happily wagging their bodies or tails.

Alex had volunteered to photograph the animals and to donate the images for use in Brightside's promotional materials. While one of the young camels leaned against me, Emma explained that she'd rescued them from a livestock sale yard where they were being sold, along with healthy horses and donkeys, for meat.

I stepped aside and Alex snapped a few pictures of the cooperative camels. Then Emma took us into a pasture where Debora and I visited with the largest cow I've ever seen and Alex lay down in the mud at the edge of a pond and took photographs of a smiling pig. Next, Emma walked us to a fenced pasture where a friendly, black horse trotted over to say hello. As I rubbed her forehead, Emma said, "This is Rosie. When I found her in a meat pen at the sale yards, she was a bag of bones. I could hear her stomach rumbling from four pens away. I'd never heard a horse's stomach rumble, and I walked over to see what the noise was. She was standing there with a little boy. The boy was wearing glasses and standing outside the corner of her pen. He had his arms through the bars, and the horse had her head resting in his arms. He was singing to her. I left and came back forty minutes later, and she was still standing there with her head resting in his arms, and he was still singing to her. I walked over and said, 'You like that horse, don't you?' He said, 'Yes, I want my family to rescue this horse.' I said, 'Don't worry, I'll make sure the horse is safe.' When the auction started, I outbid the meat buyer and brought Rosie home."

Like most advocates who rescue abandoned and discarded animals, Emma says the work is frustrating. Her happiness comes from the animals, such as Flossie, a big, white, woolly sheep who, when I met her, was lying in fresh hay, her back against the barn, her eyes closed, and her head tilted toward the sun. Emma explained that she takes Flossie to schools as an ambassador for all sheep and lambs. "The animals tell their stories better than I can," Emma says. "We've met with over fifty thousand schoolchildren together. Flossie gives them the opportunity to know, touch, and connect with an animal they typically only know as meat."

Alex called Emma to have another photograph, and I sat down

with Flossie. I placed a hand on her soft forehead and massaged it. Her eyelids fluttered, and I told her she was a good girl. When I stopped, she opened her eyes and smiled at me, imparting her gratitude.

My morning at Brightside was what I imagine heaven to be: green pastures with hundreds of animals of all species happily living together with full comprehension of the gift they've been given — to live with a human being who represents the kindest of her species.

In addition to Brightside, Emma is creating sweeping changes for millions of animals in her home state. Her quest was born from witnessing negligence at a time when she was helpless to end it.

● ● ●

Ross, Tasmania, Australia

The first animal I had a relationship with was a little crossbred dog called Minnie. She looked a bit like a monkey. Her hair was brown, wild, and wiry, and she had two rows of teeth on the bottom. I'd dress her up in clothes and put bonnets on her, and she'd lie on her back in the pram, while I wheeled her around my grandmother's garden. She was gentle, patient, and kind. She was everything to me.

I was raised in the city of Launceston, Tasmania, but I actually grew up in the country because that was where my love was, with the farm animals. My maternal grandparents had an eight-thousand-acre farm in a town called Ross, and I spent as much time as I could there. My grandfather was different to other farmers. He had a high regard for animals and would go to extraordinary lengths to find the mothers of lost lambs. He was unique that way and encouraged me to be the same way.

I was fortunate to have lots of pets growing up: rabbits, dogs, a cat, a bantam, a magpie, a lamb called Mary, and a pony named Allegro. Allegro had been a stock horse, used on the farm. I rode her without a saddle, bridle, or halter. We'd go to the beach, just me and a naked horse. I'd put my arms out as if I was flying, close my eyes, and gallop the beach with her.

My first connection with an animal who wasn't my own pet happened when I was around six years old. There was a workman on my grandfather's farm who had two dogs, including a little Jack Russell called Sweetie, whom he clearly adored. He also had a greyhound named Flash who was chained to a tin A-frame shelter on the side of a hill, far away from any houses, where the cold wind blew mercilessly.

Flash was brindled, a tan color with dark, zebra-like streaks, and she was small for a greyhound. I was strictly forbidden to go near her because my grandparents told me she'd bite. I ignored them and would sneak up the hill, sit down next to her, and pet her for hours. She was gentle, sensitive, quiet, and lonely. She was the first animal I'd ever met who was clearly sad, unloved, and destitute. She had nothing — not even a bed or hay to sleep on. I was told Flash was a hunting dog, but I never saw her off the chain, ever. She was there for years. I knew she was suffering terribly, and I knew that there was absolutely nothing I could do to help her.

In contrast, the old man who owned her loved his other dog, Sweetie. That dog was his life. She went to work with him on the farm every day and was always at his feet. She had the best life with him. She was adored, and I just couldn't comprehend how he loved Sweetie so much yet neglected Flash so terribly. I often thought of what it was like for Flash to look down from that hill and watch all the other animals having a good life.

After visiting Flash for a couple of years, I turned up at the farm one day and she was gone. I asked where she was but no one would tell me. Today I believe she'd been taken away and shot.

My experience with Flash was the first and the only time during my childhood that I witnessed such poor treatment of an innocent animal. It took two separate events, many years later, to trigger me to take action for animals the way I'd wanted to take action for Flash.

The first event happened when I was thirty-three years old, working as a veterinary nurse and living in London. I was at a dog show when I stopped at an animal rights stall. I picked up a brochure that was titled "Stop the Export of Greyhounds from Australia to Asia." I read the brochure and was horrified to learn that greyhound breeders exported live dogs to parts of Asia to race — and then be eaten by humans. That was the moment I knew I had to do something different with my life. I rang the organization that put out the pamphlet, Greyhound Action UK, and became their North London coordinator. The more I learned about what was happening to the greyhounds, the more I knew I had to return to Tasmania, to make a difference there. I also knew I needed to learn as much about the exploitation of animals as I could.

In my new quest to learn more about this exploitation, I went to a rally against primate experimentation that was being held at Cambridge University. There were two thousand people there. One of the speakers was a man named Mel Broughton, a true animal activist who conducted direct action to save animals' lives, even if it was against the law. I'd never heard anybody like him, let alone a man, speaking with so much empathy for animals that he put them before his own freedom. The speech — and the man himself — changed my life.

Growing up, I had never felt understood. I always gravitated toward animals instead of people. Because of this, I didn't always fit in socially with other kids, and even my own parents didn't understand me. When I got to this protest, I couldn't believe it. I'd found people just like me. I hadn't known they even existed. When I listened to Mel speak, I realized there was nothing wrong with me at all. My compassion and love for animals weren't odd traits. They were strengths; they were good qualities to have. I remember thinking to myself, *God, I can be who I want to be!*

When I left London, the first thing I did to stand up for animals was for greyhounds. The greyhound racing industry in Victoria, Australia, was putting on a promotional night to drum up interest. They were hosting a live greyhound racing event with a free barbecue and a plasma-screen television giveaway. They were calling it a family night.

I wrote them an email to say that Greyhound Action Australia — which didn't actually exist! — would be there and would be protesting. I attached a photo of half a greyhound on a meat market table in Asia, letting them know that I knew what they did with their greyhounds. They responded by canceling the event. That's when I realized that one person truly could make a difference.

Upon returning to Tasmania, I sold everything I owned and decided to start a sanctuary that helps all animals, not just those that are considered companions. There are more than three hundred animals living at Brightside Farm Sanctuary now. They include, at any given time, up to thirty-five greyhounds. The sanctuary also serves as an animal rights education center and adoption shelter. Life is good for those who live here. But my true goal is to make life wonderful for those who don't.

• • •

Brightside is a fifty-acre farm sanctuary located in the Huon Valley of southern Tasmania. Since its inception, Brightside has provided humane education to fifty-five thousand schoolchildren, teaching them the often-unspoken facts about factory farming, greyhound racing, and horse racing.

Behind the scenes of Tasmania's largest farm sanctuary, Emma is an active animal welfare campaigner and undercover investigator. Her work has been credited for the closure of the second-largest battery hen farm in Tasmania, the shuttering of one of the state's largest piggeries, and the banning of greyhound hurdle racing in the state.

Emma rehomes approximately three hundred dogs every year. Half of them are greyhounds.

Have you ever rescued a ladybug?

My grandmother, who taught me empathy, had rosebushes that had aphids on them. Ladybirds, as we call them, eat aphids, so there were lots of them in her garden. She taught me that they brought good luck if you gently blew them away. I've always loved them.

Name three things that make you happy.

Saving animals, rehoming dogs to amazing homes, watching the Brightside rescued animals live happily.

What one book, documentary, or speech has had a profound effect on you?

The speech I heard in London given by animal rights advocate Mel Broughton, cofounder of SPEAK, the Voice for the Rights of Animals, a campaign to stop animal testing in Britain. He is currently serving a ten-year prison sentence for conspiracy to commit arson; he was going to burn a building at Oxford University that planned to house an animal-testing lab.

Regarding your food choices, how do you describe yourself?

Vegan.

If you had one message to deliver to others, what would it be?

Become an informed consumer, not just about what you eat but about the animals we exploit and use. Find out what happens to racehorses and greyhounds. Know what happens to animals forced to spend their lives in laboratories. I believe that knowledge would change people.

If you had one wish that was guaranteed to come true, what would it be?

It would be to take everybody by the hand and walk them through a factory farm because I honestly believe most humans would not eat those poor animals if they saw where they existed before they were slaughtered.

What advice do you have for people who say that they want to help animals in need but are too debilitated by what they witness?

Go to a farm sanctuary and meet a cow or a sheep. You won't want to eat them anymore. It changes you. You realize there's no difference between a dog, cat, pig, cow, sheep, or chicken.

Jenny Desmond

CHIMPANZEE

In March 2015, the New York Blood Center (NYBC) abandoned sixty-six chimpanzees, some of whom they'd been experimenting on for more than thirty years. They left them on uninhabited islands in Liberia, Africa, without food or fresh water. The chimpanzees — who had been forced to endure invasive, painful experiments and had been injected with HIV, hepatitis, and West Nile viruses — were left to die. An American researcher who was in Liberia to address the Ebola virus crisis saw what was happening to the chimpanzees and called on friends in the United States for help. A coalition of more than thirty-five animal welfare and conservation organizations joined forces. Together with animal rights activists, they launched a global campaign demanding that NYBC honor its commitment to provide for the individuals it had discarded. When NYBC refused, the Humane Society of the United States (HSUS) stepped in with a fundraising campaign and hired Jenny and Jim Desmond to oversee the chimpanzees' care.

I first learned about Jenny while reading about the Liberian chimpanzees in an article written by Karen Lange in *All Animals* magazine. Wanting to know more, I reached out to Jenny, and over lengthy emails, we bonded.

Jenny's connection with chimpanzees began when she was seven years old and her mother gave her Jane Goodall's first book, *My Friends the Wild Chimpanzees.* Her mother inscribed it: "To my very own little Jane Goodall." Shortly after that, Jenny announced to her uncle that when she grew up she planned to live in the jungle with monkeys.

Jenny spent her childhood in Manhattan Beach, California, where she ran around the house on all fours wanting to be an animal. Her parents, though not animal lovers the way she was, still nurtured her love for and connection with animals. However, when the number of rescue animals living in the house reached an all-time high of twenty-two, Jenny and her animals moved into a cabana behind the house.

Jenny's dream of working with animals came true unexpectedly. She met a man in Boston, and they went on an around-the-world backpacking adventure. Then, in Africa, they were asked to parent an orphaned chimpanzee they named Matooke, and they both found their calling.

• • •

Entebbe, Uganda

I wanted a career where I could be around animals. There were plenty of options, but none of them worked for me. I didn't want to work in a zoo because I couldn't stand seeing caged animals. The obvious choice of veterinarian was off the table because I'd passed out three times at the vet clinic when my animals were being treated. I am definitely not a math and science person, but I still decided to study wildlife biology in college. When I realized it was all science and that job opportunities included positions like game park ranger (deciding on numbers of hunting licenses to issue each year), researcher (I am not a patient observer), or working in a lab (yuck!), that option flew out the window. I guess I gave up on an animal-related career at that point.

I ended up changing my major to social work, moving to Boston after school, and working in sales and marketing. That's when I met Jimmy Desmond at a brewery. Jimmy was a chemist. We connected over a mutual love for beer, parties, and socializing with friends. It was pretty much love at first sight. It wasn't until we got married and took an around-the-world backpacking trip that our journey with wildlife began.

It had always been a dream of mine to see great apes in the wild. So, on that trip, we visited orangutans at the Sepilok Orangutan Rehabilitation Centre on the island of Borneo, Malaysia. The experience was so exciting, we ended up volunteering there and working with veterinarian Annelisa Kilbourn. Jimmy became so enthralled with her work rescuing great apes and studying disease transmission between humans and other apes that he realized he wanted to become a veterinarian. At the same time, I was introduced to the world of wildlife rescue, rehabilitation, and conservation of wild populations and found my path. I suddenly saw there was a way for me to put my passion for animals to use. It was a true sign of fate. We had no intention of doing what we do today, and yet we met, fell in love, got married, and embarked on a journey around the world together. It is only on that trip that we found our way at the same time as one.

To get some experience as wildlife rehabilitators, I wrote to Jane Goodall for advice, and to my surprise, she wrote back! She connected us with our now dear friend Debby Cox, and we ended up in Uganda, Africa, managing a rhino reintroduction and sanctuary program at Uganda Wildlife Education Centre [UWEC] in Entebbe. And that's where we met Matooke.

UWEC works with the Ngamba Island Chimpanzee Sanctuary and has chimps on-site, as well as rhinoceros. They take in wildlife confiscated by authorities and rehabilitate and release the animals when it's possible.

One day we were called to pick up a male eastern chimpanzee who, we were told, was in poor condition. We didn't know his history. We guessed his mother was killed, likely for bush meat, because a mother chimpanzee will never willingly give up her child. By his condition and age — estimated between two and three years old — we suspected he'd been taken as an infant and kept as a "pet" for one or two years in a village. We found him in awful condition. He was in a dog crate, sitting in his own feces and urine, with a lot of hair loss. He was extremely thin and very depressed. Usually chimps like this have come from villages where they haven't been nurtured, fed, or treated well and end up physically sick and mentally unstable. He was in very bad shape, and his sadness was clear in his eyes.

When the young chimpanzee was reported to UWEC and the Ngamba Sanctuary, there was no one on-site available to care for him. He needed to be nurtured and quarantined for three months. We were asked if we would be willing to take him and give him around-the-clock care. We agreed, and our adventure with him began.

We took the little boy, still in the dog crate, to the inside of our hut at the back of the rescue center. He was no different than a trau-matized human child who'd witnessed the murder of his family, been kidnapped, then been held captive and teased for years. In addition, this had been done to him by a different species, one he didn't know or understand. He was devastated and did not trust anyone, including me. Jimmy and I took on the role of father and mother for him, and as we saw it, our job was to bring him back to life.

He wouldn't come out of the crate, let me touch him, or take much food or water from me. The only type of food he would eat was a fruit similar to a banana called *matooke*, so that's what we named him. For nearly a week, he sat at the back of the crate, and I lay at the front with the door open. Hours and hours passed, and then days and days. It took four days before he let me touch him. It took another two days before he came out of the crate. The day he came out, he let me embrace him and that was that. We connected spiritually, emotionally, and telepathically. We bonded for life.

One day, Matooke accidentally rolled down a hill, and it made me laugh. I watched him register that I had laughed. Then he went right back up and did it again and again and again. He understood he was funny and that it was fun to make someone laugh. Before long, his sense of humor became apparent. He loved being tickled and playing games, and he loved to laugh.

Matooke also loved playing tricks on the dogs who lived on the property. He'd play chase with them and then run up a tree where they clearly couldn't follow — and then laugh his head off. At night, he often wanted to go to bed before I did. So he'd climb halfway up the ladder to our loft and make crying sounds until I caved and joined him.

After the three-month quarantine period, where he was only

allowed to be with us, we began introducing Matooke to other chimpanzees. His new family was comprised of a ragtag group of individuals from various backgrounds. They had been rescued from roadside zoos, poachers, being used as entertainment, and the pet trade. It took a month of bringing him to spend time with the group for the day, then bringing him home with us at night, before he made a choice. One night he decided to stay with his new chimp family instead of coming home with us. He definitely chose to leave us, and it was a great moment.

The fact that, in the end, he chose to be with his own kind was a beautiful and important thing to see and understand. He wanted to be with people who spoke his language, knew who he was and what he was about, and could truly meet his needs and wants. Just like any one of us, he wanted choice, freedom, love, understanding, and dignity.

Matooke is living happily in Uganda at UWEC with a large chimp family. Every time we visit him, he transforms from a big, tough, alpha male to a playful, silly, happy boy. He wants to laugh, be tickled, and play chase, just like before. He has grown up and become a confident, strong, and fulfilled individual.

Matooke changed my life and the life of my husband. He sealed the deal. We were clearly on a path to work with wildlife at the time, but he made it all crystal clear. After knowing him, whenever I saw pictures of little chimp faces in tiny metal boxes in research labs, I saw him. He made all the experiments on animals real. There was no question in either of our minds that we had to act on our love for him, to help others. It was a true epiphany, and there was no turning back once it happened.

• • •

Jenny and her husband, veterinarian Jim Desmond, are the founders of Liberia Chimpanzee Rescue and Protection (LCRP), the first and only chimpanzee sanctuary in Liberia, Africa. They rescue and rehabilitate chimpanzees who are victims of the bush meat and pet trades in that country.

In addition, Jenny and Jim, working with local and international partners, helped create Liberia's first law enforcement task force and public awareness campaign on wildlife trafficking. Their goals are far-reaching and include developing education awareness efforts to combat the trade of chimpanzees, which continues in Liberia. In their work, they seek to create partnerships with international organizations and country government agencies to develop and support the sanctuary's facilities and programs. Active locally, they have established successful vaccination and spay/neuter programs. When he's not napping with chimpanzees, Jim is a researcher in emerging disease.

As a footnote, in 2017, the HSUS reached a financial agreement with NYBC to help provide for the continuing care of the remaining sixty-three chimpanzees it abandoned on islands in Liberia. Humane Society International now oversees the project and has committed to care for the chimpanzees for the rest of their lives.

Have you ever rescued a ladybug?

Of course. Hasn't everyone? How can you resist them? I was the "Don't kill it!" screamer in my household and still am.

Name three things that make you happy.

Kindness, laughter, friends/family (both human and non!).

What one book, documentary, or speech has had a profound effect on you?

There are too many to name, some fiction and some nonfiction. Almost every single book, from hardcover baby books like *My Little Puppy* and *The White Squirrel* to heart-wrenching novels like *Ring of Bright Water* and *Call of the Wild* and so many books about animals in Africa.

Regarding your food choices, how do you describe yourself?

I am a longtime vegetarian. It started with chicken and turkey when I was fifteen years old. I had a turkey someone had given me because he wasn't "right" when he was born. One day I was carrying him somewhere, cradling him on his back, when I looked down and saw our Thanksgiving dinner right there in front of me. That was the last time I ate any kind of bird. The rest followed along later in bits.

If you had one message to deliver to others, what would it be?

Take action. Do good.

If you had one wish that was guaranteed to come true, what would it be?

I'd want my mom back. She is my soul mate. Of course, I would also wish that the cruelty to and suffering of animals would end. My mom would tell me that if I only had one choice, I should choose the second.

What advice do you have for people who say that they want to help animals in need but are too debilitated by what they witness?

I understand. It took me a long time to make myself "see" the truth. Witness is the perfect word. Once you have witnessed cruelty and abuse, it can't be unwitnessed. Taking action is what gets you through. Taking action is what will empower you. And taking action truly helps you to move past the debilitation.

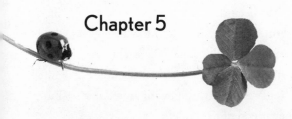

Chapter 5

PIG, CHICKEN, RABBIT
The Rewards in Leading the Way

Hancock, Maine, USA

From the time I was twelve years old until I was sixteen, I had a terrifying stepfather. His alcohol-fueled behavior, which ranged from playing Russian roulette with loaded guns to drowning innocent puppies, created a living nightmare. Although he appeared sophisticated and charming, his heart was cruel and twisted.

I never thought of him as having a single redeeming quality. But in writing this book, I discovered there was, ironically, one positive to having him in my life: His cruelty to animals served to ignite my passion to advocate for them.

The long driveway of my stepfather's estate led to a large, shingled house with a sprawling lawn and flower gardens. In front, the waves of the Atlantic Ocean lapped against a stone beach. Despite his obvious wealth and the conveniences it afforded, he chose, for a brief time, to raise chickens and pigs for food. This posed a dilemma for me. Up until then, I'd never made a clear connection between packaged meat and a living being.

My first shock came one night at dinner. My two brothers, sister, stepsister, stepbrother, and I were famished. We'd been locked out of the house all day and had been denied breakfast and lunch, which was not unusual. At dinnertime, we filed into the dining room and took our designated seats around the table, where a crystal pot containing bright yellow mustard was situated in the center of a white linen tablecloth. My stepfather was sitting, with an unusually smug grin, at his place at the far end of the table.

Mom entered the room carrying a cream-colored china platter and placed it in the center of the table. There was only one thing on the plate: a gigantic, gray tongue. So shocking was the sight that it rendered all the kids speechless. A few seconds passed before anyone spoke, but then the voices came in a flurry.

"What is it?" my six-year-old brother Billy asked.

"You mean who is it," my stepbrother Christopher said.

"That's disgusting!" my brother Jimmy added.

"I'm not eating that!" I exclaimed, followed by a chorus of "me neither!"

And so, as happened far too frequently in that house, six children went hungry and silently watched as two adults sitting on opposite ends of a table sliced into a calf's tongue and ate it.

In the months that followed, I was confronted again and again with the reality of where my meat came from. One crisp fall morning, my stepfather returned drunk from duck hunting and demanded I pluck the feathers from a bird he'd killed. I pleaded and begged not to do it, but ultimately my fear of him trumped my sadness. I sobbed as I pulled the feathers from the beautiful bird's body, my emotions flashing between rage and despair.

A few months later, two piglets arrived and were placed in a dark well house deep in the woods. My stepfather named them Pythias and Damon, and we were told they'd be raised for food. They were friendly pigs, each with a big personality. We visited them often to deliver food. When they were finished eating, they would come just close enough for us to reach over their wooden fence so that we could scratch their backs. Their happy presence brought internal conflict: I really liked the taste of bacon, but I also really liked the pigs.

One day, they disappeared. A month later, my stepfather gleefully announced that the pork chops for dinner were provided by Pythias. I stopped eating pork at that moment. And within a few years, I'd stopped eating meat altogether. My stepfather's choice to raise animals for food had caused me to see the essence of life in other animals. The experience changed me forever.

• • •

I think the connection we make with animals comes naturally and starts at birth. As toddlers, we're delighted by all creatures, from ladybugs and frogs to sheep and dogs. And then, for myriad reasons — stemming from social pressures to societal norms — we disconnect from the other species in our world. Sometimes, we're lucky enough to reconnect later in life. For many, that reconnection is welcome because it brings us back to the happy times of our childhood.

In my case, I'd always known that Pythias and Damon were going to be killed. So I'd distanced myself from them, not getting too close. It took forty more years — and a move to the other side of the world — for me to truly connect with a pig.

• • •

Margaret River, Australia

The Margaret River region, in Australia's southwest corner, is known for gentle hills that roll into the turquoise-colored Indian Ocean, never-ending white beaches, big waves that surfers dream of, and a rich, gravelly loam soil comparable to the Bordeaux wine country of France. It's a nature-lover's paradise, where kangaroos outnumber people, rainbow-feathered parakeets and pink parrots color the sky, and kookaburras announce dawn and dusk with monkey-like calls.

Jon had brought me to the region the first time I visited him in Australia, and it sang to my soul. At the time, he owned a rustic property, and every evening we would sit outside to witness a magical event. As the sun dropped below the Indian Ocean, hundreds of kangaroos would emerge from the bush to graze in the field in front of us. Every morning, we'd hold hands and walk a mile down a deserted beach before taking a plunge in the milky blue surf. There was a lot to like about Australia — especially this man with the accent.

To add to Jon's appeal, his sister, Sandra, and her husband, Ron, owned a winery on two hundred acres overlooking Geographe Bay. That's where, in 2010, more than a decade after I'd first come to the region, I met Sadie.

Sadie, a three-hundred-pound black pig who looked like an oversized bumblebee due to a twelve-inch-wide white ring around her midsection, lived with her children in the backyard of an old farmhouse on the property. It was an idyllic home for pigs, with plenty of shade trees, ample water, and two shelters. From the house where I stayed, it was a short walk uphill along a red dirt road to Sadie's pen. When I was lucky enough to stay at the winery, my morning routine involved taking CousCous and Chickpea, our small, white fluffy rescue dogs, on a mile-long walk past the farmhouse.

The first time we noticed Sadie, we stopped to say hello. She came to the fence with five piglets, all of them clearly hoping we'd brought something yummy to eat. They were friendly, snorting their hellos as I leaned over the fence to pet them. Ben, the winery's property manager, came out of his house to greet me and told me their story. He said Sadie was his new breeder pig and that he intended to raise her children to feed his family. When I asked if I could feed them, he said yes — but made sure I understood they were strict vegetarians. Their diet consisted mainly of leftover veggies from the restaurant on the property along with plenty of grapes from the vineyard.

The next day, CousCous, Chickpea, and I began a daily ritual of visiting and feeding Sadie and her family when we stayed at the winery. Each time we came, Sadie greeted us with welcome snorts, pushing others out of the way to be the first to get the bread and vegetables we delivered. When she finished eating, she would always come back to me, leaning her body against the wire fence for scratches behind her ears and on the sides of her neck. Her tough skin with its wire bristles was alien to me, yet the comfort she received from touch was not. She reminded me of the dogs, who also had favorite foods and let me know where they preferred to be scratched.

A year passed. Sadie's children disappeared from the pen, and both CousCous and Chickpea died. I found solace in my visits with Sadie, until one day I walked to the pen carrying a bag of apples and discovered she wasn't there. My heart sank.

I soon learned that Ben had left the winery to take another job, and Sadie had been moved to a temporary, secluded pen between the restaurant and a dam. I ran a quarter of a mile before spotting the fencing on a dry patch of gravelly dirt some seventy-five feet from the road.

"Sadie!" I yelled as I walked toward the three-hundred-pound pig, who was lying on the ground. Her head lifted. She stood and slowly sauntered toward me, stopping short of the electrified fence. I reached over and gave her my hand to sniff. Her pink snout touched it, inhaling the scent in short bursts. I pulled an apple from the plastic bag and offered it to her. She nudged it with her nose until it dropped on the ground and then looked back at me.

She was a shell of the pig I'd known, and it was obvious why. She'd been moved from pig heaven to a patch of dirt that even a camel wouldn't like. And it was hot. It was ten in the morning and already 95 degrees, well on the way to the predicted 110. The only shade was a small tin shed that stored heat like an oven.

I surveyed her yard, a fenced fifty-square-foot patch of red gravelly dirt. A hose held in place by a metal rod reminded me of a gerbil feeder. I touched the end with my finger. A ball moved and released a few drops of water. I removed the drip ball attachment from the end of the hose expecting a rush of water, but it didn't come. The only source of water on this barren piece of property was a feeder she had to prompt with her snout to get even a few drops.

I put the apples down and walked the perimeter in search of a water spigot. Sadie followed. That's when something unexpected happened.

I stumbled on a stick and instinctively picked it up and threw it out of the way. It landed inside the yard. Sadie took off after it, picked it up in her mouth, and ran back to me. She dropped it, pushed it toward me with her nose, and looked up expectantly. I threw the stick again, and again Sadie retrieved it, but this time she raced toward me smiling.

We played for half an hour before I went for help.

I found Jon having coffee on the terrace of the house, and when I explained Sadie's dilemma, he was quick to remind me that she wasn't my pig and I should be mindful of that.

"Yes, dear," I said sarcastically. Of course, he was right, but Sadie's situation was wrong. "She has no water and it's a hundred degrees down there," I said. "I'm going to look for a shovel. She needs a mud pool."

Despite Jon's warning not to interfere, he joined me at the pen and helped me create enrichment for Sadie by adding logs and sticks to her barren yard.

I worked inside the fence, picking at the dirt underneath the feeder, in hopes of creating a watering hole so she could cool off. Sadie hung close, taking a keen interest in my work, her blue eyes, haloed by long, white lashes, looking at me intently. While we didn't speak each other's language, we were communicating. She knew what I was doing, and she understood I was doing it for her.

After a few hours' work, Sadie had a pen with sticks and logs to play with and a bucket full of water. But my attempt to create a mud bath failed. The soil was too porous and the air was too hot. Every drop of water was sucked up by the thirsty ground.

That night, I felt compelled to call Ben — who was still Sadie's owner — to express my concerns. He explained that he didn't have a place to keep her anymore. He'd found an adequate home for her at a free-roaming breeding farm where she'd be well-fed and would spend her days with other pigs, but if I could give her a better home, he said he'd sell her to me instead.

I loved Sadie. She reminded me of the many dogs I'd known throughout my life. During our day together, when I'd played with her, it was as if the pig in the movie *Babe* had come to life. She was so much more than someone's breeding pig, doomed to give birth to litter after litter just to see her piglets taken away. She was funny and smart and inquisitive. Like all of us, she enjoyed simple pleasures: eating grapes, having her back scratched, lying in the sun, and playing in water. I wanted to take care of her, but I wasn't sure I could offer her a better situation than Ben had organized.

The next morning, after spending an hour with Sadie, I drove to a hundred-acre property that Jon and I had purchased five years earlier with the hope of one day using it for an animal sanctuary. The tenant there was something of a hippie who lived off the land. She grew her own vegetables, fed her dog roadkill kangaroo meat, and had three retired racehorses she'd rescued from meat markets. I explained my dilemma and asked if she'd consider taking care of

Sadie if I paid her. Her answer surprised me. It was an unequivocal "no." She explained that her horses were afraid of pigs and she didn't want to do anything to stress them. I understood her concerns and was forced to face the fact that my only door to helping Sadie had been shut. At the time there weren't any local rescue groups or farm sanctuaries that took pigs.

I went back to Sadie's pen, sat down next to her, and cried. I would miss her. While I knew she'd enjoy living with other pigs, I wanted a different life for her — one I couldn't give.

Like birds who sing when it rains, Sadie's spirit soared with simple gestures of kindness, the gift of a shared loaf of bread or a stick to play with. She showed me that even in the direst of circumstances, she was still capable of experiencing joy and expressing gratitude. Because of my time with her, I understood why so many of my friends were working to create better conditions for animals who were being raised for food. I would later join their army to help farm animals and would discover the rewards that come to those who lead the way to help others.

Josh Balk

CHICKEN

I first met Josh Balk when we were seated next to each other at a leadership summit dinner for the Humane Society of the United States (HSUS) in Washington, DC, in 2015. Josh, a boyish redhead with a wide and welcoming smile, was wearing an HSUS staff name tag. We introduced ourselves before sitting down to listen to US Senator Cory Booker, a fantastic orator and animal welfare advocate, speak to a room filled with HSUS volunteers. It wasn't until the next day, when we were working together on a Massachusetts ballot initiative to end the extreme confinement of calves, pigs, and egg-laying hens, that I discovered this young man in his mid-thirties was, in his own right, a world leader in the social justice movement for animals. As vice president of farm animal protection for the HSUS, he is credited with negotiating groundbreaking deals with food companies to better the lives of farm animals. He is also an entrepreneurial golden boy, having cofounded the food technology company JUST (originally called Hampton Creek).

Like many people who've chosen a career path advocating for animals, Josh was an empathic child and was especially affected by animal suffering.

"As early as I can remember," he says, "I cared about animals. I had dogs at home, and I loved them very much, but I still had a feeling that animals outside my circle mattered. I felt incredibly sad when I saw suffering — even on television programs. My dad and I often went fishing, but once I got the fish, I felt bad about the whole thing. To this day, I have nightmares about my fishing past."

After high school, driven by a steadfast sense of right and wrong concerning animals and their treatment, Josh aligned himself with like-minded people. While attending George Washington University in Washington, DC, he interned with the HSUS and later became a volunteer. Advocacy turned to activism in 2002 when Josh accepted a job with the nonprofit Compassion Over Killing. During his time at the organization, he worked undercover in a chicken slaughter plant owned by Perdue Farms. He was twenty-five years old.

• • •

Howell, Maryland, USA

I still remember my first day on the job. My shift was early morning, so it was before sunrise. The ride to work was cold and dark. I parked in the lot, walked into this decrepit building, and found my way to the locker room. I remember I was paralyzed with fear because there were a dozen or so workers there eating and getting changed and drinking coffee. I was sure they could see the hidden camera on me.

Then the supervisor came in and motioned for us to get in the shackling room. We followed the supervisor in, and I got in line with the rest of the workers, all in front of the conveyor belt. The belt was waist-high and just above it were metal shackles. I heard a noise to my left. A truck pulled up, parked, and dropped an unrecognizable white mass on the belt. Then the belt started to creak and churn a little bit and move. The shackles began swinging, and I looked over again and saw the chickens approaching, piled on top of each other on the conveyor belt heading my way. I thought, *Oh my God, this is actually happening!*

We were being trained to grab the chicken and shackle her. *That's it*, I remember thinking, *I can't believe I'm going to grab this poor animal and do an unconscionable thing: shackle her and send her to her death.* I grabbed her and she started flapping her wings to try to free herself. She was trying to scratch me and peck at my hands. She was fighting for her life. She struggled with every ounce of energy she had. Her legs were all crooked because chickens in the meat industry are genetically manipulated to grow so big their legs often cripple beneath the weight of their bodies. Her breast was featherless and bright red, burned by ammonia from the floor of the factory farm where she was raised. She was scared and screaming, and I remember saying underneath my breath, behind the surgical mask I was wearing, "I am so sorry. I'm so sorry."

It was an experience I will never forget. It's one thing to read about or watch the plight of farm animals. But nothing can match seeing the suffering and fear firsthand. Seeing this poor bird in pain for no fault of her own inspired me to fight on her behalf and the billions like her in the poultry industry.

• • •

Josh's work exposed cruelty to animals at the Perdue plant, and media coverage brought to light the abusive slaughter practices in the chicken industry. A year later, Josh transitioned into a role leading the corporate negotiation efforts for the farm animal department at the HSUS. There are currently no federal laws that regulate the treatment of the nine billion animals raised for food in the United States each year inside factory farms.

To circumvent the government's passivity in protecting animals used for food, Josh was directed to eliminate the worst factory farming abuses by convincing companies to require higher standards of care for the animals used in their supply chain. He moved swiftly, leading a team that convinced hundreds of companies to adopt strict animal welfare policies. Threatened by his success, meat producers worked against him by strengthening their lobbying force in Washington. One lobbyist, Rick Berman, went as far as to create a Facebook page and website called "HumaneWatch," which attacks the HSUS and its staff, including Josh. Instead of embracing consumers' cries for change, Berman tries to silence the good work of the organization. But the attacks have only served to strengthen Josh's resolve.

Most meat, eggs, and dairy come from factory farms where animals are raised in windowless sheds, provided no enrichments, and left to breathe an unhealthy amount of ammonia emanating from their own waste. In the United States alone, hundreds of millions of these poor animals are confined in tiny cages that prevent them from moving more than a few inches for their entire lives. As the human population increased and the standard diet included more meat, eggs, and dairy, there was a growing need for these products to be produced as cheaply as possible. As a result, small family-run farms have given way to factory farms that value the mass production of meat over the humane treatment of animals.

Witnessing this inspired Josh to start a food company.

• • •

In my work, I was being exposed to it all. The more I knew, the more it became clear that the animals needed us to be as strategic as possible during our finite time on earth if we really wanted to help them. I wanted to disrupt global factory farming, which represents the more than 90 percent of farm animals who we make suffer in the world.

Aside from the transformational work I was a part of at the HSUS, I thought that if I could form a company that produced plant-based foods that are affordable, marketed to the mainstream, and taste just as good as animal-based food, then I could make a further difference.

I pitched my idea on the phone one night to my high school friend Josh Tetrick. He had wanted to start a company that was inherently good for animals and liked my idea. So we started building a team. We hired a chef, a head of research and development, and a person to lead sales. We impressed a venture capital team enough to get a half million dollars, and we got started. Hampton Creek — named after my late St. Bernard, Hampton, who was such a love for me — was formed.

Our goal is to create the biggest company in the world that happens to be good for animals. Our values are to be innovative and aggressive, to go fast so I can have the biggest impact I possibly can in my lifetime. It's a mentality that requires thinking about mortality. I'd hate to, in my last moments, think I could have made a bigger difference but didn't give it a shot. If I was bold and acted with courage to take leaps, I think I could peacefully say good-bye to this world.

• • •

In 2011, Josh Balk and Josh Tetrick cofounded Hampton Creek, later renamed JUST, when they were both thirty-two years old. Their products — which include egg substitutes, cookies, cookie doughs, mayos, salad dressings, and even "egg" patties — are made completely from plants. Their most popular product is Just Mayo, an egg-free mayonnaise. They started selling "clean meat" in 2018 — meat grown from a small cell sample; that is, meat that has never existed in animal form. The product is expected to change the world by eliminating factory farming and the subsequent need to slaughter animals.

Proof that innovation can be rewarding, within three years of the company's inception, the two Joshes had raised $120 million to fund their venture. Within four years of its founding, the company was valued at $1.1 billion.

As vice president of farm animal protection at the HSUS — his full-time job — Josh leads a team that has persuaded hundreds of companies — including Walmart, Kroger, Kraft Heinz, Starbucks, Aramark, and Supervalu — to adopt animal welfare policies that prohibit extreme confinement of animals raised for food. He's also worked to pass laws ending the crate and cage confinement of calves, pigs, and chickens in a dozen states through successful ballot initiatives or legislative campaigns in state houses.

According to Paul Shapiro, founder of Compassion Over Killing and former vice president of policy at the HSUS, there are more laws and corporate policies protecting farm animals than ever before, and more consumers are leaving animals off their plates and eating plant-based meals instead. This colossal shift is due to Josh and other leaders in the compassion movement who confront cruelty head-on, using common sense and innovation. By exposing a food system that is inherently bad for animals and the people who eat them, they're creating positive change for everyone.

Have you ever rescued a ladybug?

I haven't, but if I saw one who needed my help, I'd be eager to do so.

Name three things that make you happy.

I love politics, movies, and football.

What one book, documentary, or speech has had a profound effect on you?

Peter Singer's *Animal Liberation* is a must-read for any person interested in animal issues.

Regarding your food choices, how do you describe yourself?

Vegan.

If you had one message to deliver to others, what would it be?

Just get started now. Start changing your diet to be more humane. Start volunteering for an animal organization. Start a company to render animal exploitation obsolete. Start donating as much as you can. Time isn't on animals' side. They need us to act now.

If you had one wish that was guaranteed to come true, what would it be?

I'd like to eliminate all suffering.

What advice do you have for people who say that they want to help animals in need but are too debilitated by what they witness?

There's no need to witness anything to change your diet or to lobby your legislator to pass an animal welfare law, or to volunteer for a farm animal organization. Animals don't need us to merely witness their suffering. They need us to take strategic action on their behalf.

Peter Singer

HOMO SAPIENS

Not everyone who has changed the world for animals had a moment with a different species that catapulted them on a mission. I discovered this when I reached out to Peter Singer, the bioethicist and philosopher credited with launching the modern-day animal welfare movement with his book *Animal Liberation: A New Ethics for Our Treatment of Animals*. In this book, he makes the convincing intellectual case that humans and other animals have shared qualities: the ability to enjoy their lives and also to suffer. He argues against speciesism, stating that human beings should not ignore or discount the suffering of other species and should give equal considerations to the interest of all beings "irrespective of their species, just as everyone agrees we should give interest to human beings irrespective of their race and sex." With this pronouncement, he gave the modern world permission to believe what we innately know — that animals are sentient and that we have a moral obligation not to exploit or mistreat them.

I reached out to Peter because he's a hero among heroes throughout the world. I was intrigued to know what sparked him to explore our moral obligations to other animals so convincingly that he triggered a sense of justice that has driven thousands of people to act. I also wanted to know if there was something that happened in his childhood that set him, unknowingly, on a path to focus on ethics, morality, and animal rights.

I learned that three of Peter's grandparents were killed in the Holocaust. His parents, both Austrians of Jewish descent, emigrated from Vienna to Australia in 1938. Peter was born in Melbourne eight years later. His earliest memory of an animal is of his pet cat, Buddy, who disappeared when Peter was five years old. He doesn't remember being especially empathic toward animals and says his mother "took no interest in animals at all." But his father, Ernst, did. "My father was concerned about animal suffering, and if we happened to be following a truck taking cattle to slaughter, he would say something about how cruel it was. He made similar remarks if we were walking along a beach or a pier, and people had caught fish who were lying flapping and dying in a basket," he said.

Peter's personal awakening came later, inspired by an interaction with his own species. His moral philosophy on animal equality was sparked when he asked a fellow student at Oxford University a simple question about his eating habits.

• • •

Oxford, England

The experience I had regarding animals that comes closest to an "epiphany" — though I don't like that word; it's too religious for me — was not in relation to any individual animal but to all animals. It happened in 1970, when I was twenty-four and a graduate student at the University of Oxford.

I was studying philosophy, with a focus on ethics. After a class on free will and moral responsibility, I started talking to Richard Keshen, a Canadian graduate student, about some issues raised in the class. It was lunchtime, and he suggested we continue the conversation over lunch at his college. I agreed. When it came time to choose our meal, the options were spaghetti with a brown sauce or a salad plate. Richard asked if there was meat in the spaghetti sauce and was told that there was. He took the salad plate. I took the spaghetti, and we continued to discuss the class. When we had said all that we had to say on that, I asked Richard what he had against meat. He said he didn't think it was right to treat animals in the way they are treated before being turned into food.

You have to remember that it was very, very rare to meet a vegetarian then. You might meet a Hindu who avoided meat for religious reasons, or perhaps a pacifist who thought that all killing is wrong, but I don't think I had ever met anyone who was a vegetarian because of a concern for the suffering of animals. Nor had I ever heard anyone challenge the ethical legitimacy of the meat industry. It wasn't a topic one thought about much.

Richard, with his wife, Mary, and their fellow Canadians Ros and Stan Godlovitch, soon opened my eyes. They told me to read *Animal Machines*, a book by Ruth Harrison and, at the time, the only book to describe the new form of animal raising known as factory farming. I had assumed that animals live good, even pampered lives, until one day they are rounded up, taken to slaughter, and humanely killed. That one bad day didn't seem such a bad deal. But now I learned that the truth was very different: Millions of chickens and pigs never got to go outside at all, but were crowded inside huge sheds. Their suffering was completely disregarded, unless it interfered with profitability — and often it didn't.

My wife, Renata, became part of these conversations, too. Initially we decided that we could not justify eating factory-farmed animal products, but we then also had doubts about the treatment of other animals — the castration, dehorning, and other mutilations — and moved to becoming vegetarians ourselves.

That experience led, over the next four years, to the writing of *Animal Liberation*, in which I argued that the only defensible ethical basis for our relations with animals is that of equal consideration of similar interests. I then described how this principle was systematically violated in our treatment of animals when we raise them for food or when we experiment on them.

I've been pleased to hear that *Animal Liberation* influenced many of the leading activists in the animal movement, from Ingrid Newkirk to Henry Spira, and from Wayne Pacelle to Steve Wise. It has thus contributed to some of the most significant victories for animals, especially for farm animals, including bans in Europe and in California and some other US states on the most severe confinement systems, as well as pressure on giant corporations to change their treatment of animals. That includes decisions by major cosmetics companies to end testing on animals. The book has also helped the spread of vegetarianism and veganism. With all the cynicism and negativity about human nature we so often hear, it's important to know that ethical argument can move so many people to change their lives for the better — better for themselves, better for the animals, and better for the planet.

• • •

Peter Singer is perhaps the world's most influential living philosopher. His thoughts on abortion, infanticide, and euthanasia have stirred controversy, while his theories on animal ethics have caused sweeping reforms that have dramatically reduced suffering throughout the world.

In 2005, the Fulbright scholar was named one of the one hundred most influential people in the world by *Time* magazine. In 2013, the Gottlieb Duttweiler Institute named him the third most influential global thought leader for that year. In 2011, *Time* included *Animal Liberation* on its all-time list of the one hundred best nonfiction books. In 2012, he received Australia's highest civic honor, the Companion of the Order of Australia.

Peter has written fifteen books, coauthored eleven, edited numerous anthologies, and been profiled in countless films, documentaries, and books. He is a professor of bioethics at Princeton University and is also a laureate professor at the School of Historical and Philosophical Studies at the University of Melbourne, Australia. Peter helps lead many organizations and cofounded the Great Ape Project, an international organization that argues for basic legal rights (life, liberty, and the prohibition of torture) for chimpanzees, bonobos, gorillas, and orangutans. He is also the cofounder of Animals Australia. The organization works for a world where "all animals are treated with compassion and respect and are free from cruelty." Targeted investigations by Animals Australia have led to government interventions, the creation of laws, corporate food policy changes, and animal cruelty convictions in Australia, Indonesia, Israel, Jordan, and Egypt.

Like most animals, human beings have the ability to reason. We also have a responsibility to ask questions, find answers, and act upon the knowledge we gain. Peter Singer has made a profession of sharing his thoughts about our relationship with other animals. In doing this, he's not only inspired world leaders to do good, but he's demonstrated by his own story how important it is for us to ask questions. Change for all animals — from the legal abolishment of human slavery to the rise in the animal welfare movement — started with questions about morals and ethics. It has been driven by those who chose right over wrong.

Have you ever rescued a ladybug?

When we were kids, if one landed on us, we would blow it away and sing "Ladybird, ladybird, fly away home, your house is on fire and your children are home."

Name three things that make you happy.

Knowing that I have contributed to reducing suffering in the world, spending time with family and good friends, and being physically active in a beautiful place outdoors, for example, hiking or surfing.

What one book, documentary, or speech has had a profound effect on you?

I read Bertrand Russell's *A History of Western Philosophy* when I was in high school, and it led me to study philosophy when I went to university — not that I thought then that I would make a career out of it, but just that it would be interesting to talk about these questions.

Regarding your food choices, how do you describe yourself?

A flexible vegan — generally vegan when I can control what I eat, occasionally vegetarian otherwise.

If you had one message to deliver to others, what would it be?

If you have a strong emotional connection to a particular animal, or a particular species of animal, try to extend your compassion to all sentient beings — all animals who can feel pain. Don't pet one animal while sticking a fork into another who has had a much more miserable life.

If you had one wish that was guaranteed to come true, what would it be?

How big and how utopian a wish can it be? An end to all suffering, everywhere? An end to all unnecessary suffering? An end to the suffering we humans inflict on sentient beings, whether human or animal?

What advice do you have for people who say that they want to help animals in need but are too debilitated by what they witness?

Focus on the positive — on the immense progress for animals that has been made in the past forty years, both in attitudes and in laws and practices. Become part of the worldwide movement to make still further progress.

Melanie Greensmith

RABBIT

Melanie Greensmith is known for designing glamorous clothes for rock 'n' roll royalty. Before retiring her international label Wheels & Dollbaby in 2017, her clothes were most often seen in the pages of magazines — not in the advertisements, but in candid photographs of celebrities.

I met the blonde, dimple-cheeked fashion icon through her generosity. It was 2007 and I was president of the Dogs' Refuge Home (DRH), an animal shelter in Western Australia. Every six months Mel would give us several boxes of clothes we could use to raise money for our homeless dogs. Before opening the sale to the public, we'd give our small staff and volunteers the opportunity to buy first. Most of them worked for minimum wage and couldn't regularly afford designer clothes. When we opened the door for the sale, they excitedly clambered in, picked out a Wheels & Dollbaby dress or cardigan sweater, and held it tightly to their chests as if it were a prize, before returning to their jobs cleaning kennels and walking dogs.

To be truthful, my friendship with Mel and her rock star partner, Mark McEntee of the Divinyls, started as an attempt to engage her in an active role with the shelter. Her brand was popular and the couple were celebrities with big hearts for animals. At home, they had three horses, a sheep, and three small white Maltese terriers they took everywhere — including to dinner parties and the hairdresser.

Mel graciously accepted an honorary role as patron of DRH and instantly raised our shelter's status from a worthwhile charity to a fashionable cause. Despite her generous engagement, I didn't feel comfortable around the star until we had a misunderstanding. One day Mel called me with an invitation. In her soft-spoken British/Australian accent, she said, "Mark and I are having a barbie party and we'd love it if you and Jon would come. It's just going to be some close friends, people from Mark's band and a few others."

My interpretation of the invitation was that it was a dress-up party and that most of the people attending would be rock stars. Eager to impress, I borrowed one of her designs from Jon's daughter, Wren — a tight-fitting, strapless, leopard-print dress.

On the night, as I squeezed into the dress and pulled it upward, my breasts — begging for room — popped over the top, instantly enlarging their appearance. Clever designer. I pulled my hair back with a band and attached a two-foot-long, blonde ponytail hairpiece to it. I then slipped on frighteningly high heels, applied some ruby-red Chanel lipstick, and checked myself out in a full-length mirror. Gone was the preppy girl from New England. I'd transformed into rock 'n' roll Barbie.

When we arrived at Mel and Mark's house, it was immediately apparent I'd misunderstood the party theme. No one else looked like a Barbie doll. When I asked Mel why, she explained that it was an Australian "shrimp on the barbie" barbecue — just an ordinary barbecue with friends.

"Don't worry," she said, giggling. "Look around. You fit right in."

And I did. That night, as I sat outside under the southern stars surrounded by horses, dogs, sheep, and a few rock stars, I realized that when compassion for other species is at your core, you have many unforeseen friends in the world.

Mel was born in London, England, to a professional cricket-playing father and a showgirl mother. Both parents loved animals. Mel was an only child — with the exception of a Great Pyrenees dog named Bell who was already on the scene when Mel arrived. Many baby pictures were taken of Mel nestled in Bell's soft fur. She remembers the dog as both a great source of pleasure and comfort and her protector.

The next pet on the scene was a rabbit named Bunnykins, and then Puff and Patch, two guinea pigs whom she remembers vividly to this day.

"They used to run around the house, and when I'd open the fridge, they'd let out an excited little scream and run to me for lettuce. They'd also sit in my lap and watch telly with me. We were very close," Mel says. "One day a dog got into our backyard and killed Puff. I remember the dog's owner, a lady, saying to me, 'I'm sorry. I'll buy you another one.' But I wanted Puff. There was no other one."

In 1987, Melanie opened her first boutique in Sydney, Australia, and her label, Wheels & Dollbaby, was born. Michael Jackson was her first customer, unwittingly christening the brand the "outfitters to the stars." Kate Moss, Katy Perry, Courtney Love, Scarlett Johansson, Jerry Hall, and other fashionistas followed.

Melanie's designs were unique, and she thought that the decisions she put into creating them were compassionately conscientious. Until a package came in the mail. Inside was a polite letter asking her to watch a video.

• • •

Sydney, Australia

When I was a teenager living in London, I was influenced by style icon Anita Pallenberg. Pallenberg was an Italian actress and model who hung out with the Rolling Stones and dated guitarist Brian Jones and then Keith Richards. She was all over the fashion magazines. Much of the time, she was wearing fur.

I loved animals and I loved fashion. It's funny, but at the time, I would never have thought about buying a new fur coat — but I did collect used fur coats at vintage clothing shops. And I wore them.

It's strange how you can love animals but sometimes not be aware of the ways humans hurt them. My transition to understanding came in bursts of connections.

I have a thirty-three-acre rural property in West Australia. One day I found a sheep caught in the wire of my fence. She was in a bad way, so I called the vet. He asked me if I wanted to put her down and I said no. So, to save her life, he amputated her leg. The vet bill was hundreds of dollars, and my friends joked that it was the most expensive leg of lamb I'd ever had. Mark called her I-lean because she had to lean on you to stand up. I called her Sheepy.

Until we rescued Sheepy, I had no idea how inquisitive and connected sheep were. She was adorable and nosy and followed me everywhere. She loved playing with the dogs and often leaned down to them and gave them gentle head-butts. Like the dogs who barked to let us know when someone was coming down the driveway, she baa-ed. I loved her personality. She was part of our family. That's when I stopped eating lamb.

Then I got two baby cows, and that was the end of beef. I changed when I realized that everyone has a personality. I didn't want to kill someone just for my pleasure in eating it or wearing it.

It was around this time I started spending time with Chrissie Hynde. Chrissie is a founding member of the Pretenders rock band. I met her because my partner, Mark, wrote one of her hit songs, and we started hanging out. She loved my fashions, and I began designing her tour wear. We had a lot in common in that we both loved and cared about animals. We talked about that a lot. Chrissie was a passionate animal rights activist and a supporter of People for the Ethical Treatment of Animals (PETA). We'd often go shopping in London together, and as we walked around she'd point out people wearing furs and call them "fur whores." It got me thinking about how some people chose to wear fur to advertise social status.

At this time, I'd been in the fashion business for about twenty years. I considered myself a conscientious designer. Despite suppliers trying to sell me everything from rabbit fur to crocodile skin, I always said no.

In 2008, I started designing a little over-the-shoulder shrug sweater. It was a fifties-inspired look, from the Brigitte Bardot sweater days. To get the fluffiness, we used angora, and I usually paired it with a high-waist pencil skirt. The sweaters were very, very popular. We produced them in lots of colors — lemon, pink, black, and blue — and they became something my clients collected. At the time, I truly hadn't realized what angora was. I was about to find out.

One day I received a padded envelope in the mail from PETA. In it was a very polite letter asking me to please watch the enclosed video showing the harvesting of angora wool from rabbits.

I watched it. Living rabbits were having their hair pulled out of their skin and they were screaming in agony. They were then thrown back into cages, raw and bloodied. It was awful. Cruel. Frightening.

I immediately rang my Chinese supplier and asked how they were getting the angora for the shrugs. She fought back, trying desperately to assure me the rabbits weren't hurt in the process. But I knew better. That was the day I stopped buying angora and refused to do anything with it ever again.

There was a big outcry from my clients who loved the shrug. I told them I was really sorry, but due to the cruelty involved, I wouldn't be doing them anymore. I never did.

It was a huge moment for me. I had been blind to the cruelty. It made me realize that the money wasn't worth it. Nothing was worth it.

I went home, opened my closet, and took out the six vintage fur coats I'd had since I was a teenager and threw them all away.

The world is filled with people who value money over preventing cruelty. Taking that approach doesn't create fashion. Creating good designs — ones that make people feel good about themselves — does. I think designers who use fur in this day and age are looking at profit over compassion. They're buying into their clients' desire for status. I see a fur coat now and I see torture. I don't see status. It makes the person wearing it look out of touch or even very cruel.

My connections with a rabbit and two guinea pigs happened when I was a child, when I realized they had wonderful, happy personalities. It took someone else to point out to me, many decades later, that I was involved in cruelty toward those same types of animals by the fashions I was creating. I hope that in sharing this story, consumers and designers will be inspired to research and make conscious decisions before using and creating products that involve animals. I truly believe that the greatest fashions aren't born from cruelty.

• • •

Melanie Greensmith has been a trendsetter in the ever-growing faux fur fashion craze through her label, Wheels & Dollbaby, and her ongoing work styling musicians and other celebrities. Her choices have created awareness and change for tens of thousands of followers and clients. She's not alone. Encouragingly, some of the most prestigious fashion houses — Gucci, Armani, Versace, Hugo Boss, Furla, and Ralph Lauren — have opted out of using fur after learning of the cruelty involved. PETA is credited for causing this trend by exposing the immense suffering to animals raised for their fur.

Have you ever rescued a ladybug?

Yes, loads of times.

Name three things that make you happy.

Security, animals, and Mark.

What one book, documentary, or speech has had a profound effect on you?

The video PETA sent me showing what happened to rabbits when their angora fur was harvested. And the book *The Road Less Traveled* by M. Scott Peck.

Regarding your food choices, how do you describe yourself?

I don't eat meat.

If you had one message to deliver to others, what would it be?

Think before you make a decision in your life that involves another animal.

If you had one wish that was guaranteed to come true, what would it be?

It would be for my Maltese, Minky, AKA Fifi L'Amour, to come back. And world peace.

What advice do you have for people who say that they want to help animals in need but are too debilitated by what they witness?

First, only witness what you can handle. Then, know there are a million ways to help alleviate suffering. Be conscious when you buy clothes, donate money to charity, deliver food to your local animal shelter, and give a stray dog or cat a home. Every act helps.

Chapter 6

BEAR, PIGEON, COW
Connections That Drive Change

Bar Harbor, Maine, USA

There's an honorable war being fought in our world for animals. In it, the good are going after the evil, the generous are taking aim at the greedy, and the kind are blanketing the cruel. I refer to it as the compassion movement because it's fueled by a desire to alleviate suffering.

It's a stormy battle. Atrocities against the innocent have been plaguing our world. We're more aware of them now because of social media, which has helped bring to light realities that traditional news outlets don't or rarely cover. However, the question is, once we know what's going on, do we look away or do we act?

For me, the path is clear. For decades, I'd been caught up in the endless, all-consuming, daily cycle of rescue — picking up after and paying for the destruction left behind by people who are legally allowed to abuse and exploit animals. I eventually reached a point where in 2012, I made a conscious decision to put my energy and smarts toward solving the problem instead of patching it. I said a simple prayer and set an intention. I asked to be used to help millions of animals at a time, and I resolved to dedicate my life to creating laws to stop the bad guys.

Within weeks, I received a call from Lisa Baker, a forward-thinking, five-foot-four powerhouse and member of parliament in Australia, who asked me to work with her to create reforms and laws to end puppy farming. Shortly after that, Wayne Pacelle, the president and CEO of the Humane Society of the United States (HSUS), reached out and asked me to build a leadership council in Maine. Part of the Maine council's role would be to work with federal and state legislators to create laws to quash animal abusers.

Over the next several years, working on the battlefield of the compassion movement was energizing because, with each commitment, I felt closer to success. However, it wasn't easy — involving meetings on Capitol Hill in Washington, lunches with politicians at Parliament House in Australia, and coffee with state legislators in Maine — and I learned a lot of sobering lessons about politics. The core problem I've discovered is this: The people who profit from exploiting animals have money; that money pays for lobbyists and political friends; and too often for politicians, money trumps common sense.

I learned to roll with the punches until one took me by surprise. In 2015, the Maine legislature passed a bill to prohibit pet stores from selling puppies and kittens from puppy mills — a big win. If passed into law, this would curb sick puppies from entering the state, lessen the strain on already taxed animal shelters, and help put unscrupulous breeders out of business. At the time, the Republican governor of Maine, Paul LePage, was angry with state Democrats for refusing to support a constitutional amendment to end the state income tax, and he had vowed to veto any bills they sponsored. True to his word, he childishly punished animals by vetoing the puppy mill bill — even though it was supported by Republicans, independents, and Democrats alike.

The move by the governor infuriated me. I couldn't believe he would include animals in petty politics. Rather than give up, though, I took the lead from other animal welfare advocates and decided to try to change the laws in my hometown, Bar Harbor, Maine, by working to create two ordinances: a ban on selling puppies and kittens from puppy mills, and an ordinance to prohibit wild and exotic animal acts.

To me, Bar Harbor is Americana at its best. We celebrate the Fourth of July with a rip-roaring parade, hold fundraisers when people and pets get sick, and meet for breakfast at the best blueberry pancake diner in the world. The community is a family.

I enlisted help from Zack Klyver, a local whale expert, who set up a meeting with town councilor Matt Hochman. Over coffee at Matt's Trailhead Café, Matt agreed to propose the ordinances and suggested we meet with the town manager, Cornell Knight.

As we built our team, I discovered once again that, on the path to do what's right for animals, we're never alone. We may think we are, but most people are usually with us. People care about animals and their welfare. Those who don't are bullies. It just takes someone to put their concerns into action, and like a snowball rolling down a hill, the momentum only builds and gets bigger.

Cornell gave us the go-ahead for a vote. Zack and Kim Swan, both animal-loving locals who were on the HSUS Maine state council, went to work talking to town councilors about the reasons for the proposals. Diana de los Santos, the director of the local SPCA and Bar Harbor's animal control officer, raised her hand to testify, and veterinarian Marc Fine wrote a letter to support the puppy mill ordinance. Katie Hansberry, Maine's HSUS director, provided a history of documented abuses by puppy mills, circuses, and traveling acts for evidence. Everything was lined up and going smoothly — until I heard about opposition to the exotic animal ordinance.

By then, it was December 2015, and we were just days away

from the vote. I was in Australia, and Zack emailed to tell me an "educational traveling show" from another state had asked a town councilor to shoot down the proposed ordinance. On its flashy website, the business described itself as an ecology center, farm school, and traveling zoo that would bring exotic animals to children's birthday parties — an act that posed health risks to both animals and kids. However, with help from a few sleuthing friends and the internet, we quickly flushed out the company's distasteful past. Horrible reviews and news stories described how the owner, who had once operated as a nonprofit, had been shut down by his own board of directors and had an unsavory history of exploiting animals for money. The business opposing the ordinance was one of the bad guys.

A few days later, still in Australia, I watched a live internet broadcast of the December 5 Bar Harbor Town Council. Soon after the meeting was called to order, the floor was opened up for comments. One member of our team, Diana de los Santos, stood up and reaffirmed her support for the puppy mill ordinance. Then there was silence. One of the councilors asked if there were any other comments. There weren't.

I sat on the edge of my office chair feeling like I was in a courtroom awaiting a verdict. When it came, I screamed out like a New Englander at a Patriots game. The council voted unanimously in favor of both ordinances.

The locals had spoken. They didn't have an agenda, nor were they motivated by money. They knew the difference between right and wrong, and they chose to move away from the dark ages of chained elephants, whipped tigers, and sick puppies to an enlightened, kinder world.

I know that, for many people, witnessing the horrors associated with animal abuse can debilitate to the point of inaction. But looking away only perpetuates suffering and even undermines personal happiness. It doesn't take much to rally the people in your own community to make a collective, conscious decision to tell animal abusers and exploiters they're not welcome. By doing so, you can participate in a global shift as one of the good guys. When you're ready to do it, contact me and I'll help.

There have been game-changing wins and heartbreaking losses in the battle to create federal laws in Washington. That's the nature of the beast. On a state level, I've been lucky to work with others to create comprehensive reforms that affect billions of farm animals. And in Australia, while the process has taken years, the government is moving ahead with recommendations to end puppy farming. Good is prevailing, but it takes an army. It takes you.

There are many leaders in the compassion movement — too many to profile in one book. These are the people we admire for their ability to see the roots of problems and develop effective strategies for fixing them, as well as for their courage to combat greed when it inevitably clashes with compassion. They are the visionaries, pacesetters, and analytical thinkers whose unexpected connections with animals are driving sweeping change throughout the world.

Jill Robinson

BEAR

A moment of profound connection between two species can sometimes reveal life's purpose. That's what happened to Jill Robinson. An unexpected touch from a bear became a turning point in her life and ignited a movement in Asia.

Jill's reputation as an animal advocate has been widely known for years. Indeed, in the late 1990s, while I was working to change the lives of five bears in Laos, she was rescuing hundreds in China and cofounding the charity Animals Asia. I met her for the first time in 2016, when she gave a talk in Perth, Australia. I eagerly purchased a ticket to the fundraising event, excited to meet the woman who is leading the compassion movement on the largest continent on earth — Asia.

When the petite blonde with a wide smile began speaking, the hundred people in the audience fell silent as she described the roller coaster of emotional highs and lows of her work. No screenwriter could have created a better thriller — from the agony of discovering bears being tortured to the joy of their rescues. I laughed and cried as she delivered the most emotive speech I've ever heard.

Jill grew up in England, and as a child she was a friend to animals — all animals. So, it wasn't a surprise to her family when, at twenty-eight years old, she took a job with the US-based International Fund for Animal Welfare (IFAW) in Hong Kong. Her duties included investigating live animal markets in China, South Korea, and the Philippines; writing reports on the use of animals in traditional medicine; and establishing relationships with government officials.

Six years into her job with IFAW, Jill was called to investigate a bear bile farm in Zhuhai, China. The experience was life-altering and fueled her passion to create global change for animals.

• • •

Zhuhai, China

In early 1993 I was telephoned by a journalist friend. He had just re-turned from a bear bile farm and described a scene of such devas-tation and misery that I felt compelled to visit and see for myself. I'd heard about bear bile farming but knew virtually nothing about the in-dustry, and certainly nothing about the species of Asiatic black bears, called moon bears (named for the yellow moon-shaped crescent of fur on their chests), that were its victims.

I asked two friends to come along with me, and pretending to be tourists, we joined a group of Japanese and Taiwanese visitors who were on a bus trip visiting the farm.

We were taken to a bear pit, where breeding bears were put on public display. The group was invited to feed the bears by placing apples onto the end of crude fishing lines and dangling the fruit down into the pit in front of the bears. The bears were ravenously hungry and stood up on their back legs, desperately trying to reach out and grab the apples. Many visitors were teasing the bears, lifting the ap-ples high into the air every time the bears were near to catching them. The more upset and stressed the bears became, and the more they fought with each other in frustration, the more the crowd laughed.

We were then ushered to a shop where the farmer and his wife were boasting about the benefits of bear bile. While the farmers and tourists were occupied in the shop, we took the opportunity to quietly break away from the group and find the basement where the caged bears were housed. As we walked downstairs into the darkness, our eyes took some time to adjust in the gloom. The stench of disease and decay was all around us, and walking around the cages I heard odd "popping" sounds that grew increasingly louder the closer I walked to a cage. Seeing the bears close up, I realized that this strange sound was their vocalization of fear: They thought I was there to harm them.

Peering miserably through the bars, the bears had long scars across their bodies. Several had the ends of their paw tips missing; their claws had been crudely hacked away to make it less danger-ous for humans to milk their bile. Several had teeth that had been cut back to gum level, exposing pulp and nerves. Others had head wounds from repetitive rocking against steel bars in their cages due to trauma-induced regression. Most shocking of all was the sight of crude metal catheters protruding from their abdomens, the horrific instruments of torture that had been surgically implanted into their gallbladders to milk them of their bile.

Feeling shocked and sick to my stomach, I must have backed too close to a cage. I felt something touching my shoulder. I spun around in fright, fearing I was about to be grabbed by an angry and aggressive bear. What I saw next just about brought me to my knees in sadness. A female moon bear pushed her paw gently through the bars of the cage, inviting me to take it. In that moment, without fear or any reason to believe that she meant me harm, I took her paw. As hand and paw connected, the bear gently squeezed my fingers, and I was staring into the most beautiful dark brown eyes. At that instant, a message passed between us, and I knew that everything about my life had changed.

From that moment, I knew instinctively that there was no going back. I made a promise to that bear that I would do everything in my power to end bear bile farming, and I set out to do just that.

• • •

Jill named the bear Hong (Cantonese for *bear*) and began educating herself about the bile trade and the reasons why it existed.

The Asiatic black bear is an endangered species, and bear bile farming is one of the reasons for its demise. The bile produced by the bear's gallbladder is high in ursodeoxycholic acid. That acid is able to dissolve gallstones in people, without surgery, and has been used to treat gallstone sufferers for thousands of years. This medicinal application has created a black market for bear gallbladders. In 2002, an article in *Legal Affairs* magazine stated that gallbladders have sold for from $1,600 up to more than $55,000. And not just Asiatic bear gallbladders. Due to an insatiable Asian market for the organs, which arose primarily in the late 1980s and early 1990s, global bear populations have been targeted by poachers, including black, brown, grizzly, sloth, and even sun bears. This has prompted wildlife officials and advocates to reinforce laws to curb the illegal trade.

In the early 1980s, China picked up the practice of bear bile extraction from North Korea. The bears are captured alive and put into wire cages or fitted with full metal jackets to prevent them from moving. According to Jill, farmers then pay hospital surgeons to implant catheters into the animals' abdomens or to perform surgical mutilation to produce the "free drip" method of bile extraction, which creates a fistula in the abdomen and gallbladder. The bears are then forced to live, hardly able to move, in "crush cages" for up to thirty years, or until they die of infection and/or disease.

Most outrageous of all, the practice isn't necessary, since drug companies make ursodeoxycholic acid synthetically.

In 1998, Jill spearheaded a revolution and cofounded Animals Asia, a nonprofit with the goal of ending bear bile farming and improving the welfare of animals in China and Vietnam. Two years later, in 2000, Animals Asia negotiated a deal with the Chinese government to release five hundred bears from the bile farms with the worst known conditions. That same year, Animals Asia established the first bear rescue center in China. Seven years later, a second bear sanctuary was built in Tam Dao, Vietnam. And in 2014, after a bear farmer's daughter convinced her father that what he was doing was wrong, Animals Asia took over the Nanning Bear Farm in Nanning, China, and negotiated the rescue of 130 bears.

All this change was a direct result of Jill's encounter with Hong in 1993.

• • •

I went back for Hong, once I had begun building the first sanctuary, but the bears had been moved. I never saw her again. The events of the day we met are ingrained on my mind. I knew instinctively that there was no going back and that the present day and future would see me make good on my promise to Hong: That whilst I couldn't help her, I'd do everything in my power to end bear bile farming in China and Vietnam.

From this experience, I've learned never to underestimate passion and the power of the individual to make change. I've learned to be brave and face adversity if you have truth and justice at the center of all you do. I've learned to ignore those who bullied me and tried to deter my most committed and devoted team from changing the plight of the bears. I've learned that good people working from within would defend the bears and be the champions they need. And I've learned to play the game — calmly when impatient, intelligently when frustrated, and pragmatically when insane with anger.

I always say to children in presentations that sometimes we receive a message in life that we can choose to listen to — or ignore. That decision can shape the rest of our lives. Hong's message to me on that day in April 1993 was strong, profound, and impossible to ignore. Her inspiration began everything we have built in China and Vietnam today: two sanctuaries filled with over six hundred happy, healthy, rescued bears, and a foundation called Animals Asia, which has progressed a long way toward the goal of ending bear bile farming once and for all.

• • •

Jill has orchestrated sweeping changes for bears across Asia. In response to Animals Asia's work, the country of Vietnam has committed to ending bear bile farming by the year 2022. Additionally, the

Vietnamese Traditional Medicine Association has agreed to remove bear bile from all prescriptions by the year 2020.

In China, where more than ten thousand bears remain on bile farms, public awareness campaigns by Animals Asia are creating change. A poll by the organization in 2011 found that 87 percent of the Chinese people interviewed disagreed with bear bile farming. In response to widespread criticism of the practice, thousands of traditional Chinese medicine doctors are moving away from prescribing medications made from bile and are now selling herbs or a synthetic version. And in a move that highlights a monumental shift, China's government is now providing millions of dollars of state subsidies for research to create alternatives to bear bile.

Jill's life changed after being touched by an imprisoned bear. Today, she is an inspirational leader — uniting people across cultures to follow their own hearts and move forward with compassion.

Have you ever rescued a ladybug?

Ah, ladybugs! Yes, of course. I do, wherever I see them. I pretty much rescue everything. If they're in my house, I take them outside and let them go. That goes for spiders and cockroaches, too. I'm a great believer in one life, and I try not to harm the life of another being in my surroundings.

Name three things that make you happy.

Daffodils, love, and being in the company of family — including animals.

What one book, documentary, or speech has had a profound effect on you?

Earthlings, the documentary.

Regarding your food choices, how do you describe yourself?

Vegan.

If you had one message to deliver to others, what would it be?

Just look at every living creature the same way we'd like to be treated or considered, with one life.

If you had one wish that was guaranteed to come true, what would it be?

To end bear bile farming because, after that, other things would flow.

What advice do you have for people who say that they want to help animals in need but are too debilitated by what they witness?

Use your anger, your frustration, and your tears, and be the champion the animals need you to be. There's so much you can do without having to look at animals in pain or distress. You shouldn't need to hurt yourself by helping animals. If it's not comfortable to help animals by being on the front line, you can still help by influencing others to lead a cruelty-free life.

Wayne Pacelle

PIGEON

If you judge superheroes by the number of villains trying to take them down, it would be fair to say Wayne Pacelle is the Superman of the animal welfare movement. The former leader of the Humane Society of the United States (HSUS) is methodical and calculated in his approach to stopping the bad guys: the people who exploit and harm animals.

I met Wayne for the first time at a coffee shop in Ellsworth, Maine, in August 2014. The six-foot-one, black-haired forty-nine-year-old greeted me with a warm smile and strong handshake. I was surprised and disarmed when he started the meeting by summarizing my life's work for animals. He thanked me and then explained why he'd called the meeting.

The HSUS was leading a ballot initiative in Maine (my home state) to end bear baiting, hounding, and trapping. Maine was the only state that allowed all three of these practices, mostly for people who wanted the heads of bears to hang on walls as trophies. Wayne asked if I'd work for the bears.

I cleared my schedule for the next three months and stepped up — only to discover I'd jumped into raging political waters. The Sportsman's Alliance of Maine was out for blood — ours — and special interest groups such as Safari Club International and the National Rifle Association were helping finance their campaign.

I didn't know Wayne personally. I had friends who did and spoke highly of him. Given the scope of his job commitments and responsibilities, I didn't expect he'd put himself on the front lines in Maine, but he did.

At our next meeting in Portland, Wayne talked to me and a few other volunteers about the key points of our message. Afterward, I shot a promotional video about the cruelty involved in hounding and trapping. On the three-hour drive home that night, I listened to Wayne being interviewed on CNN radio about a ballot initiative to block Michigan legislation that would allow the hunting of wolves and other protected species. From a phone in a guest bedroom at a supporter's house in Maine, Wayne passionately described the assault on wolves and fiercely defended their rights to live, undisturbed, in the wild.

Later, Wayne and I were teamed up to go door-to-door in Maine's biggest cities to ask for voter support for the Maine ballot initiative. Wayne was serious and directed, carefully explaining to people the extreme methods being used to kill Maine bears. As we walked, taking note of the responses, it became clear the majority of voters were against baiting, hounding, and trapping. A poll confirmed our results. We were winning.

Then came an unexpected blow. The Maine Department of Inland Fisheries & Wildlife (MDIFW), a government agency dependent on money from hunting and fishing licenses, took a side. Employees participated in misleading commercials that suggested there would be bear attacks on people if extreme kill methods were banned.

As the battle amped up into a war, our dedicated team of volunteers continued knocking on doors, writing opinion articles for local newspapers, and posting signs. Wayne hit the airwaves. At six one morning, I tuned in to a morning talk show whose hosts clearly opposed the initiative, to restrict bear hunting to actual hunters. They attacked Wayne, peppering him with propaganda disguised as fact. Under fire, he was a warrior: heated at times, yet controlled.

Soon after, I personally experienced the extreme tactics used by our opposition when I was alerted that my car, its plate number, and my home address had been posted on a social media site for trophy hunters.

The HSUS filed a lawsuit, alleging MDIFW was illegally using taxpayers' money to conduct a political campaign and influence an election. However, before a judge could review the case, it was too late. The damage had been done. Television and radio advertisements featuring state biologists had succeeded in scaring just enough voters to believe bears were a threat to children. We lost the vote by a narrow margin.

While it was a harrowing defeat, it was also an insightful experience. I learned about the perpetual onslaught against wildlife by people who take pleasure from killing, and the guts and tenacity it takes to go against them.

I spent ten weeks working with Wayne, to pass this ballot initiative, and along the way, I wondered what fueled his passion. On a crisp September morning, I got my answer. We were driving on a heavily forested road and passed a large, dead raccoon. Simultaneously, we let out the same mournful sigh. It was then, in that simple moment of truth, I realized his motivation was not the battle. He was leading with heart.

• • •

Schuylkill County, Pennsylvania, USA

For as long as I can remember, I've felt a sense of kinship with and empathy toward animals. By our conventional measures of intelligence, they may come up short in the estimation of some people. But animals have their own wonderful attributes and endowments, and serious-minded people today reject the idea that they have neither emotions nor intelligence. They are different from us, but in good ways. They deserve not only our appreciation but also our respect.

As a boy, I read about animals and drew pictures of them. I could never get enough of watching animals, particularly the wild ones in the woods behind my aunt Harriet's house in Connecticut. And the family dogs were, well, family. My girl Brandy — a blend of Labrador and golden retriever lineage — would chase a tennis ball until my arm gave out or until dinner was announced.

I didn't need anyone to tell me that harming animals was wrong. Even more than a natural feeling of fellowship with animals, I felt a visceral disgust for cruelty. It didn't take much insight to realize that we are the creature of conscience, and we should use our own power and smarts for benevolent purposes.

By my second year at Yale, in 1985, I was reading a good bit about the plight of animals. Then, on Labor Day weekend, matters came together during a trip with other advocates to Pennsylvania. What I had been feeling, and thinking, suddenly found focus in one awful firsthand experience.

To raise money for the local fire department in a rural Schuylkill County community, thousands of people gathered for a slaughter. It had been a tradition for years, a big family event complete with beer and hot dog vendors. They called it a pigeon shoot, though that hardly begins to describe the spectacle. With a cheering, laughing crowd to greet and lionize them, gunners took their places. There were dozens of crates, and organizers tugged at ropes to pull off the lids one at a time. As they yanked off each lid, two or three pigeons would flutter upward, and then just as quickly they would fall in a burst of gunfire. "Trapper boys," mere kids of eight or nine years, would scramble out and stomp on the wounded birds or twist their heads off, with more cheering and encouragement from their proud parents and the other spectators.

My first thought was that there must be a better way to raise money for the fire department. My second thought was that the cause of animal protection was very much about people. Here was a gathering centered on gratuitous cruelty, and a crowd that couldn't get enough. The adults were appalling in their own right, but to see these kids conscripted in the crushing and killing was particularly hard to take. I was watching not just a massacre but also a kind of indoctrination. Doubtless some of the children had felt a fondness for animals similar to what I'd felt as a boy, and apparently, the point of this ritual was to root out any sense of compassion so that they could grow up to be as hard-hearted as their parents.

A few lucky birds escaped the buckshot in each round, but the odds were badly stacked against them. I spent many hours that day watching pigeons flutter out of the crates before they were shot to pieces. I had become acquainted with many cruelties by then, but I had witnessed very few. That day was a coming of age for me in so many ways, not least because I came to understand the great loss that comes with the extinguishing of any life. It's something I've never forgotten. That image of a Pennsylvania field littered with maimed or stilled birds is etched into my memory.

From that moment, it was no longer enough for me to love animals or read about their plight. They needed help. They couldn't fend for themselves. Humanity held all the power in the relationship, and we could treat that asymmetry as license or responsibility.

I returned to campus and started an animal advocacy group. When I graduated, I had a single goal: to work in the movement trying to stop animal cruelty and suffering. It still hurts to have to confront and witness so much cruelty. I rise each day with a clear conviction about the urgency and necessity of my efforts. Most importantly, I am energized by the realization that I am far from alone in confronting the task.

There have been many battles in the years since then. Fur-bearing animals, as well as wandering dogs and other unintended victims, suffer horribly in steel-jawed leg-hold traps. Dogs and cats still crowd some animal shelters, while unscrupulous breeders stock the shelves of pet stores with dogs from backyard puppy mills. Trophy hunters take potshots at animals in canned hunts worldwide, and the illicit trade in wildlife products claims tens of millions of animal lives. Dog-fighting and cockfighting are age-old pursuits that still have a following today, and kill buyers scoop up homeless horses to send them off to slaughter for human consumption. Finally, and perhaps worst of all, our industrial systems of food production cause unimaginable misery for countless billions of animals worldwide.

No battle is ever easily won. But something remarkable has happened since the mid-1980s, when I threw myself into the cause. In recent years, our cause has moved from the margins to the mainstream. Yes, many of our adversaries still have money and influence and resist even the most modest reforms. But we have something better: the power of conscience and the votes of the majority. There is a sense that the winds of change are blowing in our direction and more briskly than ever.

Since 1990, I've been part of more than thirty successful ballot-initiative campaigns to end the abuse of animals — from state bans on cockfighting to restrictions on body-gripping traps to bans on canned hunts. We've seen Ringling Bros. submit to the wishes of animal advocates and shutter its operation after 145 years. We've negotiated agreements with more than 250 major food retailers — from McDonald's to Walmart to Safeway — to change their purchasing practices to phase out extreme confinement of animals on factory farms. We've made animal cruelty a felony in every state. We've ended the use of chimpanzees in invasive experiments. Each one is a game-changing outcome for animals and an indicator of our remarkable progress.

In principle, most everyone agrees it's wrong to mistreat animals. The difficulty comes in application. We need laws that reflect our principles and our best instincts, especially when the exploitation is conducted by big business or government. It's important as well that people not only care for their pets but also make humane choices in the marketplace and support animal-protection policy reforms.

For my part, over the years I have rejoiced in the gains for animal welfare, but I've taken a few losses — indeed, there are still a handful of backwoods pigeon shoots in Pennsylvania, and to take one more example, puppy mills are still too prevalent in our nation. But the trajectory is unmistakable: By ever-larger majorities, the good heart of America is showing itself. Most people are unwilling to accept cruelty anymore. Animal protection has always been a noble cause. Now it's a winning cause, too.

• • •

When he was just twenty-three years old, Wayne envisioned building a mainstream movement for animals. Throughout his life, he's worked diligently to achieve this. During his tenure at the HSUS,

Wayne led staff and volunteer advocates to enact more than 180 federal and 2,000 state protection laws and amendments. These laws have changed the legal landscape for all animals and have instigated voluntary reforms by corporations and businesses that exploit animals for entertainment and raise them for food. In recent years, some of the world's largest food producers, working with the HSUS, have created policies that benefit billions of animals each year.

The Humane Society of the United States is a collective force for good, one that's guided by an incredibly talented board of directors and a team that includes some of the most brilliant brains in business, science, and law. The organization's member and volunteer base numbers in the millions, and this army of animal lovers works on the ground to enact laws, push corporations to do better, and make the world safer for animals. In his role as head of the HSUS from 2004 to 2018 and by providing strategic guidance to advocates globally, Wayne has arguably orchestrated more positive legal change for animals than any human being in modern times.

Have you ever rescued a ladybug?

I've been a bug rescuer most of my life, and I've moved a few ladybugs to safety, for sure.

Name three things that make you happy.

Spending time with my wife, dog, and cat; family get-togethers; hiking and other experiences in protected natural areas.

What one book, documentary, or speech has had a profound effect on you?

I memorized the Gettysburg Address as a boy, and it stays with me as a reminder of the power of words to sway people's understanding. In the same vein, I used to read a dog-eared copy of *The Elements of Style* by Strunk and White to keep me thinking about clear and concise communication. Among animal books, Matthew Scully's *Dominion: The Power of Man, the Suffering of Animals, and the Call to Mercy* is the most important to me, so well-written and subtle, yet so impassioned.

Regarding your food choices, how do you describe yourself?

I'm a longtime vegan, and that's worked for me.

If you had one message to deliver to others, what would it be?

Don't be a bystander in the face of the problems that animals endure.

If you had one wish that was guaranteed to come true, what would it be?

I'd like to see ten million Americans signed up as volunteers in animal protection work.

What advice do you have for people who say that they want to help animals in need but are too debilitated by what they witness?

There is a lot you can do without having to directly confront or see difficult imagery. You can get involved in almost every advocacy action recommended by the HSUS without doing so. In addition, there is a lot of positive work you can undertake, volunteering at a shelter or a sanctuary, giving a talk, and so on, that doesn't involve having to look at harsh or disturbing images.

Temple Grandin

COW

This book is about people who didn't look away from a seemingly impossible situation involving an animal, but who were inspired to do better — to make the world better for all animals. These people didn't choose their cause. They witnessed a problem and acted to change it. Those actions have consequently empowered and educated countless others to do the same.

When Temple Grandin first witnessed flaws in livestock handling systems that caused unnecessary suffering to many animals each year, she knew how to fix them. But it wasn't easy convincing a male-dominated industry that she could see faults that others couldn't. Fighting sexism and bullying, she persevered and is now recognized throughout the world for her work minimizing harm to animals raised for meat. An animal welfare expert and behaviorist, Temple is credited with revolutionizing an industry.

Throughout my life, I'd heard whispers of Temple, most often when writing stories for CNN about food or farming. I'd also watched a news piece about her famous invention to reduce fear in animals being led to slaughter. But it wasn't until 2010, when I saw *Temple Grandin* — the fascinating biopic about her life, starring the actress Claire Danes — that I came to fully understand her brilliance.

Temple grew up in Dedham, a suburb of Boston, in the 1950s. Like most kids, she spent a lot of time playing in the woods, riding bikes, and hanging out with her golden retriever, Andy. But unlike most kids, her mind processed information visually instead of auditorily. She connected with animals because they processed information similarly. In fact, she felt so comfortable in their presence that she could touch and be touched by animals when physical contact with people made her uncomfortable. The disconnection with people — combined with long periods of being uncommunicative and experiencing sporadic tantrums — caused her mother to seek advice from doctors. The quest to help her daughter resulted in a diagnosis of autism.

Going against doctors' advice to institutionalize her child, Temple's mother resolved to encourage her talents. Temple understood how animals thought, and she was good at drawing. So her mother pushed her to pencil more than pictures of animals — she encouraged Temple to draw and design. As she grew up, these two abilities collided again and again. Then, at twenty-three years old, she experienced an awakening with two cows that would lead to the transformation of an entire industry.

The following story is a compilation derived from three sources: interviews I conducted with Temple, quotes from Temple's book *Animals in Translation*, and quotes by Temple in the book *The Animal Ethics Reader* (edited by Susan J. Armstrong and Richard G. Botzler). Reprinted text is signaled by quotation marks; please see the notes for specific sources.

• • •

Arizona, USA

My high school years were hard, and I had a tidal wave of anxiety because of constant bullying and teasing. My mother sent me to a special boarding school for gifted children with emotional problems. The school had a stable with horses for the kids to ride. All the horses at the school had been abused. "So, there we all were, up at boarding school, a bunch of emotionally disturbed teenagers living with a bunch of emotionally disturbed animals." But I was very much in love with the horses and being around them because I could relate to them.

My aunt Ann, knowing how much I was nuts about horses, invited me to her dude ranch in Arizona one summer, when I was fourteen years old. I enjoyed it so much — being around horses all day — that I became a regular while I was in high school and college, spending six summers on the ranch.

One summer when I was there, I saw a herd of cattle being put through a squeeze chute. The animals would follow each other in a single line into a chute and then walk into an apparatus that squeezed them so the vet could give them shots. "I was riveted by the sight of those big animals inside that squeezing machine." As I watched, it seemed that the deep pressure had a calming sensation on them.

As I mentioned, I had terrible anxiety. I began to wonder if a squeeze machine might help me relieve my anxiety and panic attacks. So, when I got back to high school that fall, my science teacher, Mr. Carlock, helped me build my own squeeze chute. It worked. "Whenever I put myself inside my squeeze machine, I felt calmer." That machine and the school's horses got me through high school.

Years later, when I finished studying psychology at Franklin Pierce College in New England, I went to live in Arizona. I liked it there and I liked being around animals. I enrolled in Arizona State University to work toward a master's degree in animal science, and I took a job working for *Arizona Farmer-Ranchman* magazine as the livestock editor. One day the magazine wanted pictures of black Angus steers, so they sent me out to take them.

When I got to the feed yards, I knew cattle enough to know that the only way I'd get a good picture of them was to sit in the pen because, when you stand up, they run off. So I sat in the pen. Some cattle, they're kind of curiously afraid. You sit there, and they'll come up and they'll lick and touch you, and then if you move a little, they jump away, and then they'll come back up to you again.

On this day when I was taking pictures, there were two young cattle who I became attached to. Because there were between twenty-five and thirty thousand cattle in the lots, I named them after the pens they were in. I named them A11 Blacky and A12 Blacky. They were very friendly young steers, under a year old. They had personalities. They liked having their heads and backs scratched. From that day, I called them my pet steers.

Even though the feed yards were located a little more than an hour from where I lived, I went back to visit A11 Blacky and A12 Blacky every few months. There were about a hundred cattle in each pen, but when I got there, they recognized me and came up to the fence and let me pet them. One of the things I realized was that beef cattle had personalities and weren't just things. While I knew this about mice and dogs and horses, I hadn't known it about cattle. Spending time with the two Blackys made me realize they had feelings.

As they got older, they got bigger. We're talking nine-hundred-pound animals here. And they got pushy. Every time they saw me, they wanted attention and pets. It got dangerous to get in the pen with them because they'd push me even when they were being friendly. One time, one of them put his head between my legs and lifted me up with his head because he wanted to be scratched. I quickly learned not to reward that behavior with a scratch but to wait until they calmed before giving them what they wanted.

Each time I visited I knew it was getting closer to the end of their lives. In the 1970s, the typical lifespan of a beef steer was two years. At the time, cattle handling was really bad. I got very concerned about what was going to happen to them at the slaughterhouse. I thought about it often. I didn't ask when they would be shipped. I didn't want to know.

My relationship with the Blackys got me interested in improving things for cattle. I started to hang out in feed yards, where I noticed that a lot of times the animals didn't want to go through chutes. When I saw cattle acting scared and balking, I just naturally thought, *Well, let's look at it from the animal's point of view. I've got to get in the chute and see what he's seeing.* Unlike most people, as an autistic person, I was a visual thinker — like most animals — so when I got in the chute, I was able to see what was stopping the cattle from moving. I understood what caused them fear, and it's not what most people would think. It could be shadows, chains hanging down, a coffee cup on the ground, or a jacket hung over a railing that makes animals balk. Once I discovered the problems, I worked to create moving and handling systems that eliminated fear. I had discovered, as a young girl, that squeeze machines were actually comforting, so I set out to create devices that had a similar effect.

I found that most of the problems for animals came from the handlers. "Fear is the dominant emotion in both autistic people and prey animals, such as deer, cattle, and horses." There were many problems with slaughterhouses. The worse the problems, the worse the handlers would treat the cattle: kicking them, hitting them, and poking them with electric prods. All this made their fear worse. The key was to design a system that promoted uninterrupted flow and, therefore, less abuse.

I designed a chute system to address that need. Decades on, half the cattle in the United States are handled in equipment I've designed. My systems are also used in Australia, Canada, Europe, Mexico, New Zealand, and other countries.

"If I had my druthers, humans would have evolved to be plant eaters, so we wouldn't have to kill other animals for food. But we didn't, and I don't see the human race converting to vegetarianism anytime soon.... That means we're going to continue to have feedlots and slaughterhouses, so the question is: What should a humane feedlot and slaughterhouse be like? Everyone concerned with animal welfare has the basic answer to that: The animal shouldn't suffer." He should feel no pain and handling should be done calmly and quietly.

That's how my work started. "Animal behavior was the right field for me because what I was missing in social understanding I could make up for in understanding animals.... I owe a lot of this to the fact that my brain works differently. Autism has given me another perspective on animals most professionals don't have — although a lot of regular people do — which is that animals are smarter than we think." Cattle definitely have feelings. Neuroscience shows this. We've got to give them a life worth living. They're not just blobs of meat. Someday we won't slaughter animals. Until then, we have to give them a decent life.

• • •

Dr. Temple Grandin has written hundreds of research papers direct-
ing people who work with animals — from veterinarians to farmers
— on how to be humane to those in their care. She has received
sixty-seven awards and commendations and has been given fifteen
honorary doctorate degrees from universities throughout the world
for her work creating monumental and sweeping changes for animals, as well as for revealing mysteries surrounding autism. Temple
has published more than three hundred industry papers, book
chapters, and technical reports on animal handling, sixty-two peer-
reviewed journal articles, and ten books. The inventor and educator
is also a professor of animal science at Colorado State University.

In 2010, *Time* magazine named Temple one of the most influential people in the world. For standing her ground and fighting
for change after witnessing the extreme mistreatment of animals,
Temple is rightfully recognized as a global hero.

Have you ever rescued a ladybug?

No, but I remember as a child looking at them and not hurting
them. I remember that.

Name three things that make you happy.

When someone takes my recommendation to help an animal
or an autistic kid and it works. Doing good.

**What one book, documentary, or speech has had a profound
effect on you?**

Loren Eiseley's *The Invisible Pyramid* and Jane Goodall's books.

Regarding your food choices, how do you describe yourself?

Meat eater.

If you had one message to deliver to others, what would it be?

If you want to do activism, I don't care what subject it's on, you need to get out there in the field and see what's actually happening there.

If you had one wish that was guaranteed to come true, what would it be?

I'd like to have some peace in the world.

What advice do you have for people who say that they want to help animals in need but are too debilitated by what they witness?

Pick out a specific thing. You can't work on everything.

Chapter 7

BEAVER AND DOLPHIN

Enlightening Transformations

St. James Parish, Louisiana, USA

Nature sets an eerie stage in the bayous of Louisiana. Cypress trees draped with Spanish moss take their nourishment from black water where alligators' eyeballs, floating just above the surface, watch for prey. The air is alive with the sound of shrilling cicadas, a source of food for the spiders, snakes, and turtles who live here — and also those animals who pass through. This part of Louisiana, wet from tributaries of the Mississippi River, is a feeding and resting stop for millions of birds on their yearly migration from Canada and the northern half of the United States to Central and South America. It's a heaven for birds, with plenty of food to fuel their trip. Royley Folse also made it their hell.

Royley was once a poacher, a murderer of the worst kind who killed indiscriminately, illegally, because he could get away with it. I met him in the early 1990s when I was working as an environmental correspondent for CNN and was assigned to do a story about Dave Hall, a US Fish & Wildlife agent who was having enormous success converting convicted wildlife poachers over to his side of the law. I'd been told Royley was one of the converted.

I interviewed Royley outside his modest house, where he was hosing off a small boat. He was wearing drugstore reading glasses and dressed in an oversized camouflage jumpsuit with matching cap, along with light green rubber boots that stopped at his knees. He spoke with a French-infused Cajun accent, gesticulating with his hands.

"I poached deer, alligator, birds — anything that moved. Around here it was a big tradition to just kill as many animals as you could and brag about it," he said. He sold the meat and also used it to feed his family. Like many local Cajuns, he considered the swamplands a bountiful, God-given food pantry. What set him apart was his feeling of entitlement.

That's what put him on the radar of federal law enforcement agent Dave Hall. As Royley stalked animals, Dave, a calm, directed, and patient man, stalked him, and Royley knew it.

"All I wanted to do was catch Dave Hall and bring him in that swamp and cut him up in five thousand pieces and scatter him where nobody would ever find evidence that he ever existed," Royley told me.

The worlds of the two men collided in a bayou under the cover of darkness when Royley was caught, red-handed, with 645 dead night heron. At the time, the night heron was a protected species in the United States.

Royley estimated he'd killed a hundred thousand animals before he was caught. And yet he felt his sentence was unjust.

"I went to jail six months for killing a bird," he said. "I was in a place where they had murderers, rapists, and dope dealers. I was right there with all of them because I killed a bird."

What Royley did was more than just "kill a bird," which he soon learned. Wildlife agents have blamed attitudes like his for wiping out entire species. At the time I produced the story, an estimated 303 species were endangered in the United States alone, their decline blamed in part on poachers like Royley.

A judge sent Royley to jail for six months, and as part of a plea deal, he agreed to participate in Hall's "Poachers to Preachers" program. To be in the program, Royley had to confess his crimes on camera. During the process — which included education about wildlife conservation — he came to understand the enormity of his crimes. By the end of the program, he'd been converted and became an advocate of legal hunting practices. After jail, he went on a speaking circuit, using his film to explain how his behavior had been legally and socially wrong. The program was a success. Royley became a preacher against poaching.

I met Dave Hall at the scene of Royley's many crimes, a hauntingly beautiful swamp in St. James Parish. Dressed in a navy blue windbreaker with a matching cap emblazoned with a federal wildlife insignia, Dave explained the thinking behind his program.

"The common creed of all poachers is that there was very little peer pressure exerted on them as youngsters to prevent them from poaching or telling them that it was wrong," he said. "One of the things we have to realize is that poachers have been kind of like folk heroes. They really haven't been looked down on as criminals. The philosophy is that they're heroes in their communities for maybe doing the wrong thing, but once they're converted and see the light, so to speak, they're effective educators, much more so than a bureaucrat like me."

Through Dave's program, Royley did a 180. In an unlikely twist to the story, he also became friends with Dave — the man he'd said he wanted to murder.

I learned a lot when I was producing the story, especially about people and their heritage.

Royley grew up in a hunting-shooting-fishing culture. Until he was convinced his poaching was unsustainable, he looked at it as a birthright.

While working on this book, I decided to reach out to Royley for an update. Through his son, the famous international chef John Folse, who kindly spoke to me, I learned that Royley died in 2005. However, John confirmed that Royley had never reverted back to poaching after going through Dave's video education program. He also said that, growing up, his family had a symbiotic relationship with the swamps; animals not only provided sustenance but were their friends.

"We had pet raccoons, squirrels, wild birds, snakes — anything that slithered, swam, and flew. We'd bring them home and feed them on our back porch," John said. "We were given the greatest gift in the world — a place in the swamps of Louisiana that no one else wanted. We soon realized the bounty of the swampland, and this was heaven for us. Our lives there were all about survival, culture, and tradition."

Royley's story provides several lessons: that cultures often lay the groundwork for crimes against animals, that people can change even the most extreme types of conditioned behavior, and that money often drives people to exploit animals. Even someone like Royley Folse — who once saw nothing wrong with killing animals for the sake of it — can change once the reasons for conservation laws are understood. This lesson has been confirmed many times as I have traveled the world as an animal advocate, meeting amazing people who have transformed from exploiting animals to becoming their fiercest protectors. In other cases, the catalyst is sometimes an animal who communicates a message that triggers a realization, resulting in a truly enlightening transformation.

Dave Pauli

BEAVER

Dave Pauli is one of the great human beings I've had the privilege of knowing. I have a deep admiration and respect for him. I might not have liked him thirty years ago, before his transformation from a paid trapper to a humane educator, but since the moment he connected with a beaver named Bucky, he's touched the lives of millions of animals — and probably just as many human beings — in a good way.

Dave's a teddy bear of a guy. He wears glasses, sports a beard, and is a hugger. He's a wildlife guru with the big title of senior adviser for wildlife response and policy at the Humane Society of the United States (HSUS). Years ago, we worked together on a wildlife initiative team in Maine, but even though he was a legend among animal advocates, I didn't get to know him then. So, in the summer of 2016, when I was planning a trip to Yellowstone, I gave him a call. He warmly invited me to visit him in Montana on the way and to spend a day with him riding shotgun in his truck.

Dave picked me up before dawn in a four-door pickup he calls "Big Blue." We drove ninety-five miles from Billings to the Crow Indian Reservation in Wyola, where a rancher was complaining that four feral dogs had gathered on his rural property and were begging for food. We were there to trap and rescue those dogs. Dave moved swiftly, strategically placing traps laced with open cans of cat food around the perimeter of the house. Within minutes, a door crashed, signaling a catch, and then another and another. The third dog screeched when she realized she was confined.

"She's got pups out there," Dave said, nodding toward a nearby thicket. "Let's go find them." I grabbed a plastic milk crate, lined it with a clean sheet, and set off after him. He dropped to the ground and slithered along a dirt path, and I followed.

"She's a good mama," he said. "There are two beautifully dug bank dens in here." While I turned on my camera to film, he reached into one of the holes and pulled out a cream-colored puppy, its eyes still closed. "Here's puppy one. A boy," he said, gently placing the newborn in the crate. He went back into the den until we had recovered everybody, four girls and four boys.

I hurried them to their still-crying mother. She looked at them, her eyes scanning the crate, counting, and then she calmed.

Our next stop, with the dogs in tow, was a house where unsterilized dogs had been breeding. When we got there, the owners had put ribbons around the necks of the dogs and puppies they wanted. We took those they didn't.

Wendy Hergenraeder, Montana state director for the HSUS, stayed behind to see if she could talk the owners into sterilizing the remaining dogs. After that, with all fifteen dogs packed into a four-wheel drive, including the mom and her puppies, Wendy set off for the Lewis and Clark Humane Society, a five-hour drive away, where the dogs would be vetted, vaccinated, sterilized, and offered for adoption.

Dave and I drove in the opposite direction, to a wildlife rehabilitation center where Dave introduced me to twenty-four red-eared slider turtles. They were all abandoned or discarded pets who were in his turtle boot camp program, where Dave prepared them for release. When they were ready, he would drive them thirty hours away to sanctuary ponds in North Carolina.

After meeting the turtles, who were living in muddy, concrete ponds, we picked up four mallard ducks who'd been orphaned and raised by Dave. We took the crates to a nearby pond, opened the doors, and watched them waddle down the embankment and straight into the water.

By then, I'd spent eight hours with Dave. It was 1 PM and I was scheduled to hit the road for Wyoming. Dave's day was only half over. He was going to head home to have lunch with two house-guests, Wanda the coyote and Larry the weasel, who were both re-covering from injuries.

As I drove into Yellowstone that afternoon, I felt very lucky to have witnessed one of the great defenders of animals in action. The day was enlightening — not just because of what was accomplished, but because I knew Dave's history. He was living proof that people can change.

• • •

Pasco, Washington, USA

I started hunting, fishing, and trapping for "recreation" at an early age. Growing up in a Midwestern community, we raised rabbits for meat and took time off school for the annual nine-day deer-hunting season. I especially loved trapping because it challenged my wood-craft skills and taught me to study animal tracks, feces, and activity, giving me insights into the daily life of target animals.

The trapping started for me on Christmas Day in 1965, when I was ten and received a Havahart trap. It was the rabbit/woodchuck model, but it was big enough to catch any cat, rat, or skunk who visited our pigeon loft. During the next week, I caught rabbits, a rat, a cat, and — remarkably — a long-tailed weasel, aka ermine, in its white winter coat. It was amazing, with black eyes and a black-tipped tail. I couldn't believe I'd caught it just behind my house. My grade-school trapping buddy and our trapping mentor, who was the janitor at our school, both suggested I kill and mount the ermine to have a permanent memory of the capture. But, even at ten, I felt it would be wrong to kill and mount the ermine as a trophy. Even now, fifty-one years later, I can close my eyes and vividly remember this. I still see her stark but soft eyes as she left my live trap to go back to the creek and tree-lined habitat from which she came. I was mesmerized and knew from that moment that I would rather catch things in live traps than in footholds or body-grip traps, where they would be either dead or unable to display natural behaviors.

Once word got out that I was a good live trapper, I began getting work offers from pigeon/poultry fanciers who had skunk/raccoon/fox/ coyote predation issues with their domestic animals. People paid or bartered with me, a preteen kid, to show up on my bike and trap the offending critters. The end result was most always the killing of the animal.

I continued trapping critters throughout high school and in college, when I started a business called Humane Animal Controls to make money. That was when I received my first beaver complaint calls and started doing lethal beaver control trapping. I cannot say with accuracy how many beavers I trapped over the next decade, but it was several hundred, almost exclusively caught in large body-grip traps. I was fairly efficient at it and learned to trap the whole colony by using their biological and behavioral traits against them by setting the traps underwater, near the entry to their lodge. Unlike the animals I caught in live traps, when I came to collect the beavers, they were already dead, having drowned. That gave me a comforting detachment.

All this changed when I became the executive director of the Benton-Franklin Humane Society, in Pasco, Washington [today in Kennewick]. I was thirty-four years old and had been trapping wildlife for twenty-four years. I'd already transformed to doing mostly non-lethal trapping and translocation for most species, except one: beavers. Beavers were easier to lethally trap, and the landowners always seemed more impressed with a body count of dead beavers who would not cause any more flooding or tree chewing on their property.

My personal transformation came on a warm spring day when a family brought in an apple-sized bundle of fur their kids had found by the river. It was an unweaned beaver kit. He was dehydrated and in shock from being overhandled and forcibly given cow's milk. He was in bad shape.

I'd been rehabbing orphaned raccoons and squirrels for years and knew what to do. The kit needed quiet, warmth, fluids, some digestive tract stimulation, and routine. I warmed him up by placing him under my shirt and then did warm towel stimulation of his pelvic region (something his mom would have done with her tongue). I turned a box into his den and got him to accept a formula of one cup goat's milk/canine milk replacer blended with an egg yolk and a few spinach leaves. His first feeding was 1 cc, only one-fifth of what I knew he needed four to five times a day.

The feeding was our moment of connection. He knew I was not his mamasan but somehow sensed I was trying to help. The next feeding climbed to 3 ccs, and the next to 5 ccs, and we were on our way. He survived his first twenty-four hours with me, and that was a good outcome. He was now fully hydrated — but also constipated from lack of regular fluids and from stress. I was pretty sure I knew what to do for raccoons in this situation: Give a warm-water enema and repeated navel-to-anus stroking. But this was pre-Google, and I wanted to make sure everything I was doing was right. I went to the library and checked out every book on beavers. There wasn't much, but I learned they defecate while in water.

I filled the bathtub with twenty inches of tepid water and put my new friend "Bucky" in the water after a feeding. On the second swim session, Bucky passed the hard, dry stool that had concerned me and then a series of soft, normal stools, which quickly broke up in the water. After that, he tried to climb out of the tub, so I lifted him out and set him up and on the corner. Thinking he was finished swimming, I drained the tub and was rinsing it clean when Bucky slid down the edge and started playing in the water again. *Wait*, I thought to myself. *Am I getting this right? Bucky didn't want to swim in dirty water? He wanted clean water!*

And so began our routine of feedings every four hours, a ten-minute bathroom swim, a water change, and a thirty-plus-minute clean-water swim until he told me it was time to take a nap. My first-born canine son — a German wirehair named Jocomo Luigi, aka Louie — was openly jealous of my time with Bucky. He'd walk into the bathroom to see what I could possibly be doing with this little water rat.

When Bucky sensed he was in the room, he would tail-slap the water and go under for minutes before popping up to check and see if I'd finally gotten that nasty coyote out of the room. It was like watching the PBS program *Nature* in my own bathroom.

I had the intelligent and extremely communicative Bucky under my care for almost three months, until he was old enough and fat enough to be transferred to a large wildlife rehab facility. They had other beavers, but they didn't have the staff to provide infant care.

Bucky taught me more about beavers than I had learned from trapping them for decades. He taught me about their vocalizations, their preferences, their weaknesses (eyesight), and their amazing ability to communicate. He taught me that he was not a furbearer; he was a fur-wearer — and an individual. He could be a gentleman, he could be grumpy, and he would rather have sweet potatoes than carrots. He temporarily deprived me of sleep, quality time with my other critters, and a fair amount of cash for beaver food and medications before he left. It was worth it. I felt blessed to have known him.

Despite our connection, I assumed my life would go on as before. But I was wrong. On the next beaver damage call, I set a body-grip trap but felt uneasy as I drove away. When I came back in the morning, I removed what was the last beaver I ever lethally trapped. She was a young yearling, just a little bit bigger than what I expected Bucky might be, and she was beautiful. As I held her, I noted the subtle differences between her and Bucky: the body style, the head shape, and of course the slightly different anatomy. But she was dead, and I had killed her. I could not stop at the landowner's house to show him my success. Not only because I was ashamed but because I was crying. I'd just taken the easiest path to solving a beaver conflict, and one that asked nothing of the landowner. She was the last beaver I would kill.

Bucky gave me respect for beavers and their lives. He changed my perspective by showing me that different species can communicate nonverbally. There was a lot of insight that came with knowing that. I changed my own behavior and bought live traps — Hancock, Bailey, and RAM-style — and researched nonlethal beaver controls, like Beaver Deceivers and water flow devices. Bucky had a big impact on my life.

Today when I get a call about a wildlife "conflict," I talk excitedly with the property owner about what a unique opportunity they might have to educate their kids and neighbors. I talk to them about doing something that's both green and fun. For example, a raccoon in a chimney with babies could be addressed by trapping and then breaking the family up and sending the kits to rehab. But that solves nothing. Rather, I suggest we set up a camera and watch the mom climbing up and down the chimney and the babies growing up in the chimney and finally moving out. Then we can cap the chimney and prevent future problems without negatively impacting the raccoon family. You're left with pictures and a great story for your holiday letter.

As a wildlife rehabber of thirty-six years at this point, I've been inspired by hundreds of individual animals who tell me they want to live, survive, and thrive! Bucky didn't just tell me he wanted to survive. He told me he wanted to communicate. He knew I was slow on the uptake, so he repeated his lessons. He used sign language and worked with me until I was able to figure it out. He inspired me because he knew who and what he was; he knew what he liked and didn't. He barked and thanked me for treats and also vocalized when the water in the tub was especially warm. He also tried repeatedly and daily to tell me not to trust my "coyote" Louie. Instinctively, he knew that one day Louie would eat us both. Thankfully, he didn't.

• • •

Since his transformational experience with Bucky the beaver, Dave has had personal connections with hundreds of animals, ranging from bobcats to alligators, from bullfrogs to skunks. He takes great pleasure in showing and teaching others how to relocate nuisance animals without hurting them.

As the leader of the HSUS Wildlife Response team, he travels the world, teaching governments, organizations, and everyday people how to coexist with other animals. His hands-on workshops have trained thousands of animal welfare workers and volunteers in countries from Russia to the Philippines on how to humanely capture, vaccinate, and sterilize street dogs, feral cats, and wildlife.

When people run away from natural disasters in areas devastated from tsunamis, hurricanes, and earthquakes, Dave runs in — to provide care to both animals and people. He is a true example of how one person can make a difference by educating others. He is directly and indirectly responsible for saving the lives of millions of animals in our world.

Have you ever rescued a ladybug?

Yes, and I offer them free rides to a food source. Twenty-five years ago, my wife and I planted a line of native ponderosa pine trees in our yard in Montana. We quickly discovered they'd occasionally bloom with aphids — tiny, sap-sucking insects that can wreak havoc on plants. The local food and agriculture extension agent offered several organic solutions to remove them, including the importation of commercially bought ladybugs. Instead of going that route, I just steadfastly offered any local ladybugs found on my truck, or that I met otherwise, a free ride back to our homestead with placement on one of the ten pine trees.

Name three things that make you happy.

Every early morning sunrise, witnessing my amazing daughters become citizens of the earth, watching my rescue chickens taking a dust bath.

What one book, documentary, or speech has had a profound effect on you?

I am mesmerized by good orators: John F. Kennedy, Barack Obama, John Hoyt. They capture my imagination and spirit. I think my current vision statement of "Any Critter, Any Crisis" was shaped by an informal talk given by the former CEO of HSUS, Wayne Pacelle. It was probably fifteen years ago when, as our federal legislation guy, he was talking to all the regional directors at an Animal Care Expo conference. He told us that each night he asked himself, "What have I done for animals today?" That struck a chord with me on many levels. Now, every morning, I ask myself a similar question: "What can I do for animals today?" And then I set out to help at least one animal.

Regarding your food choices, how do you describe yourself?

I describe myself as a "conscientious omnivore." I place emphasis on eating humanely and locally by supporting farmer's markets and family farms.

If you had one message to deliver to others, what would it be?

If you care, leave them there! This really means wildlife belongs in the wild. Even with the best of intentions, removing "orphans" should be a last resort because, in most situations, you are actually kidnapping the baby from a watching mamasan.

Also, lethal controls only treat symptoms. Nonlethal controls solve problems. In almost every situation, people do not have wildlife problems; they have attractant problems, habitat problems, or exclusion problems. The animal is simply taking advantage of an opportunity — and that is not cause for a death sentence.

If you had one wish that was guaranteed to come true, what would it be?

I wish that political leaders, religious spokespeople, media outlets, and all my friends and neighbors would wake up tomorrow morning with a positive outlook on what could happen if we all were better observers, better listeners, and had more compromising attitudes. Then we would be working toward peace on earth.

What advice do you have for people who say that they want to help animals in need but are too debilitated by what they witness?

Everyone can do something to help wildlife. Have a wildlife-friendly yard. Don't use poisons and glue traps. Practice non-lethal protocols. Support groups that do good wildlife projects. Comment and respond to legislation and wildlife delisting/listing campaigns. Speak up for wildlife.

Ric O'Barry

DOLPHIN

Most people I know would tell you their dream job is to work with animals and get paid to do it. That's exactly what lured Ric O'Barry into taking a job at the Miami Seaquarium in 1962. In doing so, he became one of the first captive-dolphin trainers in the world. He was twenty-two years old. At the time, he thought he'd landed the job of a lifetime. And for ten years, Ric worked in the captive-dolphin industry. He has now spent nearly fifty years working against it.

I first learned about Ric through television. Fed up with a constant stream of bad news and movies, I made a deal with myself. If I wanted to watch TV over a period of a month, it had to be a documentary. I had to be learning about something instead of being hammered with mindless violence.

One night, I happily tucked myself into bed with the dogs, turned on the TV, and purchased a documentary called *The Cove*. Within minutes I was sitting upright, taking notes. A little over an hour later, I was sobbing. The story profiles Ric as he leads filmmakers and activists in an undercover operation in Taiji, Japan, to witness and expose the horrific hunting season on dolphins. The film is gripping, educational, and heartbreaking.

I knew about dolphin exploitation. I have friends in Bali who are determined to release dolphins held in captivity there, but nothing I'd ever seen or heard had affected me like this film. In an hour and a half, I learned more about dolphins — the way they communicate with each other, their family dynamic — and those exploiting them than I'd learned in a lifetime as an animal advocate.

I also learned that Ric O'Barry, the man leading the global fight to protect dolphins, had originally fueled their popularity as entertainers. He was part of the problem until the death of his best friend.

• • •

Miami, Florida, USA

It is wrong to sacrifice another creature's well-being for our own satisfaction, despite how easily we or society justify it. To some degree, it requires willful ignorance to overlook suffering. I didn't understand this until I was thirty years old.

I grew up in Miami, Florida, where I had the pleasure of watching dolphins in the ocean in front of my house. The first time I remember seeing a dolphin I was probably three feet tall. I was standing on the powder-white sand beach. The water in those days looked like it did in the Bahamas, that turquoise color. You could look down the beach for miles and wouldn't see anybody. That was in the 1940s. The war was going on. As my mother and I watched the dolphins in the water, she told me that it was being reported that dolphins were sometimes saving the lives of US airmen. She told me that when their planes were shot out of the sky by the Japanese, survivors were sometimes helped to shore by the dolphins. That story really stuck with me.

When I was old enough, I joined the US Navy. After boot camp and before I was meant to be shipped out, I was given a fourteen-day leave. I took the leave at home, and on Christmas Day, 1955, my family went to the opening day of the brand-new Miami Seaquarium.

I remember standing by a big window with my nose pressed up to the glass. Inside was the most incredible sight. There were five-hundred-pound sea turtles, twelve-foot-long sawfish gliding along the bottom, and rays flying through the scene. There were dolphins in the tank, along with a big tiger shark and a five-hundred-pound grouper. And then, coming through the mist, was this guy in a canvas suit with a spun copper helmet and an air hose floating to the surface with bubbles streaming upward. That's when I said to myself, "When I get out of the navy, I'm going to come back and get that guy's job." And I did.

My very first day on the job, I was assigned to capture dolphins in the wild. To do this, we went into the Atlantic in a boat specially designed to haul live animals. It was called the capture boat. We put out a net about half a mile long and circled the dolphins. We then anchored the boat and got into smaller boats, working the nets until they were smaller and smaller, until the dolphins hit the deck. Many times, they drowned in the process, especially the young.

I progressed very quickly at the Seaquarium and soon became a trainer, even though I didn't know how to train dolphins. It wasn't difficult, though. You didn't feed them unless they did a trick. It was that simple. Trainers call it "positive reward," but from the dolphin's perspective, it's called "food deprivation," and that is what it is.

At the time, I was in my twenties, and the money was rolling in. I was driving a new Porsche every year whether I needed it or not. It was easy to turn a blind eye to the suffering. I was also coming from spending a few years in the military, where I was trained not to question authority and to follow orders. That's who I was then and that's what I did.

In 1964, the Seaquarium was approached to work on a TV program called *Flipper*. We would supply the set, the dolphins, and one trainer. I was given the trainer job. There were five dolphins used to play the role of Flipper, but one of them, Kathy, played the part 90 percent of the time. Kathy was young when we captured her. Her personality was cooperative, curious, and communicative.

Kathy lived in a lake that had been built around an actual tidal pool specifically for the program. It was maybe 180 meters by 180 meters (or 200 yards by 200 yards). The other dolphins were in very small steel tanks built especially for them. Looking back, it was cruel and unusual to keep them there.

I literally lived in the house on the set, and Kathy was in the pool in front of it. I lived on-site for seven years, for seven days a week. There was not a day I wasn't there. I knew Kathy's personality, and it was totally different between when the film crew was there and when I was alone with her. Like all captive dolphins, she suffered from extreme depression.

I call it Captive Dolphin Depression Syndrome. Consumers never see this because when the consumers arrive — or in the case of Kathy, when the film crew arrived — or people are there, their behavior and personality change because they're looking for food, and they know they have to perform to get it. They open their mouths, and to humans, it seems like they're smiling. They're not. It's an illusion. They're actually begging for food. As a consumer, you don't see the abuse. You *can't* see it.

After the *Flipper* series ended in 1967, all five dolphins remained at the Seaquarium. I left and began working as a stuntman and as an underwater double for other actors. I went back for a little while to train Hugo, the first orca in captivity in the eastern United States, and then returned to acting.

• • •

Ric's awakening occurred in 1969. He was living in Coconut Grove, near the Seaquarium, when he received an urgent call from its supervisor, Bob Baldwin. This is how Ric describes what happened next, in his book *Behind the Dolphin Smile*:

"It's Kathy," [Bob] said. "She's not doing well at all. They put her in one of the tanks."

"What did they do that for?" I asked.

"You should come at once," he said.

I got on my bike and pedaled over the causeway. What could be wrong? Bob Baldwin was not one to panic. If he had known what was wrong, he would have told me. If it's just that she wouldn't eat, maybe I could do something. But why did they move her? If I had been there, I wouldn't have allowed that. I pedaled furiously and, dripping with sweat, reached the Seaquarium and rode right through the gate without stopping. Somebody new at the gate yelled after me, but I kept going. I rode over to the tank where Bob said she had been put. I went up to the tank and looked in. I was stunned! It was Kathy, yes, but not the Kathy I'd known. Her back and head were black with blisters [from extreme sunburn, since she was in a small, steel tank with no shade]. Horrible! Big, ugly, black blisters covered almost her whole body, and she lay there on the surface of the water, barely moving.

I leaped in the water with her, clothes and all. She came over and into my arms. I held her for a moment and felt the life go out of her. Her tail flukes stopped moving, and she was dead. A foul white foam had formed on her blowhole. Without thinking, I washed it away. I gently forced the blowhole open with my thumb, very careful not to let any water in. I cradled her in my arm and held on to the edge of the pool so that I could use my knees to apply pressure to Kathy's rib cage. But Kathy was dead. I pressed her ribs in and out, keeping up a breathing rhythm. But I knew she was dead. How long I did that, I don't know. But she was dead, and nothing could be done about it. I let her go, and she sank to the bottom. All of a sudden, I felt very dirty. I got my bike and pushed it to Bob's office, tears streaming down my face. When I saw him, I tried to speak but couldn't.

"You don't have to say anything," he said.

I kept trying to speak but I was sobbing too much. Then, for just a moment, I cleared up and blurted out at him, "Why are we doing this?"

• • •

For me, that was the turning point. It moved me to action, that day, that moment. Up to that time, I knew captivity was wrong. While subconsciously I'd known that wild animals like dolphins don't want to be held captive and forced to perform for food, Kathy's death made that crystal clear. From that moment, I wanted to undo the damage I'd done by making dolphins such a popular source of entertainment.

Because dolphins carry the appearance of a constant smile, it's easy to believe that they are always happy and content. It's not the case. Their extreme intelligence makes them ideal candidates for captive entertainment, but it also makes their suffering that much greater. It's delusion to believe that such creatures can thrive in captive conditions.

The moment of Kathy's death changed everything. My goal became to free captive dolphins and put an end to their abuse for human entertainment. I became an activist as opposed to an in-activist. Up until that point my relationship with dolphins was all about what they could do for me. Kathy moved me to finally do something about wild captures and captivity, to educate the public to leave dolphins in the wild where they belong.

• • •

Within days of Kathy's death, Ric was arrested and jailed in the Bahamas for attempting to free a captive dolphin named Charlie Brown. On that day in 1970, the first Earth Day, Ric launched the Dolphin Project to campaign against the captive dolphin industry and to end dolphin exploitation and slaughter. It's the oldest dolphin welfare organization in the world.

Since then, Ric has rehabilitated and released captive dolphins in Haiti, Colombia, Guatemala, Nicaragua, Brazil, South Korea, the Bahamas, and the United States. He works with communities and government agencies to end dolphin trafficking in underdeveloped countries. Among other successes, he has negotiated an end to dolphin slaughter in the Solomon Islands. Working with coalitions, the organization has shut down aquariums holding dolphins and blocked imports and captures of wild dolphins in many areas. He is the coauthor of two books about his life and work: *Behind the Dolphin Smile* and *To Free a Dolphin*.

As the leading voice against dolphin hunts, Ric was the focus of the 2009 documentary *The Cove*. The film, directed by Louie Psihoyos (*Racing Extinction*) and produced by Fisher Stevens and

Paula DuPré Pesman, follows Ric to Taiji, Japan, and documents the six-month-long hunting season and mass slaughter of dolphins there. *The Cove* won the Academy Award for the Best Documentary Feature in 2010. Publicity generated by the film exposed and highlighted the brutal capture of dolphins used for entertainment in dolphinariums and aquariums around the world. The film gave Ric a platform to reach tens of thousands of students each year, many of them in Japan, to talk about dolphin captivity and how to end it by refusing to support businesses that use the animals as entertainment. He promotes the hashtag #DontBuyATicket as the simplest way people can help stop dolphin exploitation.

Have you ever rescued a ladybug?

I have rescued many ladybugs; I'm actually a big fan of them.

Name three things that make you happy.

Family, friends, a day off.

What one book, documentary, or speech has had a profound effect on you?

The Voyage of the Beagle by Charles Darwin.

Regarding your food choices, how do you describe yourself?

I'm a vegan wannabe.

If you had one message to deliver to others, what would it be?

Please do not buy a ticket to a wild animal show; their captivity is based on supply and demand. We as consumers have the power to end this abuse.

If you had one wish that was guaranteed to come true, what would it be?

For the annual dolphin slaughter at the cove to be abolished.

What advice do you have for people who say that they want to help animals in need but are too debilitated by what they witness?

There are always ways to help that do not require you to be on the front lines. Public awareness and education are hugely important; you can find your own voice and means to be an effective activist.

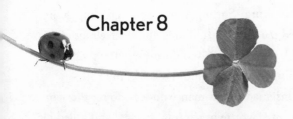

Chapter 8

SHARK AND COYOTE

From Fear to Happiness

Cottesloe Beach, Australia

I don't remember being afraid of anything until I was six years old. That's when my mother, unable to get her children inside for dinner, started a nightly ritual of yelling out the back door, "The bats are coming, the bats are coming!" Bats lived in our barn, and I'd never been afraid of them until my mother told us the story of a local boy who was bitten by one when it became entangled in his hair — at dusk. That story — most likely created over a cocktail by my parents and used as a tool for my mother to corral her children — planted the first seed of fear I had for another animal.

I blame Steven Spielberg for the second seed, planted in the summer of 1975, when he converted Peter Benchley's book *Jaws* into a heart-pounding, nail-biting, jump-out-of-your-seat movie. The film about a man-eating great white shark terrorizing Cape Cod beachgoers caused millions to flee the water and extinguished the unencumbered joy I, and many others, once felt in the ocean.

Twenty years later, I landed in Australia and was lured into the Indian Ocean's spectacularly clear, blue water. A peace washed through me as I ventured into the sea each morning, communing and connecting with nature. Surfing waves and spending hours snorkeling transported me back to childhood and the feelings of living in the moment. I became addicted to the experience: swimming with fish, the awakening of muscles, and the salt in my hair.

It ended in an instant when a man who was doing the same thing one morning at my favorite beach was attacked and killed by a shark. And then it happened again and again, in what became a string of eleven fatal attacks between 2010 and 2017 that led Western Australia to be named the deadliest coast in the world.

During this period, pretty much everybody left the ocean and hit the pools. I was one of them. But after many months out of the ocean, I received a message. It was on a 105-degree day. I was walking the dogs on the beach and feeling frustrated by the invisible chain preventing me from plunging into the water. Then a quote from Franklin D. Roosevelt popped into my head and kept repeating: "The only thing we have to fear is fear itself." It was then I made a conscious decision to conquer my fear of sharks.

The transition came in baby steps and happened over several years. It started with knuckle-swimming, when you swim so close to shore you scrape your knuckles on the sand. Eventually, I also joined a swim group made up of people who were training for open-ocean, long-distance swims. In the meantime, the Western Australian government was considering killing great white sharks, which meant overriding international and federal protections of the species. The idea of a shark cull ignited an ongoing local debate about what was causing the attacks and whether a cull would effectively stop them.

One possible cause was identified in July 2012 by Humane Society International Australia (HSI). HSI reported, "There may be a possible connection between the export of live sheep from Fremantle, Western Australia, and reported shark attacks." When export ships from Australia carry live animals — such as sheep, cattle, and goats bound for slaughter in the Middle East and Asia — hundreds of animals, and sometimes thousands, die en route, and their bodies are thrown overboard, providing a consistent food source for sharks. HSI said that six people in Australia had been attacked between September 4, 2011, and June 20, 2012, when export ships were nearby. Further, HSI reported that a similar link was found in Egypt in December 2010, when a string of five shark attacks within a single week were most likely provoked by a live export ship that threw sheep overboard while it passed through the Red Sea.

Nevertheless, the Western Australian government dismissed this potential connection, and in early 2014, the state's premier, Colin Barnett, ordered a shark cull.

Contracted fishermen set baited drum lines along the coast, and on the first day, as I stepped onto the beach for my swim, I watched as contractors pulled a drowned shark from the water. My morning joy turned to sorrow. As much as I felt empathy for the swimmers, surfers, and divers who'd lost their lives, I now felt empathy for this dead shark. Killing did not feel like the answer.

My husband, Jon, didn't agree with me. He believed the cull should happen. One morning as I set off to attend a shark rally, he suggested it would be a waste of time and that I'd be sitting on the beach with only two hundred people. To his surprise and mine, six thousand people were there, protesting to voice their opposition to the cull. A poignant sign at the rally pointed out that, the year before in Australia, twenty-five thousand people had died of obesity-related illness, twelve hundred from car accidents, ten from lightning strikes, and two from sharks. Overwhelming empathy for the sharks was shown by the very people who loved the ocean and were at the greatest risk: swimmers, divers, and surfers. Even more poignant, relatives of those who'd been killed also protested the cull, as they believed those who'd died wouldn't want the sharks to be killed.

After four months, the cull ended. Of the 172 sharks that were caught, none were great whites, the species blamed for the attacks.

Publicity over the cull brought awareness and change. Surf Life Saving Western Australia, a rescue organization, became an alert center for shark sightings and public safety warnings. Using information from helicopter beach patrols, drones, shark sightings, and transponders that detected and sent alerts when tagged tiger and great white sharks passed beaches, the organization delivered alerts via Twitter and a beach safety app. I got into the habit of checking Twitter before heading for the beach, just to see who I might be swimming with.

By 2016, my swim team coach, Ceinwen Roberts — a thirty-five-year-old, five-foot-two, sun-kissed blonde with a beaming smile and matching disposition — was training us for a 12.5-mile (20-kilometer) open-ocean race from the mainland to Rottnest Island. Ceinwen had established the race, called the Port to Pub, and she was convinced I could do it. Her own swimming history includes completing the Triple Crown of Open Water Swimming: solo swims across the English Channel, around Manhattan Island, and from Catalina Island to the California mainland. Two of those swims involve swimming through the night, and when I asked her about sharks, she said, "I don't even think about them. There's no point. If it's my time to go, it's my time to go. I'm too busy enjoying the good parts of being out there: the serenity, clarity, salt, fish, reef, and having nothing to stop me." She inspired me to enter the race.

Let me be honest: I was scared. But I was also determined. I knew what the accomplishment would do for me, spiritually, mentally, and physically. I didn't know my awakening would actually come two weeks before the swim.

It was February 22, 2016. The weather was overcast, what Australians call "sharky," due to the fact that a majority of shark attacks occur on cloudy days. I joined a group of fifteen women —

mostly mothers in their late thirties and early forties who called themselves the Aquabutts — on an ocean training swim, led by Ceinwen, from Cottesloe Beach to North Cottesloe Beach and back, a distance of over a mile.

We first swam into deep water, fifty yards from shore, and then we set off along the coast. The first leg was easy. The swell was pushing north, and we rode it up the coast. Then, as we treaded water off North Cottesloe Beach and prepared for the push back, we talked about how high the waves were getting and how much harder the return trip would be. We didn't talk about what we were all thinking: that we'd congregated in a spot where a swimmer had been killed by a great white shark years before.

To push us, Ceinwen decided to break the group up. Ten swimmers would start first, and she would go with them. The five fastest were told to hold back and start only when the others were about a quarter of the way down the coast. I was in the second group — not because I was fast, but because I was wearing flippers.

Finally, my group set off. The water was unusually murky. Schools of tiny fish moved around me like underwater tornadoes. I saw a shadow. It was at that moment my goggles lost their seal. I flipped over and floated on my back, tightening them. As I was doing this, a shark-spotting helicopter flew overhead. As I watched it buzz past, I felt comforted just knowing it was there.

I put my head back in the water and noticed that the distance between the five of us had widened. We were no longer in a pod. We were spread out in deep, choppy water. And that's when it happened.

I felt the whoosh of helicopter blades just above me, accompanied by a deafening siren. I knew immediately what it was and what it meant. Jaws was with us.

A fear like no other consumed me. Luckily, it came with a massive rush of adrenaline. I wasn't alone. I don't remember much about the time it took me to swim to shore. The five of us in the second group crawled onto the beach at the same time. Someone puked. I stood up and looked out at the angry ocean. Nine of the swimmers in the first group were almost on the beach, but two weren't heading in. We all started screaming. One of the girls was still swimming and Ceinwen was trying to get her attention. We watched in terror, screaming for the girl to stop, fearful of the potential horror that could unfold before us. Thankfully, it didn't.

The lifeguard at the nearest station told us the rest of the story. After passing us, the helicopter pilot spotted a ten-foot shark and radioed that it was heading straight for us. The species was most likely a tiger or great white.

As I walked away that morning, I was grateful and exhilarated. Grateful to have been swimming with a very big shark who had the opportunity to eat one of sixteen women and didn't. Exhilarated by the fact that the fear that had paralyzed me throughout much of my life was gone.

I still get scared swimming in the ocean sometimes, like when I'm caught up in a swirl of fish and I know that someone is causing their panic, but the fear doesn't consume me. I've had a great life. I understand that everybody's got to eat. I hope it's not me that gets eaten, but if it is, so be it.

By immersing yourself in nature, you can experience a form of enlightenment. This is when the soul is free of fear and absorbs, almost by osmosis, the energy of life. The connection between all species becomes clear. I have friends who've been given the gift of this knowledge. They've gone on to change the world.

Shawn Heinrichs

SHARK

Overcoming my fear of sharks was a personal quest. But when I was forced to helplessly bear witness to the indiscriminate culling of tiger and great white sharks by the Western Australian government, I was motivated to do more politically. I started by going to a shark rally to protest the culling. It was a sunny day on Cottesloe Beach, just outside Perth, Australia. The air was electrified with the collective compassion of six thousand people. Everyone was there for one reason — to insist that we, as humans, had no right to kill sharks. The results from the rally and research put an end to the culling. I was so excited I wanted to know what was being done on a global scale to protect the species.

I called my girlfriend Carole Tomko. She'd coproduced the Louie Psihoyos documentary *Racing Extinction*, which exposes the way humans are contributing to the mass extinction of many species. While watching it, I'd been particularly moved by underwater cinematographer and conflict-zone photographer Shawn Heinrichs. Carole kindly made the introduction.

Heinrichs was born in South Africa and raised in Philadelphia, Pennsylvania. He describes his father as a nature lover who often took him for hikes in the woods and was always trying to help birds. Both parents, he says, reinforced his own tender feelings for animals.

Armed with a camera, Heinrichs took up diving and nature photography as a hobby and went into the tech world as a financial officer for a software startup company. His life took a dramatic turn in 2006 on a trip to Indonesia. He was filming a newly established marine reserve in Raja Ampat, an archipelago known to have some

201

of the richest marine biodiversity on earth. And in a moment of what could be called divine intervention, Heinrichs captured on camera an act so heinous that it would serve as a catalyst for monumental global change.

• • •

Raja Ampat, West Papua, Indonesia

I was that kid who defended little animals. I couldn't help it. I think that's where it starts for a lot of us — I used to rescue every little bug and every little animal I could.

I especially loved my dogs, Shiba and Shane. I loved them so much I would actually eat out of their dog food bowl. But I felt kinship with all animals. I've always felt one with them and on par with them. We use the distinction between humans and animals as a hierarchy to allow all sorts of horrible things to be done to animals. But I love them as I love anything.

West Papua is the heart of the coral triangle in Indonesia. It is the most biodiverse part of all Indonesia and, in fact, the very heart of marine biodiversity. The Raja Ampat Islands are really special. You won't see more pristine reefs or a greater diversity of fish anywhere else on the planet. Its waters are home to whale sharks, manta rays, dolphins, and turtles, along with more than five hundred species of hard corals. It's an amazing place.

In 2006, I traveled there to apply my emerging underwater filming skills to creating a video for my friend Andy Miners and a group of angel investors. We were aiming to garner support for our newly established three-hundred-thousand-acre underwater marine reserve and eco-resort called Misool. The resort would support conservation efforts of the marine ecosystem by empowering local communities to reclaim traditional tenureship of their reefs, protecting them from the insatiable global demand for seafood. My role as a volunteer was to document the beauty of this new marine reserve.

From the United States, it took seven planes and twenty-four hours on a basic wooden vessel with crude bunks and a makeshift kitchen to get there. The total trip took eighty hours, which is a lot longer than even getting to Antarctica. It was way off the beaten path.

At the time, you couldn't go anywhere without seeing a shark-finning, gill-netting, or long-lining boat. People were even fish bombing, using homemade explosives dropped on fragile reefs to stun fish, turning thousand-year-old reefs into rubble. Every imaginable form of unsustainable fishing and illicit wildlife trade you can imagine — shark finning, turtle poaching, live reef fishing — you name it, it was there, strip-mining the place. It was the poster child for destructive fisheries.

What I witnessed there became a turning point in my life and cemented all the work I've been doing since.

I'd been diving for two weeks when I noticed that I hadn't seen a single reef shark over the course of the entire trip. Not one. Everything was in place — everything except sharks. I wondered if I had come at the wrong time, if I was filming during the wrong tides, if water temperatures were too warm and were keeping them away. I went through all these excuses in my head because I couldn't imagine the sharks had literally been wiped out of the entire area.

On the final day of our trip, the crew and I had just wrapped up our last dive and were making our way home to our camp. The sun was dropping below the horizon, casting its warm glow and brilliant rays across the late afternoon sky, as we glided across the glassy waters in our speedboat. We were soaking it all in when we suddenly noticed a nondescript wooden fishing boat anchored back in the corner of a mangrove lagoon. It was in the boundaries of our newly established no-take zone, an area where fishing was strictly prohibited. We wondered what it was doing there and decided to check it out. As we approached the boat, we were affronted by the smell of drying flesh and the sound of buzzing flies.

We pulled up to the boat. Juvenile reef shark fins with numbers on them were strewn all over the blood-soaked deck, the numbers obviously designating some kind of value or grade. The fins were drying in the sun. I was like, "Oh my God. Here are our sharks!" A fisherman emerged from the mangroves in his small canoe and boarded the vessel. While my friend Andy engaged him in a conversation in Indonesian, I turned my attention to the water beneath the vessel and saw something glistening on the reef below. I wondered, *What's that?* So I put my mask on and looked in and saw the body of a beautiful young reef shark who had just been finned, still bleeding out from its fins, rolling back and forth on the reef.

I was struck by the juxtaposition of this incredible ecosystem with this atrocity. I was in such shock that I felt like my whole body was electrified and shaking. I was trying to reconcile these two things because I wanted, like all of us, to find some plausible deniability: I wanted to believe there was another reason the sharks weren't around. But the answer was literally staring me in the face. This is what had happened to paradise. We had literally finned all the sharks in paradise for this horrendous trade.

At that point, I decided I had to do something about it. I grabbed my camera, dropped into the water, and began filming. I remember coming face-to-face with this beautiful shark, and all the little cleaner fish were still picking at its skin because they didn't know it was dead. There was this really horrible irony, that the fish were all going about their duty cleaning its skin, and the shark was rolling as if it was alive, but it wasn't. It had just died. After enduring its fin being cut off, the shark had been thrown overboard alive, to suffocate. I looked around. There were another dozen shark bodies strewn across this beautiful reef.

I went face-to-face with each and every one of them. That was really emotional. I started tearing up in my mask. I was just trying the best I could to document it, knowing there was some reason why I had to tell this story.

I came back to the surface and was so angry. I got back into our boat and said to my friend Andy, "Why the hell is this guy here?"

Andy asked him, and the guy showed him a permit. This itinerant fisherman had paid the local community thirty dollars to fin sharks for thirty days, so even if he caught only ten sharks a day (and he got a lot more than that), that'd be three hundred sharks for thirty dollars, or ten cents a shark. It struck me that the very birthright of this community, their incredible marine ecosystem, was being strip-mined at wholesale rates of ten cents a shark, just to feed the insatiable demand in China and Southeast Asia for shark fin soup. The soup — mainly consumed in China and Vietnam — was once believed to have health-giving properties, but that has since been debunked. In fact, reports are just the opposite. Sharks have high concentrations of mercury and beta-Methylamino-L-alanine, a neurotoxin that is linked to dementia and other brain disorders in people.

I sat on the deck of our boat as the sun set. I remember looking at the fins and looking in the water and realizing that this had to stop. I'd traveled eighty hours to find one of the last places in the ocean unspoiled by humans, and in the middle of paradise, it was basically atrocity central.

The real moment of life transition for me was when I surfaced from the water. I had witnessed and looked into the eyes of these sharks and watched the life slip from their bodies. The utter wrongness of what we were perpetuating on nature hit me like a ton of bricks. In this last great place, this epicenter of marine diversity, I realized that if I didn't dedicate myself to fixing these issues, there'd be nothing left — for me, my children, and my grandchildren. I changed my life on that very spot. Everything I would do from then on would be dedicated to ending the destruction going on in our oceans.

That was, for me, the biggest turning point in my life. I went back and made a video of what I'd just witnessed and called it *Shark Fin Frontier*. It was the first real video I ever produced, and I put it up on YouTube.

It was my first film, but it changed my life. I had news agencies and citizens from across the world contacting me when they saw it, and I realized the power of video and media. We showed the film to the regional government in West Papua, and they were horrified to realize that what was happening in their waters was being aired around the world. The film was used by Misool as a major leverage point to get stronger conservation in the area and to ultimately have Raja Ampat declared a shark and ray sanctuary in 2010.

For a long time, my most profound connection with a shark was, sadly, with a dead one, with the shark I saw floating in the ocean after being finned. But then, in early 2007, I journeyed to the Bahamas to meet some of the most feared of all shark species. In the clear blue water off the Bahamas, I would come face-to-face with a massive — and very much alive — tiger shark, and my empathy for the species would take a massive leap — and cement my desire to help them.

I'd been a diver for sixteen years at that point and was one of those people who preached to everyone not to worry about sharks. That was all good — until I was in a boat in the Gulf Stream in a place called Tiger Beach, looking down off the dive step at several sixteen-foot-long tiger sharks swimming below me, right where I was about to dive.

It was a moment of truth. I had to reconcile the last of the deep-seated and unfounded fears programmed into me over a period of decades by the media with my conviction about what I intellectually knew to be the truth about sharks. I thought, *This is my mortality. This is my life. I'm putting it on the line now.*

I dropped down and descended to the sandy bottom. And then this massive tiger shark appeared. It was circling cautiously, and then it decided to come in and give me a closer look. My heart was pounding. It came directly up to me and sort of nosed right into my camera, really gently. I remember it looking directly into my camera lens, and I watched its eye as it rolled up and down, checking me out. It slowly circled away, and when it came back, it circled three times. I gently rubbed my hand along its side because it was almost pushing into me, like when a kitty wants to rub your leg.

The shark's name was Emma. My friend Jim Abernethy had dived with her for years. She was an incredibly gentle, curious, beautiful tiger shark. Jim said that every year she showed up pregnant and had her babies somewhere in the area.

It was amazing because, in that moment, all the myths and media programming in my head about how terrifying the tiger shark was and how it was going to try to eat me vanished. I realized how intelligent and sentient Emma was. She was tactile, using all her senses — including touch — to figure out who I was. She wasn't coming to eat me. She was just curious about what I was, and not once did she show any form of aggressive behavior. I realized that everything I'd been taught by the media about sharks was wrong. Yes, they were impressive predators, but they had no intention of attacking and eating me. It took coming face-to-face with a shark the size of a small car to vanquish that irrational fear and replace it with a dedication and passion to protect them.

To describe sharks, I now use the model of a dog, which makes more sense than comparing them to some mindless, senseless killing machine because they simply are not. They're super-intelligent animals. The giant sixteen-foot predatory shark named Emma behaved like a puppy dog, with the same curiosity and gentle interactivity. When you're in the presence of an animal and you make that connection, they're no longer abstract. They're a sentient being that has a spirit, a soul. Meeting her was a moment when I realized I could speak about the true nature of sharks, not with my mind, but from my heart.

• • •

Since his first film, *Shark Fin Frontier*, exposed the horror of shark finning, Heinrichs has gone on to become a full-time cinematographer and marine conservationist. As an undercover journalist, he risks his life by exposing the often-illegal slaughter of marine life that is causing the desecration of the world's oceans.

Through his television and film production company, Blue Sphere Media, Shawn Heinrichs has successfully blended work with passion to expose atrocities in places we can't see ourselves.

Heinrich is a volunteer for the global conservation organizations WildAid, Manta Trust, the Safina Center, and the International League of Conservation Photographers. His photographs and film footage have been used to help create conservation treaties, laws, and marine-protected areas and to educate communities and governments to protect their own waters and those who inhabit them.

Through his work with the Misool Foundation, in partnership with indigenous communities, Shawn has helped to successfully create the Misool Marine Reserve, protecting three hundred thousand acres of the world's most biodiverse reefs.

Due in part to his prolific work documenting shark finning at Misool and the trade in general, shark fin consumption in China has decreased by an estimated 50 to 70 percent, and there are now twenty-five times more sharks found inside the Misool Marine Reserve than directly outside of it.

Have you ever rescued a ladybug?

I rescue all the little bugs. I especially love ladybugs because they're so pretty. I have memories of warm, summer days, watching them on blades of grass, marveling at what beautiful, vulnerable, little creatures they are. They're such anomalies, little buttons bouncing through nature.

Name three things that make you happy.

My family and friends. Nature. Acts of kindness. Acts of kindness make me very happy.

What one book, documentary, or speech has had a profound effect on you?

The Lorax by Dr. Seuss.

Regarding your food choices, how do you describe yourself?

Vegetarian and conscious eater.

If you had one message to deliver to others, what would it be?

In the words of Dr. Seuss in *The Lorax*, "Unless someone like you cares a whole awful lot, nothing is going to get better. It's not."

If you had one wish that was guaranteed to come true, what would it be?

I would like to see the restoration of the balance of nature, where humans embrace and accept that we are part of nature and no longer wage war on it.

What advice do you have for people who say that they want to help animals in need but are too debilitated by what they witness?

Nowhere is sacred anymore. The fight is happening on all fronts. Ninety percent of the ocean's large predatory fish have been depleted since 1950, which means their functional roles in ecosystems have almost been lost. Either you decide you're going to put a stop to it or you close your eyes and look away, but it's going to keep happening if you do that. You can't hide from it. Imagine it was your child under imminent threat. Would you close your eyes so you wouldn't have to face it, or would you act now in your child's defense?

Zoe Weil

COYOTE

It's strange how people can sometimes be in your midst but you walk past each other like ghosts, never truly crossing paths until the timing is perfect. This was the case with Zoe Weil. We lived twenty minutes from each other for decades. I frequently passed the sign for her Institute for Humane Education (IHE) in Surry, Maine, wondering who lived down the driveway. Yet I never turned down it myself, ignoring the instinct that told me I should learn more. It took a mutual friend from Washington — and a battle to protect bears — to bring us together.

In 2014, I was introduced to Zoe by Wayne Pacelle at a meeting to end bear baiting, hounding, and trapping in Maine. As we talked I learned that Zoe — a five-foot-one woman with muscle-toned arms and long, gray-salted brown hair — was the cofounder of IHE and lived just beyond the road sign I'd passed for years. I instantly regretted not having taken the time to meet her sooner.

We became fast friends, meeting for engaging discussions on the phone and on Skype, and when we were lucky, in a lake or near the ocean. I'd been asked to build a state council for the HSUS in Maine. Zoe answered my call to join it. And I answered hers: to help build awareness for IHE, the international school she'd started with the purpose of creating a just, humane, and sustainable world through education.

Zoe's own education began in New York City, which for her was a wildlife wonderland. Where others saw pavement, Zoe discovered caterpillars, rescued injured birds, and marveled at the living tree roots that upended cobblestones. She made weekly visits to the

Central Park petting zoo and bonded with a sheep. Wooly Baba, as she fondly called him, greeted her each week like a long-lost friend and their friendship would be the catalyst for her decision to exclude lamb and eventually all meat from her diet.

Despite her love for most animals, Zoe was, like most people, afraid of some. It would take a close encounter with coyotes to overcome those fears.

• • •

Adirondack Mountains, New York, USA

We all have vivid memories of the ghost stories of our childhood, and some of them leave lasting marks. I never developed a fear of werewolves or vampires — instead, I became afraid of coyotes. When I was seven or eight years old, I was hanging out with my best friend and two older boys who were telling scary stories about coyotes. I didn't know anything about coyotes. I didn't know that they are canids like dogs or that they're the size of a small border collie. The image these boys painted was of vicious, conniving, werewolf-like beasts. I was terrified.

I couldn't stop thinking about the coyotes in the days, weeks, and months that followed. In my mind, they became the epitome of what is most ferocious in the world.

Nearly twenty years after I heard those scary stories, I signed up as an apprentice to learn how to guide vision quests. My first ten-day vision quest a couple years earlier had been life-changing. I was a city girl. I'd spent the first eighteen years of my life growing up in Manhattan; had gone to college in Philadelphia; had lived in Washington, DC, for the better part of a year; and had attended graduate school in Boston. I was used to bright lights, loud noises, and crowds. Being still in nature and celebrating life as a human animal on this planet were largely unfamiliar to me, even though I loved nature. But I was transformed by those ten days, truly at peace in the natural world, fully myself, and bursting with love for nature and the people I was with. I wanted to gain the skills to lead people on their own journeys of personal transformation.

During a vision quest, each person spends three of the ten days alone. During my first quest, I chose a spot near a brook, just off a clearly marked trail and not far from our base camp. As soon as it got dark, I retreated into my tent because I was scared to be in the wild at night. I didn't come out until the sun rose.

This time, as an apprentice eager to test my own limits, I chose a spot well off the trail and on a ridge high up in New York's Adirondack Mountains. Although I set up my tent in case it rained, I never entered it. Instead, I chose to sleep on the bare rock, under the stars. But when I climbed into my sleeping bag that first night, I didn't sleep.

Shortly after I lay down, I was startled to hear cries like human screams. They began far off, but soon the creatures making these sounds surrounded me on three sides. As I parsed the cries, I heard barks, howls, yips, and keening, and I realized I was surrounded by coyotes. Theirs were the eeriest, yet most awe-inspiring sounds I'd ever heard. Yes, my skin tingled, but knowing these weren't human screams, I was not afraid.

How ironic. Screaming humans would have sent me running down that ridge as fast I could, but screaming coyotes? I didn't want them to stop! In fact, as their voices became louder and closer, my initial alarm changed to excitement. I even found myself wanting them to join me on my rocky outcropping. I felt so alive and fortunate to hear these incredible sounds and to know that I was among wild animals privileging me with their voices. I was disappointed when they eventually moved on, even as I basked in the feeling that I'd been graced by wildness.

We can so easily be made to fear wildlife, which often leads us to harm them. In the case of coyotes, these wild relatives of our dogs are still vilified and killed by the hundreds of thousands annually. Even worse, our fear extends beyond individual predator species like coyotes and encompasses all of nature.

We have a name for this fear of nature: biophobia. Biophobia is dangerous. It prevents us from spending time in the natural world and keeps us from learning about other species. And it leads us to destroy, sometimes unwittingly and sometimes wantonly, what we do not understand.

Yet our fears can be transformed through knowledge, and our lives and the lives of other species can be enriched as we learn to live harmoniously. I was once terrorized as a child by a bat flying in my bunk at camp. Then a kind counselor taught me about bats, their impressive use of sonar, and their desire to avoid me — while eating the mosquitoes that really did want to bother me. My counselor slowly transformed my fear into appreciation, and I grew to love bats. To this day, I cannot wait to welcome the bats from their winter hibernation and watch them eat their fill of mosquitoes in summer.

During the years between being frightened of coyotes as a child and blissfully lying on a rock surrounded by them, I learned about them. I learned that coyotes don't harm people, except in the rarest of cases. I learned that the cruelty we've inflicted upon them, and our relentless efforts to destroy them, have not diminished their numbers in any significant fashion. My learning about coyotes led to my appreciation of them, which set the stage for the awe-inspiring, reverence-inducing, wonder-filled night on that ridge.

Knowledge and the understanding and compassion that can flow from it are the most important keys to discovering how to live justly, compassionately, and sustainably on our beautiful planet and in relation to the other creatures with whom we share it. In an instant, knowledge can eradicate phobias and fears born of ignorance.

Soon after my experience on that ridge, I became a humane educator. For the past thirty years, I've helped people gain understanding, appreciation, and reverence for all species, including humans, and the environment that sustains us. My focus is now on transforming our education system so that all young people learn to be excellent researchers and critical, creative, systems thinkers who strive to find solutions to complex, interconnected problems in ways that are good for people, animals, and the planet. My goal is to educate a generation of solutionaries who will solve problems at their root in ways that do the most good and least harm to people, animals, and the environment.

My experience with the coyotes is illustrative of this important process. We can all seek out accurate information to counter not only our fears and biases but the stories we hear that may not be true, like scary stories that paint coyotes as vicious and dangerous. We can strive to think critically and creatively and recognize the various systems that contribute to problems — and thus find solutions to conflicts, including those between people and animals. We can foster reverence by heading into nature with awakened senses, where we'll sometimes have once-in-a-lifetime encounters like I did, ones that transform us and fill us with wonder. In so doing, we have the opportunity to move toward more humane and wise choices and to participate in the unfolding of a more just and healthy world.

• • •

Zoe Weil is dedicated to transforming our education system into one where a generation of "solutionaries" are armed with the skills needed to find solutions to our greatest problems.

This educational pioneer is the cofounder and president of the Institute for Humane Education (IHE), where she's created the first graduate programs in comprehensive humane education, linking human rights, environmental preservation, and animal protection.

Zoe's infectious, upbeat presence and common-sense approach to education have led to several acclaimed TEDx talks and numerous awards. She is the author of seven books, including *The World Becomes What We Teach: Educating a Generation of Solutionaries*; *Most Good, Least Harm*; *Claude and Medea*; and *Above All, Be Kind*. Through her work with the IHE, she's spoken to more than a hundred thousand students, and she suspects that millions of young people have been touched by the institute's work — learning to solve problems effectively, humanely, and sustainably.

Have you ever rescued a ladybug?

Of course! I also pet bumblebees and rescue worms from puddles.

Name three things that make you happy.

Being in nature, improvisational comedy (doing it and watching it), kindness.

What one book, documentary, or speech has had a profound effect on you?

Sapiens: A Brief History of Humankind by Yuval Noah Harari.

Regarding your food choices, how do you describe yourself?

Vegan.

If you had one message to deliver to others, what would it be?

Do the most good and the least harm to people, animals, and the environment. Be kind. Be wise. Be strategic. Be a solutionary.

If you had one wish that was guaranteed to come true, what would it be?

That we live in a *Star Trek* future, with a healthy planet earth, no more war among people, no more poverty and prejudice, and no more exploitation of animals.

What advice do you have for people who say that they want to help animals in need but are too debilitated by what they witness?

Try not to refuse to see with your eyes what they have to endure with their bodies. Witnessing is such a powerful component to educating others. Be willing to see in order to teach. In the words of singer Joan Baez, "Action is the antidote to despair."

Chapter 9

SNAKE, JAGUAR, OWL, SALAMANDER

Answering the Call

Seal Cove, Maine, USA

Some people love snakes. My mother is one of them. I didn't get the gene. According to my grandmother, from the time she was five years old, my mom was a romper-wearing tomboy who preferred trees to toys and dogs to dolls. She spent most of the day outside exploring marshes in her hometown of Wakefield, Massachusetts. When she did arrive home, it was often with a pocketful of garter snakes.

Twenty years later, with four children and a dog in tow, Mom was a bird-calling, four leaf clover–picking, ladybug-rescuing naturalist: a scout leader with her own troop. We climbed mountains, chewed on spearmint leaves, and lifted logs in search of the orange salamanders we called newts. When a snake crossed our path — and one inevitably would because Mom knew where to look for them — she'd pick it up and coo like it was a baby. We were encouraged to stroke and hold it while Mom gave us her usual tutorial about its habitat, behavior, and diet before she let it go.

These experiences were magical but didn't extinguish the anxiety I felt in the company of snakes. While I knew these feelings were a form of irrational fear, they weren't something I felt the need to conquer until I bought a dream property in Maine.

Seal Cove — named after the gray seals who frequent it — is a nature-lover's paradise on Mount Desert Island. Its shores are rocky and alive with barnacles, crabs, and periwinkles. Overhead, bald eagles and seagulls surf air currents, while on the ground, field mice scamper from under bushes of sweetly scented sea roses and rabbits make their homes in holes under pine trees.

Here, in this natural Eden, Jon and I purchased a piece of land with a two-room cabin on it. Leading up to the cabin are five exceptionally wide granite steps that seem to have been placed in anticipation of a grand house that was never built.

On our first day in the cabin, I woke to a sun-soaked morning and set off for my usual chilly swim in nearby Echo Lake. Upon my return, as I was climbing up the steps, I was startled by a brown snake coiled in the grass next to the top stone. I screamed and simultaneously leaped over the step before running inside.

Jon was very excited to hear we had company and was eager to see the snake. So we walked out to the deck and peered over the edge.

"There it is!" I said, pointing. The snake hadn't moved.

"Is it poisonous?" Jon asked, having grown up in Australia where most snakes are deadly.

"No," I said. "It's a garter snake. It can't hurt you."

"Then why are you screaming?"

"I don't know," I responded. And I didn't.

The next morning, I came up the steps after my swim and the snake was there — again! My response was the same. I screamed and jumped past it. Over coffee that morning, Jon, a medical doctor specializing in psychiatry, decided to conduct an intervention.

"It's obvious that snake isn't going anywhere," he said. "He's been living here long before us."

"I'm sure of it," I said.

"So what do you want to do? Do you want it to be killed?"

"What?" I exclaimed. "Of course not!"

"Then you're going to have to live with it," he said. "Jenny, your fear of this harmless creature is illogical. I've got a suggestion. Why don't we name him? I think if you start seeing him as a friend, you'll be a lot happier."

"I'll try."

"Good," he said. "Our pet snake is hereby named Cecil."

Jon is a very smart man, and I liked his idea. But it didn't quite work. Now, whenever I saw Cecil, I screamed out his name while jumping over the top step. This went on for a few weeks — until the morning everything changed.

I was weeding around the raspberry bushes on a corner of the property, twenty feet from the steps, when I noticed something unusual in a piece of garden netting. As I looked closer, I was horrified to see Cecil's body caught in the nylon squares. He was in bad shape, having obviously moved through one tiny hole after another only to become trapped. He looked like someone had placed rubber bands around him in a dozen places.

"Jon!" I screamed. "Cecil's in trouble. Come quick!"

After a quick assessment, Jon carried the tangled netting to the top granite step. He sat down and pulled the section containing Cecil into his lap.

"Poor Cecil. We'll help you, buddy," Jon said, examining him. "Jenny, I'll need tweezers, nail scissors — the tiny kind — and also regular scissors. You'd better bring some cotton, alcohol…and a coffee would help, too!"

I collected everything and sat down next to Jon and Cecil.

"It's serious," Jon said. "After going through the holes, he must've realized he was getting caught and tried to back out. This nylon thread has become wedged under his scales and can't be pulled out easily. Getting him extricated is going to be hard."

"I'm sorry, Cecil," I said, regretting having placed the netting and sorry for the dozens of times I'd greeted him with a scream instead of a hello.

Cecil was calm and pliable as Jon moved him around, determining where to start. When he was ready, he asked for the tweezers and then the tiny scissors. The job was painstakingly slow. But Jon was meticulous, determined not to harm Cecil while trying to save him.

Cecil accepted the help and didn't fight. He wasn't vicious or defensive. If anything, he was the opposite. It was obvious to me that he knew his life was in Jon's hands, and there seemed to be trust.

The surgical procedure took over an hour, and when the last thread was finally removed and the netting dropped, Cecil stayed in Jon's lap. He didn't slither away until he was placed on his favorite spot on the grass and sent forth with a "Good luck, buddy."

The next day, I realized that a bond had been forged during the rescue. As I returned from my morning swim and walked across the lawn, I noticed Jon sitting on the top granite step talking to someone. It was extraordinary. A few inches from Jon on the step, Cecil was coiled with his head in the air, looking inquisitively at his heroic human friend.

The rescue of Cecil created an unexpected cross-species friendship, and it awakened me to the fact that despite our differences, we have similarities and can communicate if we're receptive. Some people, like my mother, are open to these connections from the start and understand the symbiotic, natural relationship of all species. They empathize with underdog species and are impassioned to protect them by answering the deafening call they hear that is silent to others. And in their quest to help one animal, they provide better lives for all of us. They restore rainforests, create biosphere reserves, and preserve ecosystems. They produce documentaries to alert us to our own destructive paths, and they teach us why we must nourish our empathy and compassion for others. Their mysteriously inspired connection with animals may start with a simple act — like rescuing a snake or a ladybug — but their work for other species may be what leads to the preservation of our own.

Leandro Silveira

JAGUAR

The largest cat in the Americas is the jaguar. It's the third-largest cat in the world after the lion and the tiger. The jaguar has a rich cultural history and, sadly, a bleak future. The species once roamed in the southern United States, where it is now endangered. In Central and South America, the jaguar — also known as *Panthera onca* — is threatened from loss of habitat due to human encroachment and persecution. Even in Brazil, the jaguar has become endangered. But there is hope for the preservation of the species. His name is Leandro Silveira.

When he was a young boy, Leandro didn't know the history of the big cat that roamed freely in his native country of Brazil. He loved being around wild animals and had opportunities to spend time with them that most children didn't. His father was a veterinarian and often took him to the zoo, where he saw the animals from a different perspective. Considered by his parents to be the most sensitive of their four children, Leandro preferred taking care of the animals his father brought home on weekends rather than playing with toys or other children. His first pet was a blackbird he raised from a hatchling. The fact that he released the bird — and that it always came back to him — served as a reminder as he grew up that humans and other animals can live in close association while also being free.

When he was thirteen years old, Leandro had a glimpse of a powerful and mysterious animal that would create his destiny. His connection with a black-spotted jaguar became the catalyst for the creation of the Jaguar Conservation Fund, the first organization in the world devoted exclusively to protecting the species and its natural prey and habitat through research and conservation.

• • •

Goiás, Brazil

I was raised in the state of Goiás, in central Brazil, where agriculture and cattle ranching move the economy and cover the fragmented landscape of the Cerrado, a vast savanna. In this state, the most popular vacation for city dwellers is to camp on the beaches of the Araguaia River during the school break in July. I was introduced to this river in 1983, when I was thirteen years old. I joined a couple of uncles and cousins for a month of camping on the white-sand beaches of the river. The plan of activities and things to do were very clear: Men would go fishing, women would bathe in the sun, and children would swim in the shallows or play football or volleyball on the beach.

The wilderness of the Araguaia River enabled me to connect to nature in a unique way. There was no electricity, water pumps, or human noise. We were virtually isolated from modern civilization. As we slept in tents on the beaches a few meters from the river, we had the rare opportunity to connect with different sounds from nature. Those deep, silent nights taught me the sound of the howler monkeys, the splashes of the river dolphins feasting on schools of sardine-like fish, and the call of the jaguar.

My epiphany happened on the first day. We set off from the small town of Luiz Alves in three six-meter-long aluminum canoes equipped with forty-horsepower motors and loaded with twenty days' worth of camping gear and supplies. Halfway into the three-hour river trip, our canoe pilot — a local Indian who worked as a guide — suddenly pointed the bow of the canoe toward the river bank and increased its speed. Then he started shouting, "Jaguar! Jaguar!" It took a while for everyone on the canoe to spot the animal, and as far as I remember, I was the last one to see it. But there it was, a black jaguar standing on the river bank, staring at us with the same curiosity as ours. After a while the cat calmly turned and left. The event lasted all of about thirty seconds, but for me that moment was magical, and it came at a point in my life where every second lasted minutes.

That moment started my obsession with the jaguar. At the time, I knew little about our native wildlife. I think most Brazilian kids of my age valued African wildlife more than their own. After all, it was animals from Africa we saw on TV, in movies, and in books. The wildlife from Brazil was virtually undocumented on TV.

For the next twenty days of the camping trip, I tried to control my intense interest in the magnificent cat, but I had so many questions. No one at the camp could answer my questions, and no one seemed to care about the jaguar as much as I did. This moment of loneliness over the feeling I had for the cat made me want to learn more.

Five years later, I found myself going to college to become a biologist. However, in 1988, to become a biologist meant to become a teacher. Everyone who learned I was taking the biology course would say, "I didn't know you wanted to be a teacher." By then, Brazil was focused on development, which meant clearing native habitats to expand agriculture and cattle ranching. Conservation wasn't an issue and environmental NGOs were virtually nonexistent worldwide. It was very confusing and frustrating for me at that age. I wanted to be a biologist just to study jaguars, but I had no single reference in the country on which to mirror my goals. The closest I could get to my future jaguar research was to assist as a trainee on primate projects in the Amazon. Every time I mentioned to a professor or supervisor I wanted to study jaguars, I was persuaded to give up on the idea because such study would be too difficult or too costly. Who would give money to study jaguars? Why study them? These were the kinds of questions I would hear and to which I had no answers.

Being discouraged to study jaguars never made me give up. In fact, I believe that it encouraged me even more. I became more intrigued by the idea that we knew so little about the species and yet there was no natural support to study it. During college, the only literature available to learn about the jaguar was through the history and culture of ancient people of the American continents. During my studies, I found that all major Mesoamerican civilizations prominently featured a jaguar god, and for many, such as the Olmec, the jaguar was an important part of shamanism. At the time, this was the support I needed to continue pursuing my goal. Even if my species had no ecological importance, I could prove it had cultural importance.

My path changed when I was still in college. In the eighties, if you wanted to be a wildlife biologist, Dr. George Schaller, the mammologist and biologist, was an inspiration. I was watching Dr. Schaller on TV one day as he talked about initiating the first-ever jaguar study to be carried out in the Brazilian Pantanal. I was glued to the screen. That's when everything clicked. That's what I wanted to do. I wanted to research jaguars!

Before long I was training on a Schaller project in the Amazon. But I didn't meet him until a year later when I traveled to New York. That's when I told him that he was the reason I became a biologist who studied jaguars. His work had inspired and energized me to follow my dream. He responded by opening doors. He recommended I train with Peter Crawshaw, who was a PhD student initiating a jaguar study in Brazil. I took his advice to work with Crawshaw and I never stopped.

In 2002, I married biologist Anah Jácomo. We shared a similar vision, interests, and life goals. We both had PhDs in jaguar ecology and conservation and were planning the next steps of our life. It did not take long for us to decide to create the Jaguar Conservation Fund [JCF], the first organization solely devoted to studying and protecting the largest cat of the Americas. Through JCF we started jaguar studies in all Brazilian biomes with the goal of discovering their conservation demands under different scenarios, cultures, and landscapes. Through JCF we were able to attract the media to the cause. That's when I had my second jaguar epiphany.

I was working on a BBC documentary called *Jaguars: Born Free*, and we were at the end of two years of filming the first-ever attempt to introduce orphaned jaguars back into the wild. Anah and I had been raising three newborn jaguars whose mother had been shot by cattle ranchers. We fed them from the time they took milk from a bottle until they took live, wild prey. The only male of the three, named Xavante, was the largest, but at the same time the gentlest and most attached to me. When it was time, they were all released wearing GPS tracking collars. We watched them as they slowly adapted to their freedom.

Seventeen days after his release, Xavante's GPS collar was sending a no-movement signal. Concerned, the crew and I investigated to see if he was still alive. As we tracked the signal, we found it was coming from the middle of a swampy area we couldn't navigate. As we weren't able to reach the site, I decided to call Xavante to see if he could respond. If he was alive and could move, the collar would activate the signal.

After a few loud calls, Xavante answered from very far away. His roar-like meow got closer and closer until he finally appeared and jumped on me for a hug, taking me to the ground. I confess that I was nervous; I didn't know for sure if he would recognize me. But he did, and if it weren't recorded by the BBC film crew, one might think it was fantasy.

When we finished hugging, I saw that Xavante had been severely wounded by white-lipped peccaries, a kind of wild pig. He lay down and let me and Anah treat the wounds. And when we were finished, he left.

This moment was magical and will be stuck in my mind for the rest of my life. How could a 110-kilogram [240-pound] jaguar respond to your call, give you a hug, lie down, stay still to have wounds treated, and walk away again? Xavante taught us a lot that day. We learned about respect, gratitude, and compromise. I felt honored for the opportunity. After all, I was given the chance to literally embrace the animal that was worshipped, feared, and respected by ancient people such as the Maya and Aztecs.

When I look back at my career, I try to balance frustrations with goals achieved in order to not be disappointed. This is because I still feel that there is so much still to be done and I have so little time. In this context, what I have done does not represent much for the species. Yet at the same time, I realize a lot has changed since my first childhood epiphany with the jaguar. The changes have happened at all levels and scales.

And I've changed personally. I've come to respect and tolerate others' perceptions, cultures, and attitudes toward the species. In the end, I'm proposing the protection and conservation of a species that may kill someone's livestock or even take someone's life. So, in order to engage people who are literally living close to jaguars, I have to find ways to balance their losses and fears with the necessities for the survival of the species. I have to find a way to teach others how to live with this big cat without thinking they have to kill it. It's definitely not an easy task for any conservationist.

Looking back over the years and making a balance of the progresses and changes in general, I am more optimistic today than I was a few years ago. But we need to make changes in perceptions, values, and attitudes. We need to reconnect modern society to nature and species. City populations need to understand that the depletion of jaguar habitat happens in response to their consumption and demand. At the same time, I believe that advances in communication are a tool that can favor jaguar conservation. After all, we can now disseminate information, raise awareness, and involve society in our mission in a much easier way. If we do this well, younger generations can participate in saving this magnificent cat — not only for themselves, but as a living symbol for their children and the world.

• • •

Since his first jaguar sighting on the banks of the Araguaia River, Leandro has led conservation efforts for the species in Brazil and beyond. In 2002, he cofounded the Jaguar Conservation Fund (JCF), and in 2006, he also established Criadouro Onça Pintada (the Jaguar Breeding Project), the first wildlife sanctuary in Brazil designed specifically to rehabilitate and release orphaned jaguars (while also providing care to hundreds of other native Brazilian animals). Through JCF, Leandro initiated the Araguaia River Biodiversity Corridor

Project, which established a partnership among scientists, NGOs, the government, and local citizens to protect a main watercourse in Brazil to support conservation, biodiversity, and local livelihoods.

Today, the jaguar is legally protected in most countries where it remains. Leandro works to conserve the species by monitoring populations and establishing alliances. To understand biological and habitat requirements, JCF monitors jaguar populations using scat-detector dogs, live jaguar capture/collar/release, radio telemetry, and camera trapping. The organization has also successfully formed partnerships with cattle ranchers. Together, they've created jaguar reserves that promote the diversity and abundance of prey species to avoid conflict with cattle.

Looking back on his groundbreaking work for jaguars, Leandro feels his most impactful accomplishments have come from inspiring others to become involved in animal conservation. Leandro says that, to date, more than eight hundred volunteers and four hundred students have traveled from different countries to participate in Jaguar Conservation Fund projects in Brazil. Their experiences, he says, have not only affected their lives but have caused them to be advocates for change.

Have you ever rescued a ladybug?

Yes, I have. It was a common thing to do when I was a child.

Name three things that make you happy.

Wild animals. Talking to and living close to traditional communities. Living where I live — beside a national park, an hour drive from the closest town, where I am able to take care of many species.

What one book, documentary, or speech has had a profound effect on you?

Watching David Attenborough on TV, when I was a little child, presenting all kinds of species. Later, learning the stories of people such as Jane Goodall, Dian Fossey, and George Schaller inspired me into a career as a conservationist.

Regarding your food choices, how do you describe yourself?

A true omnivore.

If you had one message to delivers to others, what would it be?

Try to live closer to animals, no matter the species, and look them in the eyes. Animals connect us to the real meaning of our existence on this planet.

If you had one wish that was guaranteed to come true, what would it be?

A true balance between people and nature with no wars.

What advice do you have for people who say that they want to help animals in need but are too debilitated by what they witness?

First, we have to remember that individual animals are re-placed. So, as much as it impacts you to see an individual an-imal suffering, we also need to put our efforts into stopping the causes that led to the suffering. This may be frustrating because results may come in the medium to long term, but it is essential for the species. Therefore, I believe that everyone can and should do their part in helping animals, no matter where they are. If you are not close enough to physically help, you can always campaign to change people's attitudes and bring awareness to the cause.

Barbara Royal

OWL

If you believe in divine intervention, you know people don't come into your life by coincidence. I understood this when I met Dr. Barbara Royal in Chicago while on tour for my book *The Divinity of Dogs*. During the tour, my publisher had organized an unusual event for me: a day of shared appearances with Peter Abrahams — aka Spencer Quinn, the prolific *New York Times* bestselling author of the Chet the Dog series — and Dr. Barbara Royal, Oprah's personal veterinarian and author of *The Royal Treatment: A Natural Approach to Wildly Healthy Pets*. It was an appearance I won't forget.

The day started when my minder, a middle-aged man in a suit, picked me up at the hotel and drove me to the two-hundred-seat auditorium. As I walked through the lobby, I felt a flush of anxiety as I saw three tables stacked high with books. What if no one bought any of my books? What if they lined up to shake hands with the bestselling author and the celebrity vet but not me?

After making my way on stage, I introduced myself to the other authors and sat down, still stewing in a self-induced panic. Soon, a woman warmly introduced each of us to the audience, then she turned to us and asked, "Who wants to read first?"

My hand shot up. "I'll go," I said, desperate to get it over.

I read a couple of stories from my book, received an unexpectedly generous round of applause, and instantly felt relieved. I glanced at the other authors and noticed Dr. Royal was nodding her approval while applauding enthusiastically and smiling at me. I felt another wave of relief, thankful for the blonde-haired, close-to-my-age veterinarian's generosity.

Still, as Peter read next, I couldn't help conjuring visions of the crowd stampeding past my table to buy Dr. Royal's book. I was glad we'd been paired to promote our books together, but I felt like the odd man out. I was like a local musician tapped to follow Bruce Springsteen on stage. It was a no-win situation.

Once Peter finished reading to laughter and applause, it was the doctor's turn. She immediately stumbled and made fun of herself, and at that moment, I liked her — a lot. As she continued, her words transported me around the world as she saved the lives of an elephant, a zebra, and many, many dogs. She described a house fire during which she nearly died trying, in vain, to save her pets. And she talked about her spiritual connection with animals. By the end of the twenty-minute talk, I wanted to be first in line at her table. I hoped she would be a sellout.

After a final question-and-answer period, the reading ended, and Barbara and I beelined for each other, agreeing to meet up again after the book signing. Signing books for readers is my favorite part of being on tour. I was surprised and chuffed when the crowd split into three similarly sized lines to meet the authors.

Afterward, Barbara and I fell into nonstop chatter as if we were long-lost sisters. When my minder approached to take me back to the hotel, Barbara and I looked at each other and smiled.

"She's coming with me," she said. "I'll deliver her to tonight's event, and if you don't mind picking her up there, that would be great."

Barbara and I then canceled our individual plans for the rest of the afternoon and spent three hours in a little Italian restaurant somewhere in the suburbs of Chicago, laughing like old friends and questioning the purpose of our connection.

Ten months later, I returned to Chicago to shadow Barb at her veterinary practice. In reading her book and researching her work, I'd come to understand she is a superstar in the field of integrative medicine, the practice of using both Eastern and Western medicine to achieve optimum animal health. She is also an expert in animal nutrition. No wonder she was Oprah's vet! Then a director of two animal shelters, I was indirectly responsible for thousands of dogs and cats a year, and I was keen to learn how Barbara approached dogs with allergies and cancers, two of the most common problems I saw. She didn't disappoint.

For two days, I worked alongside Barbara in the examination rooms, as dogs and cats streamed in for hydrotherapy, massage, and acupuncture. They were treated with herbs and vitamins and put on raw food diets. Careful X-rays were taken without sedation, and medication was given when warranted. Human clients were sent home with detailed instructions on how to change their own life-styles in order to help their pets. When Barbara left the room, I often stayed behind and asked people what they thought of the practice's integrative medicine approach. Every person responded the same way: They loved it. Most of them told me that Barbara had saved their pet's life when other veterinarians had recommended euthanasia.

Some veterinarians will tell you that they learned about healing in vet school. Barbara has a different story. The direction she took in medicine, she says, was imparted telepathically by an owl.

• • •

Roslyn, Washington, USA

My right arm has always gotten me into trouble, or at least interesting situations — I volunteer for unusual assignments with it. I've had it completely inside a rhino during an hour-long ultrasonic reproduction exam. It is trained in acupuncture and can deftly place needles without me having to look, so I can watch the eye of an African elephant for signs of irritation at each sharp point. It has been the play toy for a baby Sumatran tiger. In this instance, it was a perch for a wild owl.

It was 1994. I was thirty-two years old and in my last year of veterinary school at the University of Illinois. As part of an internship with the Woodland Park Zoo in Seattle, I was with a group of wildlife biologists on a banding mission in Roslyn, Washington. We were part of a team whose goal was to protect the spotted owl, a highly endangered species, and their whole habitat by registering active nests so that the immediate surrounding area would be considered off-limits to loggers. Instead of the loggers clear-cutting the whole forest, the trees around a registered nest would be legally protected.

When I heard about the wildlife assignment I'd volunteered for, all I could think was how improbable it all was. I was expected to call in a male owl by hooting, then offer him some food, and then follow him — leaping over trees and careening down a hill at twilight — through the forest as he flew overhead to bring the food to the babies in his nest. Once there, we would count, band, and gently examine the baby owls to keep track of them and protect their forest.

Amid the long hours spent in the forest, my epiphany took just a few seconds — and it happened on my right arm. The owl, whom I'd called with some clever mimicking of another male owl, flew in close to see if I was an interloper in his territory. He landed just a few feet away on a branch above my head. He seemed to size me up, and then without hesitation flew off the branch and onto my outstretched arm, where I had the food. He was unbelievably light and sure-footed. I had on a leather glove, so his sharp talons didn't leave an impression, but his unexpected gaze certainly did. For a moment, he stood on my arm, with a calm focus, and we looked at each other eye to eye. His thoughtful gaze was riveting. Shiny black eyes, slowly blinking, set in circles upon circles of tiny neat brown feathers, expressionless but full of intent.

Looking directly into his eyes, I saw deep into the forest and sensed the profound relation between him and his food, his evolution, and our planet. I felt the gentle shock of this unexpected and timeless connection with him, the forest, and everything in it. I understood that we are all intimately and inextricably connected to each other and to our environment and planet. I barely had time to accept his wisdom before he took off noiselessly into the sky.

Something about that moment stuck with me. It is a memory that seems like it only happened yesterday, even though it has been decades now. Once I started practicing medicine, I often would be brought back to the image of those eyes in the forest. The owl's message guided me to learn more, connect more, and open my eyes more. I felt that with the knowledge he imparted, I could be more than a doctor: I might find a way to be a healer.

Every time I look at a new animal in my practice or see a health issue that seems unsolvable, I remind myself of the beautiful intricacy of nature and its incredible power to connect and heal. I look at every complicated case with the excitement of knowing there are options to help. I'll take a moment to grab my stethoscope with my left hand, but I also remember that moment when my right arm held the wise owl who spurred my natural education.

The wild health of that owl was a product of being in sync with his environment. Everything — from the density and humidity of the air, to his hunting and food choices, to the way he preened his feathers — all played a role in maintaining his vigor and connection to his home. That realization changed the way I treat my patients, and in fact, the way I treat my clients. Today, the focus of my medical practice is a holistic one. I am not satisfied with the status quo of health care. Instead, I expect my patients to be wildly healthy.

• • •

Barbara Royal, DVM, is credited for making sweeping changes in the way veterinary medicine is practiced by integrating nutrition with holistic and pharmaceutical medicine. She has led the American Holistic Veterinary Medical Association and the American Holistic Veterinary Medical Foundation and is the author of *The Royal Treatment* and coauthor of *One Hundred & One Reasons to Get Out of Bed* with Natasha Milne. She was featured in the 2016 documentary *Pet Fooled*, an investigative film about the pet food industry and its unseen and unregulated dangers.

In 2017, she cofounded the Royal Animal Health University to provide the professional tools for everyone from veterinarians to guardians to achieve optimum "wild" health for the animals in their care.

Barbara's practice, the Royal Treatment Veterinary Center in Chicago, treats thousands of patients each year, from pets to wildlife. She is a strong voice leading the charge to improve animal health and veterinary care globally.

Have you ever rescued a ladybug?

When I swim in Lake Michigan, I often run across ladybugs treading water helplessly. When that happens, I swim them to shore for a safe release. I was taught they are good luck and have magical powers and that they were friends with the fairies in our garden.

Name three things that make you happy.

Aside from animals, music. I'm always inspired by the way a music conductor can raise his hands and beautiful music happens. This is what I hope I can do when I raise and move my hands over my patients. Lake Michigan — I am happiest near, on, or in water. And my children, Sean and Sophie, who constantly delight and surprise me.

What one book, documentary, or speech has had a profound effect on you?

Charlotte's Web and *The Trumpet of the Swan*, both by E. B. White.

Regarding your food choices, how do you describe yourself?

Conscientious omnivore. Source and quantity matter.

If you had one message to deliver to others, what would it be?

If you eat meat, be a conscientious omnivore. If we love animals, we should love the animals that feed us and demand more humane and sensible treatment for food animals.

If you had one wish that was guaranteed to come true, what would it be?

I would wish for composting toilets, to stop us from wasting beautiful clean water in our toilets, and to allow us to properly replenish the world as we use its resources. My training has taught me that every animal on the planet uses resources from the earth, benefits from them, and then gives back. Why don't we?

What advice do you have for people who say that they want to help animals in need but are too debilitated by what they witness?

Stop worrying about yourself, and remember that the best way to feel invigorated is to help someone else. Animals count, and being an animal lover simply means you are connected to your own ancestry. Give them a hand.

Andrew Sabin

SALAMANDER

Some people never grow up. Andy Sabin likes to think he's one of those people. His unending quest to protect salamanders, turtles, and snakes has given him cause to continue exploring the great outdoors — the place he's been happiest since he was a boy. Today, in his early seventies, he's undeniably one of the most passionate animal philanthropists in the world.

I met Andy when I stumbled into native tiger salamander territory in Bridgehampton, Long Island. I was in town for a twenty-four-hour getaway with my girlfriend Susan Rockefeller. I'd envisioned a night curled up in pajamas, in front of a fire, with takeaway. But on the three-hour bus trip from Manhattan to Bridgehampton, it became clear that wasn't going to happen. Keen to show me what she called her "magical place," Sue had a plan.

"First, we'll stop at the house. Then we'll go into town and have a veg-o lunch, then I want you to meet my neighbor — Jane — she's so nice. After that, I'll show you Sagg Beach and then we'll have dinner with Andy," she said.

"Who's Andy?" I asked.

"Andy's the Salamander Commander. He needs to be in your book."

A few hours later, I was sitting across a table from Andy Sabin at Pierre's restaurant in Bridgehampton. The seventy-one-year-old, sporting a five o'clock shadow of black hair to match his bushy eyebrows, greeted me like an old friend: warmly. He was wearing a gray-striped Oxford shirt and a Tibetan Buddhist bracelet made of nuts the size of macadamias. I sized him up as a conservative Buddhist. I was right.

A proud Republican, Andy didn't hesitate to tell me he had supported Trump in the 2016 presidential election, but he wasn't happy with a recent vote in the Republican-controlled Senate to permit extreme kill methods of bears and wolves on national wildlife refuges in Alaska. Neither was I. We'd both contacted legislators and asked them to side with animals on the vote. They hadn't, but Andy and I had found our connection.

"How long are you in town for?" he asked. "I'd like to get you over to the house. I live with two dogs, a cat, eighty chickens, four peacocks, eight rabbits, four goats, about eighty pheasants, a chameleon, a couple of lovebirds, and a pig who's a pain in the ass. He bites when he's grumpy. Oh, and I've got two boa constrictors in my office. Most of them are rescues."

"We have to leave midday tomorrow," Sue said. "I'm going to take her over to SoFo."

"Oh, great," Andy said, grinning. "You'll love that! I wish I could be there, but I leave at four AM on a fishing trip."

The next morning, Sue and I stopped at SoFo, or the South Fork Natural History Museum and Nature Center, an educational retreat cofounded by Andy and three of his friends to teach people about the flora and fauna of Long Island's South Fork. Sue is an adviser and supporter.

Upon entering the converted barn turned living museum, I felt like I'd been sprinkled with fairy dust, my mind awash in memories of a childhood spent lifting logs and searching for orange-colored salamanders in the mossy woods of Maine. Frank Quevedo, the nonprofit's executive director, greeted us.

The first and most memorable resident Frank introduced us to was a fifteen-year-old, ten-inch-long tiger salamander, named for its tiger-like stripes on an otherwise gray-colored, shiny-skinned body.

The unnamed amphibian lived in one of a dozen terrariums on the lower level of the museum. He slightly resembled a frog and was the biggest salamander I'd ever seen.

Outside, to the sound of birdsong, we watched a pair of ospreys through binoculars as they carried fish to their nest on the sanctuary property. Frank explained that the property is part of a nature preserve with eleven hundred contiguous acres called the Long Pond Greenbelt, a chain of coastal plain ponds, wetlands, and oak forests that support the highest concentrations of rare species in New York State. It's also home to endangered plants and animals. One of the endangered amphibians here is the eastern tiger salamander. And one of the reasons it still exists, Frank explained, is due to conservation efforts by Andy. A summer hot spot for the who's who of society, Long Island has long been under threat from intense development. Andy purchased habitat and opposed new development in known salamander habitat. He then created SoFo to help others — especially kids — understand that, to preserve a species, you have to understand its connection to the air, soil, and water.

The visit to the center took me back to when I was eleven years old and my science teacher brought the class on a field trip to a nearby marsh. That day — learning about beavers, pollywogs, minnows, and ecosystems — remains my favorite memory of grade school.

Andy's passion to protect some of our least-popular species was inspired by an interconnectedness he felt with all wild animals. It started when he was a young boy and began with snakes and frogs. He has since dedicated his life to driving global protection for these underdogs by funding millions of dollars of research to preserve them, their habitats, and in essence, us.

• • •

Long Island, New York, USA

My grandfather, Abraham, immigrated to America from Russia in the late 1800s. He came through Ellis Island in New York, where he was given the last name of the city where he came from, Seratov. He moved into a tenement house on the Lower East Side of Manhattan and supported his family by collecting junk.

My father, Samuel, went into the family business at the age of twelve. And when I was nine, I began helping out. By then, it had transformed from a junk shop to a factory that was boiling down scrap metal to aid in World War II efforts.

I grew up in Brooklyn, New York, and always had a relationship with another animal species. My family was never without a German shepherd or a dog that we loved. You've got to understand, I came from a mother who would take in any stray dog or cat on the street, whether she had room for them or not. I can't remember a day growing up when we didn't have a dog. Everybody in my family — brother, sister, mother, father — loved animals, especially dogs and cats. But I was the one who, although I loved all animals, strayed toward reptiles and amphibians.

When I was eight years old, my family started taking trips to the Catskill Mountains, about a hundred miles north of New York City. Up there, surrounded by ponds, streams, and lakes, I fell in love with nature and everyone in it. I was particularly fascinated by frogs, toads, and snakes and was always looking for them. I loved catching and playing with them. When the weekend was over, I often brought them home to keep as pets. At one point, the house in Brooklyn had about 120 snakes, mostly because two or three of them had had babies. My parents were really good about it and never disliked anything. They may not have been in love with snakes, but they never told me not to play with them, and they were always supportive of me keeping them as pets.

Eventually I grew up — physically, but never mentally. I never stopped spending time outside, looking for critters.

In 1967, I took over the family business and converted Sabin

Metal to a precious metal recycling company and grew it to be the largest independently owned precious metals refiner in North America. It has been very successful.

In 1972, I started going to the South Fork of Long Island, an area known by many as the Hamptons. I didn't go there for the parties and shit. I went because I like being in the ocean, walking on the beach with the dogs, and exploring in the woods. It's peaceful.

When I was thirty-two, after years of being intrigued by salamanders, I became really interested in protecting the species. The tiger salamander, the world's largest land-dwelling salamander, was endangered in New York and was thought to be extinct on Long Island. So I was always on the lookout for them. Then, one day, I found one.

It was March 13, 1986. I was on the Sag Harbor turnpike at night, looking in the woods around there. That's when I saw it: a dead tiger salamander in the middle of the road. I picked it up and sent it to the Department of Environmental Conservation [DEC] laboratory upstate and, a few days later, received confirmation that it was a tiger salamander. I got so excited at that point that I started searching the ponds close to where I'd found the dead salamander, to see if I could find one alive.

After spending decades learning about salamanders, I knew they migrated in February and March to breeding ponds. While they can stay underwater for a while, they eventually need to surface for air. So, I positioned myself in a pond with my waders on and a net in my hand and waited for hours. I was looking around carefully when all of a sudden I saw this little head pop up. I scooped the salamander up with my net. I was sure it was an endangered tiger salamander.

The DEC came down and confirmed its identity, and I returned the salamander to its pond. That was the beginning of a lifelong effort to protect New York's endangered tiger salamander. The truth is, I knew that if I didn't protect the species, nobody else was going to do it.

Since then, I've fought a lot of battles not only in the name of tiger salamander preservation but also to protect the biodiversity of the South Fork of Long Island. I realized early on that once an area is developed, that's the end of a species because that's the end of its habitat. For the past forty years, I've been searching for and find- ing tiger salamanders and then reporting my findings to the DEC. Because they're still endangered in New York, those findings often cause problems for developers: Legally, you're not allowed to do any construction within a thousand feet of 50 percent of a tiger pond, or five hundred feet around the whole pond.

Fighting to protect the species' habitat has become a passion and I've put my money behind it. Most developers haven't gone against me because they know I have the money to fight them. So they work with me instead. I try to encourage them to look for properties to develop that have already been disturbed, and most often they do. I show them what they can do while still preserving the salamander. That's been my way of conserving the beauty and nature of the area I call home. And that's how I became known as the "Salamander Commander" — for rediscovering the species on Long Island, for leading the charge in protecting areas where the salamander lives, and I suppose, for teaching others about why they should care about it, too.

In doing this type of preservation, you have to believe that a species, once it's gone, is gone forever. If you believe in the world of biodiversity and the importance of all species, you want to protect them, regardless of what's going on. If everybody took the attitude that the world is coming to an end, and helping is pointless, we'd get nowhere. As for why I focus on helping amphibians and reptiles, I see them as the underdog. They are the creatures that nobody cares about because they're not furry. They're not a tiger. They're not a lion. They're not an elephant. They don't cuddle. They're like the forgotten people.

I have a bunch of commodity and precious metal–related businesses, but in the end, that doesn't matter. I don't want to be the richest guy in the cemetery. My greatest ambition now is to endow my four sons with a strong, responsible, and growing family business and a safe and thriving planet for future generations.

• • •

While amassing a fortune in the precious metals industry, Andy Sabin says it's been a pleasure to give more than $100 million back to the world. Through the Andrew Sabin Family Foundation, the philanthropist awards grants for environmental protection, the preservation of amphibian and reptile species and their habitat, and cancer and genetic research.

Among many gifts, he endows the Sabin Center for Climate Change Law at Columbia University and the Emmett Institute on Climate Change and the Environment at UCLA School of Law. He provides scholarships to international students at the Yale School of Forestry and Environmental Studies and the Yale Center for Business and the Environment in hopes that they will take what they've learned back to their home countries to teach and practice conservation. Separately from specific schools, Andy gives annual environmental fellowships and conservation prizes to students throughout the world.

Andy's passion and generosity have been acknowledged by the scientists whose work he's supported through the naming of four species: *Centrolene sabini*, the seven-thousandth amphibian species discovered in the world, in Peru, and also known as the Sabin glass frog; *Aphantophryne sabini*, a frog endemic to Papua New Guinea; a pigmy chameleon called *Rhampholean sabinii* from Tanzania; and a dwarf lemur named *Cheirogaleus andysabini*, discovered in 2005 in Madagascar.

While Andy's gifts to the world are many, perhaps his greatest achievement has been in finding the fountain of youth and enthusiastically sharing it with others. He sums it up this way: "The purpose of life is to find something ennobling to live for, and then — enjoying the journey — to live honorably, joyfully, courageously, compassionately, usefully, and in the end, to make a difference that one lived at all."

On weekends, Andy can be found on the South Fork of Long Island, taking children on nature walks in search of salamanders.

Have you ever rescued a ladybug?

I have not rescued them. I used to buy them because they eat aphids. I believe in natural pest control, and ladybugs are a beautiful way to keep the roses thriving.

Name three things that make you happy.

Buddhism. Helping people with cancer. Taking kids for nature walks and seeing the smiles on their faces.

What one book, documentary, or speech has had a profound effect on you?

The speeches given by Teddy Roosevelt and the work he did as a Republican conservationist. Conservation is conservative, and I wish we had more conservatives concerned about conservation.

Regarding your food choices, how do you describe yourself?

I'm a healthy eater. I grow all my own organic vegetables. I don't spray, so I share with the bugs, and I also give away a lot of the vegetables from my garden to the food pantry for poor people and senior citizens.

If you had one message to deliver to others, what would it be?

Every day above ground is a good day. Feel blessed that you're alive and able to do things and make a difference in the world.

If you had one wish that was guaranteed to come true, what would it be?

I'd love to see a healthy, less-polluted world where we protect biodiversity and get rid of pollution by planting trees. I'd like to see everybody smile. That's the universal language, a smile. Everybody understands a smile.

What advice do you have for people who say that they want to help animals in need but are too debilitated by what they witness?

You don't have to have money to help animals. You can volunteer at a shelter and be hands-on. There are a million things you can do for animals that don't require any money; they just require your time and love of animals.

ACKNOWLEDGMENTS

August 2016, Long Pond, Maine, USA

I woke at 4 AM to the haunting sounds of loons echoing across Long Pond. Their morning revelry sang to my soul, and as I lay in bed with my eyes closed, their voices lifted me from slumber. The day before, I'd reached an agreement with New World Library to write a book called *Rescuing Ladybugs*. I was content and peaceful. I looked out the window at the water and noticed that the dark night sky was making way for an orange-hued sunrise. I jumped out of bed and ran to greet it — barefoot and wearing only a white nightgown. The path to the dock was lined with a soft cover of pine needles. A squirrel greeted me with a nervous chatter as I passed his tree. As I reached the moss-covered dock, the sky was turning a deep, multicolored, layered red. I walked to the center of the dock, sat down, crossed my legs, and waited for the show. As the loons sang, the squirrel chattered, fish jumped, and the sun rose, I gave thanks for the day. Little did I know that at that moment my life was about to change forever.

• • •

Eight weeks later I realized that the spider bite I thought I'd received that morning on my foot had actually been a tick bite. I had Lyme disease. Within months, I could barely walk or talk. It would take the support of some very special people to get me well enough to write this book.

As I worked to swim to the surface of a very rough sea, I kicked toward a beam of light created by the amazing people who inspired and supported me through the process of completing this book. They include my New York literary agent of twelve-plus years and loyal friend Susan Raihofer, London co-agent Kate McLennan, and mentor Elisabeth Luard. I'm forever grateful to Kelly Williams for being my right arm, and to Naama Grey-Smith, Elaine Tselikis, and Natasha Milne for their input. It's been a privilege to work with Georgia Hughes — my dream editor. I'm grateful to her for keeping the faith and for enthusiastically publishing this special book and with it, its message. The team at New World Library has been awesome. I'm thankful to Barbara Fisher for designing a special cover, Art Director Tracy Cunningham, Managing Editor Kristen Cashman, Publicity Director Monique Muhlenkamp, and copyeditor Jeff Campbell for pointing out the wrongs to get it right.

The wind in my sails was provided by Aaron Praba, Annette Fredrickson, Frank Spear, Isabella Clark, Dr. Hugh Derham, Dr. Charles Bro, and Dr. Harald Bennefeld. #Lifesavers

The smile on my face was caused by my twelve-year-old niece, Alice Skiff, who inspired me every day with her strength as she underwent hundreds of treatments for brain cancer. A day didn't pass when Alice didn't impart the type of wisdom that gives pause. #Hero

The laughter in my life is caused by friends. I'm grateful to those who supported this project and kept me smiling in 2017: Amy Bennett, Anne Bright, Jeanne and Peter Bowen, Grant Castle, Katie Chapman, Patti Chapman, Janet Field, Ali Franco, Ita

Goldberger, Carolyn Hartz, Taylor Hood, Russell James, Dianne Laurance, Becky Madeira, Jackie Montfort, Carolyn O'Neil, David and Susan Rockefeller, Marisa Tribe, and Guy Warwick. The highlights of being hospitalized for treatment in Germany were the other patients — whom I now call friends. There were tough moments, and I thank Daniela Simon for sympathy-crying with me during an excruciating foot infusion and David Kennedy for making me laugh hysterically. In Australia, my fearless coach Ceinwen Roberts motivated me to keep going every single day, and Michael Berry, David Hobbs, and Alex Jolly kept me afloat while offering themselves as shark bait when storm clouds prevailed. In Maine, I thank Kathy Shields for turning around on the lake when my legs gave up; and the "swimmah girls," all of whom I love dearly. I thank Diana Ansley, Nancy Dawson, Dorothy Feeley, Sara Fraley, Ali Thompson Kassels, Shelly LaFond, Becky Madeira, Elizabeth Montfort, Anne Pomeroy, Betsy Uhlman, and Paula Vogel for their enduring friendship and laughter on foggy mornings, sunny days, and moontini nights. #Youneverregretaswim

The fuel that nourishes my soul has been provided by those who have encouraged me. I give thanks to the teachers who inspired confidence: Miriam Pyle; Betsy Found; Sandra Modeen; and Barbara Brack, who showed me that it's not only okay to lead with compassion, it's the only way. Kimmie Ross catapulted me to another level of understanding when she persuaded me to climb a mountain barefoot. On that unforgettable day, she bestowed a gift of enlightenment, and I'm eternally grateful. My brother, Jim Skiff, is my biggest fan. His confidence and loyalty will never be lost on me. I adore him and love his special knack for inciting laughter at the most inappropriate times — especially in the company of Bill Skiff and Kate Hood. And, for welcoming me into their warm hearts two decades ago, I'm thankful for Sandra, Ron, and Winnie Wise — true gifts in my life.

The peace within me comes from being engulfed in a blanket of love by Jon Sainken — my favorite human being.

The joy in my heart undoubtedly comes from dogs. Their unlimited love for and devotion to me — I can only hope — is mirrored through my eyes back to them. Darling Honey, sweet Sunny, always jubilant Happy, and devoted Tootsie and Hope gave me a reason to keep going while writing this book.

The sunshine in my day has always been provided by people who have bravely chosen to right the injustices inflicted on the innocent. It has been my privilege to walk amid their light as they radiate all that is good about humanity. My passion has been reignited by and I'm extremely grateful to the leaders highlighted in this book. They're all amazing, and I feel very fortunate they allowed me to share their personal stories. Over the years, I've particularly loved working alongside the inspirational volunteers and staff of the Humane Society of the United States, the SPCA of Hancock County, and the Dogs' Refuge Home. I'd like to take the opportunity here to acknowledge the steadfast dedication of friends: Lisa Baker, Debora Brown, Alex Cearns, Ian Coombes, Jayne Finlay, Gina Garey, Cynthia Griffin, Katie Hansberry, Karen Lasasso, Ginny Millner, Kari Nienstedt, Lynn Nobil, Jamie O'Keefe, Chris Osborn, Joan Reimers, Karen Rhodes, and Stillman Rockefeller. I'd also like to thank Orfeh and Marc Bekoff — for the good they do in our world.

The dawn of each day brings hope. During my life I've witnessed progressive, positive change. I'm grateful to you, the people I admire — many of whom I've never met — for being part of that change. It's a team effort. May good prevail. #Rescuingladybugs

ANIMAL WELFARE ORGANIZATIONS

Animals Asia: www.animalsasia.org
Animals Australia: www.animalsaustralia.org
Blue Sphere Foundation: www.bluespherefoundation.org
Borneo Orangutan Survival Foundation: www.orangutan.or.id
Brightside Farm Sanctuary: www.brightside.org.au
Campaign Against Canned Hunting: www.cannedlion.org
Dolphin Project: www.dolphinproject.com
Great Ape Project: www.greatapeproject.uk
Great Elephant Census: www.greatelephantcensus.com
Humane Society of the United States: www.humanesociety.org
Institute for Humane Education: www.humaneeducation.org
Jaguar Conservation Fund: www.jaguar.org.br
JUST: www.justforall.com
Liberia Chimpanzee Rescue and Protection: www.facebook.com
    /liberiachimpanzeerescue.org
Manta Trust: www.mantatrust.org
Misool Foundation: www.misoolfoundation.org
Oceana: www.oceana.org

People for the Ethical Treatment of Animals: www.peta.org
Peter Singer website: www.petersinger.info
Protect What Is Precious: www.protectwhatisprecious.com
Royal Animal Health University: www.royalanimalhealth
    university.com
South Fork Natural History Museum and Nature Center:
    www.sofo.org
Temple Grandin website: www.templegrandin.com
Vulcan Productions: www.vulcanproductions.com
Wildlife Friends Foundation Thailand: www.wfft.org
We Animals: www.weanimals.org
World Animal Protection: www.worldanimalprotection.org

NOTES

Introduction

Page xiii, *"Never, never be afraid to do what's right, especially if the well-being"*: This quote is often attributed to Martin Luther King Jr., but according to professor Dan Farber, he never said it. For details, see "What Martin Luther King DIDN'T Say" at LegalPlanet, http://legal-planet.org/2014/01/19/what-martin-luther-king-didnt-say.

1. Buddha and Bear

Page 3, *nearly 500 million people around the world who consider themselves Buddhists*: "Buddhists," Pew Research Center, April 2, 2015, http://www.pewforum.org/2015/04/02/buddhists.

2. Porcupine, Monkey, Elephant, Pteropod

Jo-Anne McArthur: Monkey • Baños, Ecuador

Page 38, *Jo-Anne McArthur is an award-winning photojournalist, author*: "About We Animals," We Animals, accessed November 1, 2017, http://weanimals.org/about.

Carole Tomko: Elephant • Okavango Delta, Botswana

Page 41, *one of the "most influential women in cable television"*: "2010 Most Powerful Women in Cable: The Top 50," Cablefax, November 1, 2010, http://www.cablefax.com/archives/2010-most-powerful-women-in-cable-the-top-50.

Page 42, *The mission of Vulcan is to "find smart solutions"*: "About: The Vulcan Story," Vulcan, accessed November 12, 2017, http://www.vulcan.com/About/The-Vulcan-Story.

Page 43, *a place called Abu Camp, located in the Okavango Delta in Botswana, Africa*: "Abu Camp Elephant Program," Abu Camp, accessed November 12, 2017, https://www.abucamp.com/pdf/6-ABU-ElephantProgramme.pdf.

Page 45, *Vulcan released the results in September 2016. The data showed*: Tony Banbury, "Great Elephant Census Reveals Dramatic Declines in Populations," Vulcan, August 31, 2016, http://www.vulcan.com/news/articles/2016/great-elephant-census-results-are-in.

Page 46, *Within three months, the Chinese government vowed*: Jani Actman, "China to Shut Down Its Ivory Trade by the End of 2017," *National Geographic*, December 30, 2016, https://news.nationalgeographic.com/2016/12/wildlife-watch-china-legal-ivory-market-african-elephants.

Susan Rockefeller: Pteropod • New York City, USA

Page 52, *reading "The Darkening Sea," an article by Elizabeth Kolbert*: Elizabeth Kolbert, "The Darkening Sea," *New Yorker*, November 20, 2006, https://www.newyorker.com/magazine/2006/11/20/the-darkening-sea.

Page 53, *Alongside two close friends, I decided to coproduce a film called* A Sea Change: *A Sea Change: Imagine a World Without Fish*, Bullfrog Films, accessed October 30, 2017, http://www.bullfrogfilms.com.

Page 54, *Since its founding in 2001, Oceana has achieved close to*: "About Us," Oceana, accessed October 30, 2017, http://oceana.org/about-oceana/about-us.

3. Dragon, Manta, Orangutan

Page 62, *In 1977, Komodo and the islands and water surrounding it were designated*: Details on Komodo National Park come from the following: "Komodo," UNESCO, accessed December 23, 2017, http://www.unesco.org/new/en/natural-sciences/environment/ecological-sciences/biosphere-reserves/asia-and-the-pacific/indonesia/komodo; Komodo National Park, accessed December 23, 2017, http://www.komodonationalpark.org; and

"Komodo National Park," UNESCO, accessed December 23, 2017,
http://whc.unesco.org/en/list/609.

Guy Stevens: Manta • Hanifaru Bay, Maldives

Page 66, *He kindly gave permission to reprint this story from his book*: This story
is an excerpt from Guy Stevens and Thomas Peschak, *Manta: Secret Life of
Devil Rays* (Dorchester, UK: The Manta Trust, 2016), 34, 35.

Page 69, *In 2011, his work was further rewarded when the Baa Atoll*: Mohamed
Sajid, "UNESCO Declares Baa Atoll a Biosphere Reserve," Maldives Insider,
June 30, 2011, http://maldives.net.mv/1656/unesco-declares-baa-atoll-a
-biosphere-reserve/1346414145000.

Page 69, *That same year, Guy and Thomas Peschak cofounded the Manta Trust*:
"The Manta Mission," Manta Trust, accessed October 14, 2017, www.manta
trust.org/about-us/the-manta-mission; and Guy Stevens and Thomas P.
Peschak, "Manta: Secret Life of Devil Rays," www.mantabook.com, accessed
May 4, 2018.

Page 69, *In 2013, Manta Trust, as part of a coalition of charities*: Wildlife
Conservation Society, "CITES Makes Historic Decision to Protect Sharks
and Rays," ScienceDaily, March 14, 2013, accessed December 19, 2017,
https://www.sciencedaily.com/releases/2013/03/130314110258.htm.

Page 69, *A year later, the organization won another victory*: Wildlife Conservation
Society, "New Listing to Protect 21 Species of Sharks and Rays," Science-
Daily, November 10, 2014, accessed December 19, 2017, https://www
.sciencedaily.com/releases/2014/11/141110110209.htm.

Page 69, *In 2016, the Manta Trust, working with nonprofits Planeta Océano*: Douglas Main, "Peru Enacts Protections for World's Largest Manta Ray Population," *Newsweek*, January 7, 2016, http://www.newsweek.com/peru
-enacts-protections-worlds-largest-manta-ray-population-412945.

Willie Smits: Orangutan • Kalimantan, Borneo

Page 72, *the extinction of the orangutan, a species that shares 97 percent of our DNA*:
"NIH-Funded Scientists Publish Orangutan Genome Sequence," National
Institutes of Health, January 26, 2011, https://www.nih.gov/news-events
/news-releases/nih-funded-scientists-publish-orangutan-genome-sequence.

Page 80, *Willie Smits has been called the one person on the planet who understands*:
"Willie Smits: KIN Global 2016," Kellogg Innovation Network, YouTube,
August 18, 2016, https://www.youtube.com/watch?v=kkXm-wHLEE4.

Page 80, *Over the past thirty years, Willie has established 114 conservation projects*:
Willie Smits, email correspondence with author, December 1, 2017.

Page 80, *Willie has been named one of the top ten greatest social entrepreneurs*: Award details are from the following: "The 10 Greatest Social Entrepreneurs of All Time," Online College, June 26, 2012, http://www.onlinecollege.org/2012/06/26/the-10-greatest-social-entrepreneurs-all-time; "Willie Smits," Masarang, accessed December 19, 2017, http://masarang.nl/en/about-masarang/willie-smits; and "Masarang's Palm Sugar Factory Receives the Presidential Paramakarya Award," Masarang, accessed December 19, 2017, http://masarang.nl/en/articles/masarangs-palm-sugar-factory-receives-presidential-paramakarya-award.

Page 81, *up to 80 percent of the remaining orangutans living in the wild*: "Pongo pygmaeus," IUCN Red List of Threatened Species, accessed December 21, 2017, http://www.iucnredlist.org/details/17975/0.

4. Dog, Cat, Chimp

Chris Mercer: Caracal • Northern Cape Province, South Africa

Page 100, *France banned the import of captive and wild lion trophies in its country*: Adam Vaughan, "France Bans Imports of Lion Hunt Trophies," *The Guardian*, November 19, 2015, https://www.theguardian.com/environment/2015/nov/19/france-bans-imports-of-lion-hunt-trophies.

Page 100, *And in 2016, the US Fish & Wildlife Service (USFWS) announced restrictions*: Rachael Bale and Jani Actman, "U.S. Hunters Banned from Importing Trophies from Captive Lions," *National Geographic*, October 21, 2016, https://news.nationalgeographic.com/2016/10/wildlife-watch-canned-lion-hunting-trophies-banned.

Emma Haswell: Greyhound • Ross, Tasmania, Australia

Page 107, *Her work has been credited for the closure of the second-largest*: "About," Brightside Farm Sanctuary, accessed December 21, 2017, http://brightside.org.au/about.

Jenny Desmond: Chimpanzee • Entebbe, Uganda

Page 115, *As a footnote, in 2017, HSUS reached a financial agreement*: James Gorman, "New York Blood Center Reaches a Deal to Help Care for Research Chimps," *New York Times*, May 30, 2017, https://www.nytimes.com/2017/05/30/science/chimps-new-york-blood-center.html.

5. Pig, Chicken, Rabbit

Josh Balk: Chicken • Howell, Maryland, USA

Page 126, *I still remember my first day... billions like her in the poultry industry*: This
story is adapted, with permission, from a 2015 speech Josh Balk gave when
he was inducted into the Animal Rights Hall of Fame. For the original,
unedited speech, see "Erica Meier Inducts Josh Balk to Animal Rights Hall
of Fame — Animal Rights Nat'l Conf. '15 AR2015," Farm Animal Rights
Movement, YouTube, January 28, 2016, https://www.youtube.com
/watch?v=J7aXhk-Ek4I.

Page 127, *There are currently no federal laws that regulate the treatment*: "Industrial
Food Animal Production in America: Examining the Impact of the Pew
Commission's Priority Recommendations," Johns Hopkins Center for a
Livable Future (Fall 2013): vii, https://www.jhsph.edu/research/centers-and
-institutes/johns-hopkins-center-for-a-livable-future/_pdf/research/clf
_reports/CLF-PEW-for%20Web.pdf.

Peter Singer: Homo sapiens • Oxford, England

Page 132, *He argues against speciesism, stating that human beings*: "Peter Singer,
Animal Equality," Carnegie Council for Ethics in International Affairs,
YouTube, posted on October 26, 2011, https://www.youtube.com
/watch?v=av22cRQNBiQ.

Page 135, *In 2005, the Fulbright scholar was named one of the one hundred most
influential*: The honors in this paragraph are from the following: Arthur
Caplan, "The 2005 TIME 100: Peter Singer," *Time*, April 18, 2005, accessed
December 19, 2017, http://content.time.com/time/specials/packages/article
/0,28804,1972656_1972712_1974257,00.html; Karin Frick, Peter Gloor, and
Detlef Gürtler, "Global Thought Leaders 2013," Gottlieb Duttweiler Institute, accessed December 19, 2017, http://www.gdi.ch/de/Think-Tank
/Global-Thought-Leaders-2013; Alexandra Silver, "ALL-TIME 100 Nonfiction Books: *Animal Liberation*," *Time*, August 16, 2011, http://entertainment
.time.com/2011/08/30/all-time-100-best-nonfiction-books/slide/animal
-liberation-by-peter-singer; and Gemma Breen, "Controversial Bioethicist
Tops Queen's Honours," *ABC News*, June 11, 2012, http://www.abc.net.au
/news/2012-06-11/queens-birthday-honours-revealed-2012/4057484.

Page 135, *The organization works for a world where "all animals are treated"*: Animals Australia Facebook page, accessed December 5, 2017, https://www
.facebook.com/pg/AnimalsAustralia/about.

Page 136, *Targeted investigations by Animals Australia have led to*: "Media Centre,"

Animals Australia, accessed December 6, 2017, http://www.animals
australia.org/media. Also, Reid Dearson of Animals Australia, conversation
with author.

6. Bear, Pigeon, Cow

Page 146, *In 2015, the Maine legislature passed a bill to prohibit*: "An Act to Prohibit
the Sale of Dogs and Cats in Pet Shops," 127th Maine Legislature, Sec. 1. 7
MRSA §4164, accessed January 14, 2018, http://www.mainelegislature
.org/legis/bills/bills_127th/billtexts/HP022901.asp.

Page 146, *At the time, the Republican governor of Maine, Paul LePage, was angry*:
Mario Moretto, "LePage: I'll Veto Every Democratic Bill until Legislature
Agrees to Kill Income Tax," *Bangor Daily News*, May 30, 2015, https://bangor
dailynews.com/2015/05/29/politics/lepage-ill-veto-every-democratic-bill
-until-legislature-agrees-to-kill-income-tax.

Page 149, *On a state level, I've been lucky to work with others to create comprehensive
reforms*: For details, see "Massachusetts Question 3 — Minimum Size Requirements for Farm Animal Containment — Results: Approved," *New York
Times*, August 1, 2017, https://www.nytimes.com/elections/results
/massachusetts-ballot-measure-3-improve-farm-animal-confines; and "Government Moves to Stop Puppy Farming in WA," *West Australian*, November
12, 2017, https://thewest.com.au/news/wa/government-moves-to-stop-puppy
-farming-in-wa-ng-b886579692.

Jill Robinson: Bear • Zhuhai, China

Page 152, *That acid is able to dissolve gallstones in people, without surgery*:
G. Stephen Tint et al., "Ursodeoxycholic Acid: A Safe and Effective Agent
for Dissolving Cholesterol Gallstones," *Annals of Internal Medicine* 97, no. 3
(September 1982), http://annals.org/aim/article-abstract/695862
/ursodeoxycholic-acid-safe-effective-agent-dissolving-cholesterol-gallstones.

Page 153, *In 2002, an article in* Legal Affairs *magazine stated that gallbladders*: Kim
Todd, "Bear Market," *Legal Affairs* (November/December 2002), http://
www.legalaffairs.org/issues/November-December-2002/story_todd
_novdec2002.msp.

Page 153, *This has prompted wildlife officials and advocates to reinforce*: Robert S.
Anderson, "The Lacey Act: America's Premier Weapon in the Fight Against
Unlawful Wildlife Trafficking," *Public Land Law Review*, no. 16 (1995),
https://www.animallaw.info/article/lacey-act-americas-premier-weapon
-fight-against-unlawful-wildlife-trafficking.

Page 153, *In the early 1980s, China picked up the practice of bear bile extraction*: Jasmin Singer and Mariann Sullivan, "Interview with Jill Robinson," Our Hen House (podcast), November 2, 2013, http://www.ourhenhouse.org /JillRobinsonEpisode199.pdf.

Page 153, *And in 2014, after a bear farmer's daughter convinced her father*: "Nanning Bear Farm — Background," Animals Asia, accessed December 18, 2017, https://www.animalsasia.org/us/our-work/end-bear-bile-farming /what-we-do/bear-sanctuaries/new-rescue-china.

Page 154, *In response to Animals Asia's work, the country of Vietnam has committed*: Jason Daley, "Vietnam Commits to Shut Down Bear Bile Farms," Smithsonian.com, July 21, 2017, https://www.smithsonianmag.com/smart -news/vietnam-agrees-end-trade-bear-bile-180964130.

Page 155, *A poll by the organization in 2011 found that 87 percent*: "Five Things You Need to Know about Bear Bile Farming," Animals Asia, October 28, 2014, https://www.animalsasia.org/uk/media/news/news-archive/five-things -you-need-to-know-about-bear-bile-farming.html.

Page 155, *China's government is now providing millions of dollars of state subsidies*: Jennifer Ngo, "Biggest Chinese Producer of Bear Bile Seeks Synthetic Alternative," *South China Morning Post*, July 31, 2014, http://www.scmp.com /news/china/article/1563054/biggest-chinese-producer-bear-bile-seeks -synthetic-alternative.

Wayne Pacelle: Pigeon • Schuylkill County, Pennsylvania, USA

Page 159, *The HSUS filed a lawsuit, alleging MDIFW was illegally using taxpayers' money*: Deirdre Fleming, "Supporters of Bear-Baiting Ban Sue Maine Wildlife Agency over Ad Campaign," *Portland Press Herald*, September 30, 2014, https://www.pressherald.com/2014/09/30/bear-baiting-ban-proponents -sue-state-wildlife-agency-over-campaign.

Temple Grandin: Cow • Arizona, USA

Page 166, *"So, there we all were, up at boarding school, a bunch of emotionally disturbed"*: Temple Grandin and Catherine Johnson, *Animals in Translation: Using the Mysteries of Autism to Decode Animal Behavior* (Orlando, FL: Houghton Mifflin Harcourt, 2005), 2.

Page 167, *"I was riveted by the sight of those big animals inside"*: Ibid., 4.

Page 167, *"Whenever I put myself inside my squeeze machine"*: Ibid., 5.

Page 168, *"Well, let's look at it from the animal's point of view"*: Ibid., 19.

Page 169, *"Fear is the dominant emotion in both autistic people and prey animals"*: Temple Grandin, in Susan J. Armstrong and Richard G. Botzler, eds., *The Animal Ethics Reader,* 3rd ed. (New York: Routledge, 2016), 251.

Page 169, *My systems are also used in Australia, Canada, Europe, Mexico*: Details about the system are from author communication with Temple Grandin and "About us," Temple Grandin Livestock Handling Systems, accessed November 7, 2017, https://www.grandinlivestockhandlingsystems.com /aboutgrandinlivestockhandlingsystem.

Page 169, *"If I had my druthers, humans… The animal shouldn't suffer"*: Grandin and Johnson, *Animals in Translation,* 179, 180.

Page 169, *"Animal behavior was the right field… animals are smarter than we think"*: Ibid., 7.

Page 170, *Dr. Temple Grandin has written hundreds of research papers*: "About us," Temple Grandin Livestock Handling Systems, accessed November 7, 2017, https://www.grandinlivestockhandlingsystems.com/aboutgrandinlive stockhandlingsystem.

Page 170, *In 2010,* Time *magazine named Temple one of the most influential people*: "The 2010 TIME 100," *Time,* accessed November 5, 2017, http://content .time.com/time/specials/packages/completelist/0,29569,1984685,00.html.

7. Beaver and Dolphin

Page 175, *At the time I produced the story, an estimated 303 species*: US Department of the Interior Fish & Wildlife Service, "Box Score Listings and Recovery Plans," *Endangered Species Technical Bulletin* 18, no. 4 (November/December 1993): 28, https://www.fws.gov/endangered/news/pdf/1993%20Nov-Dec%20 Vol%20XVIII%20No%204.pdf.

Ric O'Barry: Dolphin • Miami, Florida, USA

Page 190, *"It's Kathy," [Bob] said. "She's not doing well"… "Why are we doing this"*: Richard O'Barry and Keith Coulbourn, *Behind the Dolphin Smile: One Man's Campaign to Protect the World's Dolphins* (San Rafael, CA: Earth Aware Editions, 2012), 229–30.

Page 192, *It's the oldest dolphin welfare organization in the world*: "Our History," Ric O'Barry's Dolphin Project, accessed November 2, 2017, https://dolphin project.com/about-us/history.

Page 192, *Working with coalitions, the organization has shut down aquariums holding dolphins*: O'Barry and Coulbourn, *Behind the Dolphin Smile,* xxv.

Page 193, The Cove *won the Academy Award for the Best Documentary Feature*: "The 82nd Academy Awards," Oscars, accessed November 2, 2017, http://www.oscars.org/oscars/ceremonies/2010.

8. Shark and Coyote

Page 196, *in what became a string of eleven fatal attacks between 2010 and 2017*: "Shark Attack Data for Western Australia," Shark Attack Data, accessed January 10, 2018, http://www.sharkattackdata.com/place/australia/western_australia.

Page 196, *One possible cause was identified in July 2012 by Humane Society International Australia*: "HSI Identifies a Possible Connection between Shark Attacks and Live Export Vessels," Humane Society International Australia, July 18, 2012, http://www.hsi.org.au/go/to/2410/18-july-2012-hsi-identifies-a-possible-connection-between-shark-.html.

Page 197, *Further, HSI reported that a similar link was found in Egypt in December 2010*: "Egypt to Reopen Beaches after Deadly Shark Attack," Reuters, December 13, 2010, https://www.reuters.com/article/ozatp-egypt-shark-20101213-idAFJOE6BC00920101213.

Page 198, *After four months, the cull ended. Of the 172 sharks that were caught*: Courtney Bembridge and David Weber, "WA Shark Cull: 172 Caught on Drum Lines off Popular Beaches," *ABC News*, May 7, 2014, http://www.abc.net.au/news/2014-05-07/shark-catch-and-kill-data-released/5435682.

Shawn Heinrichs: Shark • Raja Ampat, West Papua, Indonesia

Page 201, *Raja Ampat, an archipelago known to have some of the richest marine biodiversity on earth*: "Indonesia," Nature Conservancy, accessed December 17, 2017, www.nature.org/ourinitiatives/regions/asiaandthepacific/indonesia/placesweprotect/raja-ampat-islands.xml.

Page 205, *Sharks have high concentrations of mercury and beta-Methylamino-L-alanine*: Sandra Anne Banack, Tracie A. Caller, and Elijah W. Stommel, "The Cyanobacteria Derived Toxin Beta-N-Methylamino-L-Alanine and Amyotrophic Lateral Sclerosis," *Toxins* 2, no. 12 (December 2010), https://www.ncbi.nlm.nih.gov/pmc/articles/PMC3153186.

Page 208, *Shawn has helped to successfully create the Misool Marine Reserve*: Details about the Misool Marine Reserve are from "Misool Marine Reserve," Misool Foundation, accessed December 17, 2017, https://www.misoolfoundation.org/misool-marine-reserve.

Page 208, *shark fin consumption in China has decreased by an estimated 50 to 70 percent*: "Sharks," WildAid, accessed December 17, 2017, http://wildaid.org /programs/sharks.

9. Snake, Jaguar, Owl, Salamander

Leandro Silveira: Jaguar • Goiás, Brazil

Page 221, *The species once roamed in the southern United States, where it is now endangered*: Jaguar classifications are from the following: "Jaguar (Panthera onca)," US Fish & Wildlife Service, Environmental Conservation Online System, accessed November 29, 2017, https://ecos.fws.gov/ecp0/profile /speciesProfile?spcode=A040; "Panthera onca," IUCN Red List of Threatened Species, accessed November 29, 2016, http://www.iucnredlist.org /details/15953/0; and "Distribution, Genetics and Oral Health in Free-Ranging Jaguar Populations in Brazil," Jaguar Conservation Fund, accessed November 29, 2017, http://www.jaguar.org.br/en/projects/jaguar-distribution /index.html.

Andrew Sabin: Salamander • Long Island, New York, USA

Page 243, *Andy's passion and generosity have been acknowledged by the scientists*: "Andy Sabin," New York League of Conservation Voters Education Fund, accessed December 19, 2017, http://nylcvef.org/people/andy-sabin.

BIBLIOGRAPHY

Adams, Douglas, and Mark Carwardine. *Last Chance to See*. New York: Ballantine Books, 1990.

Armstrong, Susan J., and Richard G. Botzler, eds. *The Animal Ethics Reader*. 3rd ed. New York: Routledge, 2016.

Bekoff, Marc. *The Animal Manifesto: Six Reasons for Expanding Our Compassion Footprint*. Novato, CA: New World Library, 2010.

Courtenay, Bryce. *The Power of One*. New York: Ballantine Books, 1996.

Eiseley, Loren. *The Invisible Pyramid: A Naturalist Analyses the Rocket Century*. New York: Scribner, 1970.

Galdikas, Biruté M. F. *Reflections of Eden: My Years with the Orangutans of Borneo*. Boston: Little, Brown, 1995.

Goodall, Jane. *My Friends, the Wild Chimpanzees*. Washington, DC: National Geographic Society, 1967.

Grandin, Temple, and Catherine Johnson. *Animals in Translation: Using the Mysteries of Autism to Decode Animal Behavior*. Orlando, FL: Houghton Mifflin Harcourt, 2005.

Grosz, Terry. *Wildlife Wars: The Life and Times of a Fish and Game Warden*. Boulder, CO: Johnson Books, 1999.

Harari, Yuval N. *Sapiens: A Brief History of Humankind*. New York: Harper, 2015.

London, Jack. *The Call of the Wild*. New York: Grosset & Dunlap, 1903.

Malan, Rian. *My Traitor's Heart: A South African Exile Returns to Face His Country, His Tribe, and His Conscience*. New York: Atlantic Monthly Press, 1990.

Maxwell, Gavin. *Ring of Bright Water*. London: Longmans, 1960.

McArthur, Jo-Anne. *Captive*. New York: Lantern Books, 2017.

———. *We Animals*. New York: Lantern Books, 2014.

Mercer, Chris, and Beverley Pervan. *Canned Lion Hunting: A National Disgrace*. Kuruman, South Africa: self-published, 2005.

———. *For the Love of Wildlife*. Kuruman, South Africa: Kalahari Raptor Centre, 2000.

———. *Kalahari Dream*. Self-published, CreateSpace, 2011.

Milne, Natasha, and Barbara Royal. *One Hundred & One Reasons to Get Out of Bed: Small World Steps, Big Planet Heroes*. Allambie Heights, Australia: TWIG², 2015.

O'Barry, Richard, and Keith Coulbourn. *Behind the Dolphin Smile: One Man's Campaign to Protect the World's Dolphins*. San Rafael, CA: Earth Aware Editions, 2012.

———. *To Free a Dolphin*. Los Angeles: Renaissance Books, 2000.

Pacelle, Wayne. *The Bond: Our Kinship with Animals, Our Call to Defend Them*. New York: HarperCollins, 2011.

———. *The Humane Economy: How Innovators and Enlightened Consumers Are Transforming the Lives of Animals*. New York: HarperCollins, 2016.

Peck, M. Scott. *The Road Less Traveled: A New Psychology of Love, Traditional Values, and Spiritual Growth*. New York: Simon & Schuster, 1978.

Royal, Barbara. *The Royal Treatment: A Natural Approach to Wildly Healthy Pets*. New York: Emily Bestler Books / Atria, 2012.

Russell, Bertrand. *A History of Western Philosophy*. New York: Simon & Schuster, 1945.

Scully, Matthew. *Dominion: The Power of Man, the Suffering of Animals, and the Call to Mercy*. New York: St. Martin's Press, 2002.

Seuss, Dr. *The Lorax*. New York: Random House, 1971.

Singer, Peter. *Animal Liberation: A New Ethics for Our Treatment of Animals*. New York: Avon Books, 1977.

Skiff, Jennifer. *The Divinity of Dogs: True Stories of Miracles Inspired by Man's Best Friend*. New York: Atria Books, 2012.

———. *God Stories: Inspiring Encounters with the Divine*. New York: Harmony Books, 2008.

Smits, Willie, Gerd Schuster, and Jay Ullal. *Thinkers of the Jungle: The Orangutan Report*. Potsdam, Germany: H. F. Ullmann Publishing, 2007.

Stevens, Guy, and Thomas Peschak. *Manta: Secret Life of Devil Rays*. Dorchester, UK: The Manta Trust, 2016.

Strunk, William, and E. B. White. *The Elements of Style*. New York: Macmillan, 1959.

Weil, Zoe. *Above All, Be Kind: Raising a Humane Child in Challenging Times*. Gabriola Island, BC: New Society Publishers, 2003.

———. *Claude and Medea: The Hellburn Dogs*. New York: Lantern Books, 2007.

———. *Most Good, Least Harm: A Simple Principle for a Better World and Meaningful Life*. New York: Atria Books, 2009.

———. *The World Becomes What We Teach: Educating a Generation of Solutionaries*. New York: Lantern Books, 2016.

White, E. B. *Charlotte's Web*. New York: Harper & Brothers, 1952.

———. *The Trumpet of the Swan*. New York: Harper & Row, 1970.

INDEX

ABOUT THE AUTHOR

J ennifer Skiff is an award-winning journalist, author, and animal
advocate. Her bestselling inspirational books, *The Divinity of
Dogs* and *God Stories*, are published in seven languages.

For more than a decade Jennifer traveled the world as an investigative environmental correspondent for CNN. Her independently
produced programs about animals have aired on the Discovery
Channel and other networks throughout the world. Among other
honors, she has received the prized Environmental Media Award.

Passionate about animals and their welfare, Jennifer works with
charities throughout the world to bring relief to abused, exploited,
and abandoned animals. She led the successful campaign to build
the first bear sanctuary in Laos and initiated and supervised the
release of twelve chained monkeys back into their natural habitat
in Indonesia. Jennifer is chair of the Humane Society of the United
States Maine State Council and of the SPCAHC Trustee Council.
She is also an adviser to Animal Aid USA and the Institute for Humane Education, and is a trustee of the Dogs' Refuge Home in
Australia. In 2015, she was featured in the book *One Hundred & One*

Reasons to Get Out of Bed: Small World Steps, Big Planet Heroes along with Dame Jane Goodall and Sir Richard Branson. In 2018, she was celebrated for her contribution to animal welfare at Parliament House, Western Australia.

With her favorite Aussie and beloved dogs, Jennifer spends her life in perpetual summer between Maine and Australia.

Jennifer gifts 50 percent of after-tax profits from her books to animal charities of her choice.

Other Books by Jennifer Skiff

The Divinity of Dogs: True Stories of Miracles Inspired by Man's Best Friend

God Stories: Inspiring Encounters with the Divine

Have you had an encounter with an animal that changed your life? Please submit it for consideration in one of Jennifer's next books at her website:

JenniferSkiff.com

179

JUL 1 6 2019
P7/19'

NEW WORLD LIBRARY is dedicated to publishing books and other media that inspire and challenge us to improve the quality of our lives and the world.

We are a socially and environmentally aware company. We recognize that we have an ethical responsibility to our customers, our staff members, and our planet.

We serve our customers by creating the finest publications possible on personal growth, creativity, spirituality, wellness, and other areas of emerging importance. We serve New World Library employees with generous benefits, significant profit sharing, and constant encouragement to pursue their most expansive dreams.

As a member of the Green Press Initiative, we print an increasing number of books with soy-based ink on 100 percent postconsumer-waste recycled paper. Also, we power our offices with solar energy and contribute to non-profit organizations working to make the world a better place for us all.

Our products are available in bookstores everywhere.

www.newworldlibrary.com

At NewWorldLibrary.com you can download our catalog,
subscribe to our e-newsletter, read our blog,
and link to authors' websites, videos, and podcasts.

Find us on Facebook, follow us on Twitter, and watch us on YouTube.

Send your questions and comments our way!
You make it possible for us to do what we love to do.

Phone: 415-884-2100 or 800-972-6657
Catalog requests: Ext. 10 | Orders: Ext. 10 | Fax: 415-884-2199
escort@newworldlibrary.com

 NEW WORLD LIBRARY
publishing books that change lives   14 Pamaron Way, Novato, CA 94949